D0345231

CRH

MAY 2 3 1992

NOV 1 4 1992

Bill Roorbach

Summers with Juliet

Houghton Mifflin Company

Boston New York London 1992

Library of Congress Cataloging-in-Publication Data
Roorbach, Bill.
Summers with Juliet / Bill Roorbach.
p.   cm.
ISBN 0-395-57323-8
1. Roorbach, Bill.   2. Karelsen, Juliet, 1962–   .   3. English
teachers — United States — Biography.   4. Outdoor
life — United States.   I. Title.
PE64.R66A3   1992
974'.043'092 — dc20   91-34838
[B]   CIP

Printed in the United States of America

AGM 10 9 8 7 6 5 4 3 2 1

For Juliet

ACKNOWLEDGMENTS

With thanks to Betsy Lerner, John Sterling,
Amanda Urban, and the many friends
who appear in this book.

CONTENTS

Summers with Juliet

Hot Tin Roof

At eight I was interested in fishing, reading, and the diligent scavenging of fabulous pieces of glass, and metal, and sometimes wood. I have clear memories of specific finds: a blue glass insulator from a fallen telephone pole; a railroad spike from the tracks behind Mead Park; an old cast-iron witch's pot with sticks and mud and snails inside. I found coins and bike pedals and spoons, collected pieces of wire and strips of metal, dug up hand-cut nails and fossils and bits of old bone. I even had a weathered board with Chinese writing on it, which I'd found floated up at the beach on Long Island Sound. How far had it come? (Well, probably from Stamford or Norwalk or New York, but I had a grander vision.)

At eight I knew about an old truck in the woods way back behind our house, a Model A, I thought, the lord of all treasures, with speedometer and steering wheel intact. I also knew about an old steamer trunk that sat half buried in leaves just off Jelliff Mill Road. I had spied it from the height of the school bus, kept it secret from all but Mike Didelot, convinced it was full of jewels or some poor prince's head or a giant gladiator's outsize armor. When Mike and I finally broke into the trunk, the flower pots were treasure enough, three of them, at least a little bit ancient, and broken.

And, when I was eight, unbeknownst to me, Juliet Karelsen was born — June 15, 1962 — away off in New York City, that tall town where my father worked and where a penny could kill. By the time Juliet herself had turned eight she was already an independent little New York girl, owner of an elaborate dollhouse, maker of two hundred faces, eater of ice cream, seller on the street of homemade greeting cards, rogue child of Central Park West, in charge of her parents, in love with her teacher, in cahoots with the doormen, going steady with a black boy from school, studying ethics, playing guitar, husbanding a hamster named Willy. So sensitive, said a family friend, that she could feel the grass grow under her feet. That summer, Juliet, bearing her hamster and in league with her little sister Eva, deigned to accompany her parents to Wellfleet, Massachusetts, on Cape Cod. I was sixteen by then, about to turn seventeen, and Juliet and I had kept our relative distance. New York City, New York, to New Canaan, Connecticut, is about forty-five miles. Wellfleet, Cape Cod, to Edgartown, Martha's Vineyard, is also about forty-five miles, and in Edgartown I was on vacation with my own family.

I had to go to bird sanctuaries and dumb museums and clothes stores and nature walks and church. We went to the beach in the mornings for a prescribed number of hours, then back to the hotel for lunch. At least I got to be the oldest for a while; my big brother, Randy, was a college boy that summer and off on his own someplace, free. I kept an eye on my younger brother and sisters, coddling little Janet while picking on Dougie and Carol, then in the afternoon was set loose for three or four hours. I knew just where to go: in Edgartown, you hung out on the lawn in front of the Old Whaling Church with cool kids from every suburb in the Northeast, kids who knew what it was all about. And on the Vineyard, when it wasn't all about how long your bleached hair was getting, it was all about James Taylor. There was always a party being rumored, and J.T. was always going to be at the party.

On the Cape, meanwhile, Juliet would have been building a beach house for her doll family, a group made up of little European dolls: Hans and Bridget, the parents; Susie, Debbie, Peter, David, Frank, Louisa, and Christopher, the children; and Uncle Nick, their live-in dentist. Juliet and Eva and their friends sawed boards in the basement of her family's rented cottage until the dollhouse was done. There was no workbench in the basement and no vices, just a saw and a hammer and a pile of lumber, so Juliet made the other three hold on to the old boards, six skinny arms taut and trembling, as she sawed and hammered, intent on the work. When the other girls wanted to stop, Juliet said no. The doll family must have a beach house!

So Juliet and I lived the summer of 1970 — she a little girl barely older than my baby sister, I about to turn seventeen, both of us sifting fine sands, a world apart (at least). As a treat on her birthday, Juliet got to play miniature golf. As a treat on my birthday, I got to go out on my own, was given a midnight curfew, a wild luxury, especially since I knew of a party at which not only James Taylor was guaranteed to show but his brother Livingston, too, and probably Carole King. I dressed in my tightest black jeans and my hippest BVD undershirt (that brand had a *pocket*) and flipped my hair many times in front of the wavy hotel mirror.

The party was in progress at an elegant old house, clapboard, square, white, the home once of a whaling captain and now, having remained unsold all these two hundred years, the summer home of his progeny. Its door, painted red, was open. The music of Jimi Hendrix blared forth.

I gulped, gave my head a shake, marched up the steps of

the austere porch. No one asked who I was. I accepted a mug full of wine, lit up a cigarette and found my way into the living room and then to the hearth, where I could lean under the great mantelpiece and watch the proceedings. James Taylor did not yet seem to be in attendance. Indeed, no one older than eighteen seemed to be in attendance. I drank more wine, smoked another cigarette. I had a beer someone handed me, smoked a little pot, tried a slug of Jack Daniel's as the bottle passed my way. I never moved from my spot. On the mantel was an array of objects, all of which held real interest for me: An antique sextant. A large marine vertebra. An old, well-used bos'n's pipe. A real harpoon. A walrus tusk, scrimshawed. A baleen comb, made from the great plankton-screening maw of a humpback whale. Gradually I got drunk enough to remember myself and forget the party and to pay attention to the treasures. A shark's jaw with triple rows of teeth. When had this shark swum? A little stone Buddha. How far had Captain Pendergast (for that was the name engraved on a brass box) sailed? A pair of brass and leather binoculars. A glass float, blue as the earth and as round, escaped from a fisherman's net in Portugal, I knew, but when? And around the room, photographs and paintings and etchings: grinning second mates, sheets of blubber, boats under full sail and adorned with flags and fresh paint and men in the rigging, leaving Edgartown Harbor. Doom or success? How far did they go?

The Pendergasts also had a clock collection, thirty or forty old things, well kept and tocking. They all struck at midnight, a prolonged concatenation of bongs and dings and whistles and tweets. I stayed. Silly curfew! The party was going strong, doors closed, windows closed, music very low in fear of the ever-watchful Edgartown police. James Taylor on the stereo, as close as we would get to him that night. Someone had handed me a full jug of wine and I clutched it, staring up at a trio of rudely carved, life-size wooden geese. Full of wine I spoke my first words of the night: "I wonder what those geese were for?"

Soon a knot of us were sharing the wine and discussing the well-kept birds. Too unmarked to have been used by any hunter as decoys. "Too top-heavy, anyway," someone said, poking at one, "not weighted at all." Each goose had a reddish glass eye and feet painted onto its bottom. We argued the possible uses for the birds, the motives of their maker. A young woman came up, the young woman who was throwing the party, a good forty or sixty pounds overweight, somewhat older than I, eyes brown and slightly occluded by her chubby cheeks as she smiled. "They're boredom geese," she said. "My great-great-great-grandfather made 'em whenever he got stuck on land for too long."

The clocks, all thirty or forty of them, struck one. Ms. Pendergast, our hostess (her first name, I think, was Roberta), showed me a box of scrimshaw tools. And two narwhal tusks, the likes of which were once sold as unicorn horns. And a coconut-shell mask from Tahiti made at the time Gauguin lived there. And a block of wood with leather straps, once some ancestor's replacement foot. The log of the frigate *Margaret,* dated 1807, which my hostess wasn't supposed to open but did. The handwriting was faded and loopy, pure romance. Upstairs, Roberta showed me her bed, which had been the captain's bed on the good ship *Eleanor Alison,* circa 1830. Quickly, as if her mother were about to catch us, she got me out of her room and down the back stairs. In the kitchen were thirty more carved geese, a flight of them on two long shelves that met in the corner over the stove. "A vee," as she pointed out, "like a real flock."

Downstairs, the party had dissipated to a few drunks and

my tour guide's younger brothers. The latter were busy bouncing the former. The house was a mess. Soon, I noticed, everyone was gone but the two brothers, Ms. Pendergast, and I. My head was beginning to spin, the prelude to a night of vomiting in the shower while my father, disgusted, held me upright in the stall. "Mom's going to kill us," the younger brother said.

"Who is this guy?" the other said, pointing at me with a back-flung thumb.

Spinning or not, I lifted the big green jug of wine to my lips.

"My friend," Roberta said. She certainly was fat, a good deal bigger than I.

"Well, Mom's going to kill us," brother number one repeated with special emphasis. The brothers were not fat, not at all.

I pressed on, undaunted. "What's that thing?" I said, pointing.

"Blubber knife," the bigger brother said, annoyed. "Time to go."

Ms. Pendergast and her brothers walked me out on the porch. She shooed the boys inside and, apparently having mistaken my interest in her family artifacts for an interest in herself, she took my head in her hands and kissed me *smack smack* on the lips. Her hands on my head seemed to contain the spinning somewhat, and her lips gave the whole fuzzy world a warm, wet focus. I put my arms around some of her, for support, and there we stood, lip to lip, till the littler of her brothers came out and pulled her inside.

On the Cape, Juliet must have been asleep, hugging her pillow, dreaming of dolphins and sandbars and clam rolls and sun, after an evening spent at one of her family's ritual vacation shrines. (On a recent camping trip to North Truro she showed me everything: the Drive-in, the Dairy King, the Puritan Shop in Wellfleet; the houses of her friends, Meyer, Winkelstein, DeCarlo, Waters; the Howard Johnson's her family always stopped at; their various rented houses; their favorite beaches; the place she bought her best bathing suit *ever*.) During the day, Juliet and Eva preferred the Buzzards Bay side of the Cape, where low tide made miles of flats to play on and everyone bragged of knowing a boy who had walked to Provincetown across the sandbars before high tide came to drown him. The sisters played marina, using shells as boats and digging channels that the tide would fill, rising. They stole *Once Is Never Enough* from their mother, read the sex scenes to each other as they lay under their towels in the sand. They took Willy the hamster to the dunes, so he could see the ocean, and to Howard Johnson's, so he wouldn't be lonely at home or too hot in the car. In the cool Cape evenings Willy got to come out of his cage for a cuddly minute in Juliet's palms before bed.

My father at midnight was miffed. At one o'clock he was furious and worried, both, each emotion escalating the other. At two o'clock he went out looking for me. He got in the car (a wood-paneled station wagon that soon enough, newly licensed, I would wreck) and crawled the streets of Edgartown with his lights off. Earlier he and Mom had taken note of a party at one of the old captain's houses, so he slunk over to that neighborhood and found me, sure enough, on the porch in the near dark kissing someone as big around as he was.

The next ten years took me through a lot of territory: Weston, Connecticut, where I worked for a crazy electrician; Ithaca, New York, where I made my way through college; Trumansburg, Interlaken and Newfield, New

York, where I lived in old farmhouses for a couple of wild postgraduate years of playing piano and singing in bands; Beaver Crossing, Nebraska, where I worked on two cattle farms; Seattle, Washington, where I waited on tables and bartended and where I started writing in earnest. My path came nowhere near Juliet's again until 1980, when, at the behest of my old musician friend Jon Zeeman, I returned to Martha's Vineyard.

I could afford the trip because I'd spotted a classified ad in the *New York Times* looking for someone to write a question-and-answer-format home repair book. (I got to New York four hours early for my appointment, stumbled through the interview, talking very seriously about my short stories and novel-in-progress, actually *fell* on my way out of the publisher's office, but got the job. Ten dollars a page for a 256-page book, $2,560 — not much for a whole book, even at the time, but to me a fortune.) By that time I was living in Madison, Connecticut, working unhappily as a free-lance handyman and sharing a classically depressing suburban house with my girlfriend Susan, who was a graduate student in music at Yale. I told her I wanted to write the home repair book on Martha's Vineyard. Maybe by myself. She cried. I cried. Everybody cried, but I was determined to go and she was determined to let me.

When Jon pulled into our driveway, I was ready. He had rented a U-Haul for his PA system and his amps and his Hammond organ. He meant to have a band and play for the summer tourists. We emptied my little house of everything I owned, which wasn't much — mostly odd bits of pipe and lumber, my typewriter and boxes of books — and headed for the Vineyard. In Oak Bluffs, fresh off the ferry, we took possession of 222 Circuit Avenue, a rickety old gingerbread cottage with six bedrooms, which would make room for Brian Hess and Jeff Young (the other two thirds of Jon's jazz trio) when they turned up and leave room over the summer for three or four oddball roommates who would help pay the rent.

On sunny days our little household banded together and went to the beach. On the rare rainy days, Jon and the boys rehearsed upstairs, thumping the floor. I typed in the basement one or two frantic days a week, making the book: *Fix-It! Tips and Tricks for Home Repair*. Every fifty pages I'd stop and retype, send a package off to New York, then haunt the general delivery window at the post office until my check ($500!) would arrive. I tried to make the questions sound like real people talking, used a lot of exclamation points to show their excitement at the task ahead. *Q: My darn faucet is driving me crazy! How can I get it to stop dripping all night?* Like that. Or, *Q: I'd like to build a bookshelf to keep* this *home repair book in! How do I go about it?* or *Q: My son Jonny* [I always used my friends' names] *just had a snowball fight to end all snowball fights! How do you repair a broken window?* All the writing practice didn't hurt, I guess, and at last I could call myself a writer without inviting derision.

At night Jon's trio, the Circuit Avenue Band, played around the island — at bars, at restaurants, at parties. I went along, and the four of us managed to meet a lot of women, which, after all, was the idea.

Juliet, being only eighteen, may or may not have been too young for our notice, though she was on Martha's Vineyard for a week that summer, visiting a college friend who was working as an up-island au pair. Jules was about to start her freshman year at the University of Michigan, had spent most of the summer working as a counselor at a camp for disturbed kids, had there found not a few suitors to send packing, had had her own heart broken, too, had learned what all those lyrics to all those James Taylor songs she liked to play on her guitar were really about. When her week's visit was up, she went back to New York, vowing to return to Martha's Vineyard. In September she flew off to Ann Arbor.

It was October before the island got too bleak and empty for Jon and me, but finally we got on the ferry to Wood's Hole, then headed west to New York, where we hoped to find a place to live. We spent some miserable weeks on people's couches. Then, at Puffy's (a bar in TriBeCa), we ran into a miracle: our old actor friend, Van Santvoord, who invited us to build rooms for ourselves and share his enormous loft on West Broadway in Soho. We moved in immediately, just before Thanksgiving. Around Christmas I got a job playing piano in the Mike Corbin band, which nearly paid enough for rent, an oppressive $150 a month. In January, I put a handyman ad in the *Village Voice,* and that got me enough jobs to pay for food and quite a lot of beer. Done with the home repair book, I wrote furiously, seriously, an obsessed apprentice to fifty favorite writers, no fame or fortune in sight.

The next year, after a fine summer on the Vineyard (Juliet bicycling through Europe), I built cabinets for neighbors in Soho, worked for a contractor, played piano in three bands. (Thanks to Jon, I even got an audition with Chubby Checker's touring band. I showed up at the classy S.I.R. studios in my tattered workclothes looking like an urchin and was so nervous I could barely play. When my songs were done, Mr. Checker crossed the stage and hugged me. He's a big guy, and sweet.) And yes, I went out with women, one after the next. Many couldn't understand my life; the ones who could seemed a little nuts to me.

And so to the Vineyard, summer of 1982.

Jon and I found a cheap enough house near the sewage treatment plant on the outskirts of Edgartown, which sounds worse than it was; the sewage plant only smelled when the wind came our way, one night out of a week, or two. By now I was singing in Jon's summer band, which had somehow evolved into a jazz/rock/oldies/rhythm-and-blues/country band. He already had a keyboard player (much more versatile than I), and since I sang only a handful of songs, I was paid half what the other musicians were paid. We hadn't enough money for restaurant meals, much less enough for a decent beach towel or enough to fix our old bomb cars when they broke, but we had plenty of money for drinks at the bars, and plenty of money for admission to the Hot Tin Roof, which had been Carly Simon's place, a seventies-style disco in an old airplane hangar up in the scrub oak forest by the airport.

On the evening of July 20 I looked up from the bar there and spied a pretty young woman passing. She was blond and flushed and had an aquiline nose (which word until recently I thought meant straight, but no, it means like an eagle's, hooked) and fairly glowed with aplomb. I kept my eye on her as she glided her way across the dance floor and up the stairs through the crowd to the bar. It wasn't so much her good looks. It was her insouciance. She seemed to have no idea anyone was looking at her, least of all I. Holding my place at the bar, I waited for her to pass again. Soon enough she did. She'd cadged a cigarette somewhere, and now she brought it inexpertly to her lips, blinked hard to keep the smoke out of her eyes as she puffed, passed me by without a glance. I watched as she made her way back up into the balcony area and sat at a table with three other young women.

Jon came waltzing by, holding a beer.

"Have a look," I said.

He peered brazenly into the balcony, found the table in question. "Blond?" he said.

I pretended not to look. "Right."

"Nothing special." And off he went.

I danced with friends nearer my age then — Sally from the Rare Duck, Messina from the beach, Ellie Winters from the bookstore — hoping to give the impression of my own popularity and insouciance. I drank beer. I danced. I went to the bathroom. When I came out, the blond stood exactly in my way, having bypassed the line for the ladies' room. Her eyes were blue as the sky over Nantucket Sound, blue as the edge of the ocean. Her face was bright with intelligence, bright as the planets on a moonless night.

"Anyone in there?" she said.

"I'll check."

She followed me in, scooted into a stall. "Could you watch the door?"

I deliberated. Then, not wanting to seem too easy, I abandoned my post.

Later, when I found her near the dance floor with her friends, she pretended not to know me. "The men's room?" I said, to sharpen her memory.

"You!" she said. "There was a crowd of pissing guys in there when I came out!" It seemed she found this funny. She accepted my invitation to dance. We did so. She told me she lived with her sister and a couple of friends in Vineyard Haven. She told me she was from New York. She told me she worked at Cozy's, dipping ice cream. She told me she played guitar. She told me her name: Juliet.

I told her my name, which on the Vineyard was Billy.

"Oh," she said with real feeling, "I had a hamster once named Willy!"

*

Autumn comes early to the Vineyard. Leases expire on Labor Day. Flocks of geese start assembling for the flight south.

Juliet and I had formed a tenuous union that was about to be sundered by her trip back to Michigan for the start of her junior year. We'd danced at the Roof, kissed on the beach, climbed in the cliffs at Windy Gates and Gay Head. We'd taken clay baths and body-surfed and walked in the rain. And though I was in love, she was less sure. It had been a few weeks before we got around to *making* love (one late night at the Hot Tin Roof she kissed me nicely, and — full of beer and the heat of dancing — I asked her home. "No," she said firmly, and went back to her friends. I stood out in the parking lot then, cooling off under the stars, cursing my temerity. All lost! All ruined! After a long twenty minutes Juliet appeared beside me in the dark. "Changed my mind," she said simply, and took my hand); after that we'd stayed occasional nights at my house, in the bottom bunk of the child's bed I'd been stuck with, and even fewer nights at hers, where she and her three roommates shared two small bedrooms. She valued her privacy, wanted nights to herself, guarded her freedom, stayed always tentative on the issue of love. Insouciance itself, she seemed not the least troubled by the dark prospect of our separation.

Late on one of our last nights, she decided we should sleep on the beach, away from the crowd of superannuated teenagers in my house and away from her sister and friends. Beach sleeping is not allowed on Martha's Vineyard, but we surreptitiously borrowed her roommate Joanna's car and headed to South Beach, where I was sure we'd be caught and arrested. Jules knew a place, a dirt road that ended high over a salt pond near a darkened house. We took along all the blankets from her bed, and one pillow, and several beers, and tramped like sleepwalking children across the dunes to the beach. We walked up-island a long way, past another couple who were already asleep. Finally we stopped and spread out our blankets and felt the cold wind and watched the surf coming in under the brilliant Milky Way, Venus coruscating near Mars at the horizon, enough light despite the new moon to illuminate the spray and the crests of the marching waves and to silhouette flock after flock of night geese arriving at the pond behind us. We shivered in our blankets, sipping beer, talking softly, kissing.

After a brief hour we saw flashlights coming. We held our breaths, watching the couple down the beach get arrested. We waited, Juliet calmly, I pumping adrenaline. But the flashlight beams could not reach us and the cops turned back, satisfied with their catch. By five in the morning we had slept very little, had made sandy love and had decided to head back, to be warm in the car as the dawn arrived in pink and mist.

The pond, when we got there, was covered, acre after acre, with Canada geese. There were thousands, and new flocks arrived moment by moment: a busy airport. Juliet and I watched them from the windless warmth of the car for an hour. At sunrise the flocks began to depart out over the ocean, big flocks, then lesser ones, away in a chorus of honks from their fellows. I have never seen so many geese in one place; in fact, I have never seen so many of any single animal gathered such in one place, except humans, perhaps, and bees. I thought of Captain Pendergast's geese, unliving on their shelves.

I had always thought of geese as the end of things, flying off in melancholy Vs. I grew sad sitting there on the big bench seat of that old car, overlooking the salt pond, which had become the very heart of endings, sitting away from tousled Juliet. Hard to separate endings from beginnings at times like that. Hard to think, *Oh, time will tell,* as my bright new Juliet waved from the ferry two days later. Hard to keep the melancholy out of the letters I wrote to her nearly daily, some on birchbark from New Hampshire (anything to impress), some on my brand-new letterhead from New York (anything, anything). Hard to recognize the beginning of something, but there it was. The multitudes of geese, oblivious, leapt to the air, circled above us forming flocks, then headed out over the ocean and away.

Berkshire Turkeys

My first fall with Juliet was characterized by the nine hundred miles between Ann Arbor and New York. I wrote her daily love letters; she wrote back weekly, convinced I was insane. I paid her way back to New York for Halloween, of all the miserable holidays; in the crush of the Greenwich Village parade we fought. The problem was that she'd flown home secretly, hadn't told her parents, and for Juliet the notion of them seventy blocks uptown thinking of her, picturing her, devoted to her, *paying* for her in Michigan, was too much. Was I trying to break up her family? At Thanksgiving she came home for a legitimate visit just as Jon Zeeman and I were moving into our new place in the Meat District — a raw loft, colossal, empty, pointily wedge-shaped, a former furniture factory with nothing in it whatsoever but a single, exposed toilet.

I'd found a reasonably steady job with a contractor named Charlie Hudson, who paid very well and freely allowed me time off for music, or writing, or working on my loft. Charlie was an affable boss, didn't want to be responsible for full-time, fully dependent employees; we suited each other. By December I'd managed to accumulate a little cash, felt pleasantly wealthy and secure, but just before Christmas, Charlie Hudson left town. Though he'd warned me from the beginning, I was surprised: he'd finally closed on an inn in Western Massachusetts. And though he offered me a job up there, I refused. Who wanted to leave New York?

So much for steady income. I turned to matters closer to home. The loft took most of my time. Against the advice of nearly everyone, Jon and I installed heaters and built walls for five bedrooms, two bathrooms, two kitchens and a long hall and entryway. We made a music room in the point of the wedge, fixed the windows, patched the floor. We added lights and homemade cabinets and shelving and paint. The place was rough to live in at first — dusty and chilly and dark — but it was ours. The five years of the lease yawned before us like eternity itself.

During her January break Juliet came along on dump-stering runs with Jon and me, late-night scavenger hunts in which we sought out sinks and stoves and cable and pipe and lumber with which to build our place. We drove all over Manhattan, stopping to crawl around in fifty-yard dumpsters, liberating desks and doors and bathtubs and carpet. For Juliet and me it was a kind of working date.

Jules was in love with me, as she often said, but took pains to make it clear that she was not to be possessed. I was happy enough being around her, didn't get too loud when an old boyfriend came to town. "Just dinner," she told me. "No big deal." Late on the night of their date Jon and I went to pick her up at her folks' place as planned — midnight dumpster run! — but arrived just as she was getting out of a taxi. She was barely recognizable, dressed in a sleek winter coat over a long blue dress; she wore white gloves; her hair was in French braids. The fellow was tall and thin and dark. In jacket and tie, he looked like an ambassador's aide.

"Fag," Jon said as we waited unseen in our dark car, a trashed Wagoneer borrowed for the occasion.

The ambassador's aide took Juliet's arm, kissed her

cheek, walked her past Sam the doorman, who nodded and fawned in a way he never did for me. Jon shrugged, failing for once to think of a rational explanation with which to soothe me.

I was cool. I was calm. I leapt out of the car and raced across Central Park West and past the potted cedars beneath the canopy of the building's big entry. Sam at the door raised his eyebrows up to his hairline — *trouble* — but didn't try to stop me. At the polished walnut elevator doors I found Jules and her man friend waiting. I looked at her closely (eye shadow?), then grabbed her date's hand, shook it and barked: "Bill Roorbach. Good to meet you."

He turned to Jules, astonished.

"Back in an hour," I said.

In precisely sixty minutes, Jon and I returned with an excellent bathtub tied to the roof. Juliet was ready, waiting on the sidewalk in blue jeans and workshirt. She kissed me and squeezed my hand. She had mascara on her eyes, still, though she'd tried to wipe it off, and a little lipstick on her nose.

In mid-January Juliet took off for Paris, a semester at the Sorbonne. Jon Zeeman took off for Norway, a tour with a country-and-western band. Left behind in New York, I did some odd plumbing jobs for ready cash, worked desultorily on the loft, drank ferociously at the Corner Bistro and the White Horse Tavern and the No Name Bar and generally moped around, missing Jules (whom I pictured kicking her legs up at the Moulin Rouge or studying Camus with some sad-eyed French smoothie in a beret) and missing Jon (whom I pictured hugging big, happy, intelligent Norwegian women twice as tall as he was).

After a couple of weeks of this, I called Charlie Hudson.

My timing was perfect, he said. The job was still open, he said. He was about to start the renovation; could I be there day after tomorrow?

So suddenly I was in the Berkshires, where February is bleak and dark falls early, and suddenly I was walking around an enormous old inn by flashlight, Charlie explaining all the work that had to be done. In the middle of what had once been a farmhouse dining room was a rudimentary, walk-in wine refrigerator. Apparently, it was the former owner's idea of a classy addition to the place, but it was so amateurishly homemade that it was an eyesore, a chunky plywood booth nailed roughly to the fine old farmhouse columns and roof beams. "That goes first," Charlie said.

Restaurant tables filled what had been the parlor, some of them still set for service: wineglasses covered with dust, neatly folded napkins, cheap china plates and coffee cups in place, even menus. Charlie scoffed (in his polite manner, always polite), showing me the menu. Too many items, he said, too eclectic, too inexpensive. Unwise. Practically a diner, in this elegant house. And look at the name. Porto di Mare, in the mountains. No wonder they'd gone under!

Already I was composing that evening's letter to Juliet, telling her all about the place. To see each new thing was to describe it; I was living for two. Charlie's big plans were all well and good, but my mission of the moment was to make enough money to get to Europe to join my one true love. Charlie knew this, knew I wouldn't be with him long, probably also knew — he was full of kindly wisdom — that I'd be back.

The big parlor fireplace was boarded up with plywood, the plywood covered with peeled contact paper. A smaller fireplace hidden behind the wine cooler sported shelves built into it for glassware and, worse, a red-and-white-checked tile job over its original fieldstone hearth.

"You'll find it's less spooky when it's warm," Charlie said. It was forty degrees outside, but in there it felt like ice.

Upstairs, the four main bedrooms were in shambles, a shambles dating from well before Porto di Mare days. The ceilings had collapsed in places; 1930s wallpaper hung down over doorways; ornate moldings had been chopped up to accommodate phone wires and jerry-built closets; fine old mantelpieces had been rudely painted, had lost their grips on the chimneys. In the master bedroom an old safe stood empty, its door open, gaping in the beam of the flashlight. Wires ran to buttons and speakers, a ridiculous alarm system; the bedroom door had three locks on it. Charlie explained that according to local wisdom, the alarm system and safe and locks were the legacy of a paranoid Alice, the Alice of Alice's Restaurant fame, who had opened her second restaurant here, the failure just before Porto di Mare.

Next we clunked up a hidden stairway into the creaking black attic. Up there employees had lived under the eaves in poorly kept rooms. A cramped shower chamber had three stalls, a bathroom had three sinks and three toilets. In a crawl space, later, while renovating these rooms into normal baths, I would find a peephole some Tom had made to watch the girls shower, or maybe the boys.

"Let's make a fire," Charlie said. We trundled down to the second floor, then down the back stairs, making enough noise to chase away ghosts, down into the enormous Porto di Mare kitchen, where giant spoons and enormous paddles and pots and pans still hung. In the taproom (once some gentleman farmer's billiards hall) we built a fire in the six-foot-high fieldstone fireplace, pulled up barstools and warmed our knees.

"I saw a fox out in the front orchard," Charlie told me. "Tiny little thing. And wild turkeys, too, two distinct flocks. They poke around on the lawn very early in the morning. *You'll* never see them!"

"Sure I'll see them," I said, acting hurt to keep the joke going. "These days, I'm often up that late."

I thought of Jules, half listened while Charlie outlined his plans for the place. He would have a thousand rose-bushes. *Flowers for Juliet.* We'd restore the barn to its former enormous splendor, even though the town inspector thought it would have to be torn down. Eventually we'd have a swimming pool back on the hill behind the barn. Had I seen the view back there? Imagine! *Jules in a bathing suit.* The barracks-like motel rooms this side of the barn would be individualized as much as possible, the cinder blocks covered with drywall, the place painted. It would never be pretty, but with some landscaping . . . Ah, but the main house. Each room in the main house would be remodeled in a different style, and each would have a fireplace and a bathroom. (That's where you come in, Bill.) The kitchen would be brought up to date. A piano in the parlor. Antiques everywhere. Dinners in the circular dining room! Breakfast in the taproom! *Breakfast with Juliet. Where was she, and with whom was she sharing a glass of French wine?*

Next morning the Elliott brothers (Dave, Don and Sandy, mutual friends of Charlie's and mine, all blond, all freckled, all jolly) came over from Albany, and the five of us started in on the wine cooler. By lunchtime it was gone, rubble in the driveway, dust in the parlor air.

I missed Juliet badly, but it took me till the end of March to save enough money for a cheap one-way ticket to Belgium. After a drunken and exhausted train ride, I waited in the

Gare Austerlitz for twenty minutes before Juliet arrived. Our reunion was more complicated than I'd expected: Jules was so full of trouble from her new life that there wasn't room for me, not really. She gave me a wan smile, a tepid hug, and commented on my preposterous haircut. I thought she looked thin, but didn't say so. In the taxi to her place (I splurged, using fully five percent of my spending money), she warned me about her roommates. She was living with two young American women, and they weren't very nice.

During the next week I decided they were all quietly going nuts. Roomie number one was holed up in her room — I never even saw her. Roomie number two, Ellen, had appointed herself guardian of the bathroom, was worried about the gas bill, was worried about those pesky French hand showers, called out when you bathed too long or if she thought she heard splashing on the floor. Even so, I liked her. Once she went to Notre Dame Cathedral, hoping the quiet there and the ornate beauty would lift her out of her depression, but as she walked out of the church (feeling better!) a suicidal churchwoman, naked save a fur coat and a feathered hat, fell from the sky, splat on the paving stones at poor Ellen's feet.

Juliet was culture shocked and uprooted and over-whelmed by the troubles of everyone around her, and over-whelmed by my sudden presence, too. I tried to cheer her up. We bought cheap-o sandwiches and bottles of good wine and roamed around Paris, bought a foam mattress to bridge her twin beds, saw the Eiffel Tower on fire (or scaffolding up there, anyway, a huge blaze in the night, which didn't make a single French newspaper).

We looked forward to Juliet's spring break, planned a trip to romantic Venice, but Venice was a disaster. We got there in the middle of the Feast of the Gondoliers, or some such exuberance, not a hotel room in the place and not enough money between us to try one of the famous restaurants. We argued, not out of animosity but out of fear and exhaustion and disappointment. Juliet cried in my arms, standing (I'm serious) on the Bridge of Sighs, the first time she'd shown me her tears.

When we got back to Paris, Juliet took me to her favorite café in the Latin Quarter and said she wanted me to leave. Paris was complicated enough without me. I wept and grew angry. She railed at me, then wept herself, resolute. Our waiter found the whole scene charming and announced that we needn't pay.

Next day I spent the last of my money for a train to Norway, where Jon Zeeman was still playing country-and-western music. Soon I was invited to join a band, too, the Black Leather Bikers, starring Lars Luggarrød, a six-foot-four ex-con who smuggled liquor and tape decks and loved Willie Nelson. Lars had made an album and had a following of some of the lowest lowlife in northern Europe. His former piano player had been stabbed to death onstage in Stavanger. I took the job anyway. Lars extorted an electric piano from some sap who owed him, and I was in business.

I finally got back to New York three months later, dead broke but unstabbed. My loft full of crazed subtenants was in turmoil, the guy I'd left in charge having moved out. The city was a million degrees. Juliet, her parents told me, was in Greece, would be joining them in Sweden before long, would be arriving home in time for school. I barely stopped, hitchhiked back to the Berkshires and the inn, put Juliet out of my mind.

What a cast of characters as the inn's new summer progressed! Wait staff, bartenders, gardeners, chambermaids, suicides, busboys, chefs, prep cooks, dogs and cats, sons and daughters, girlfriends, boyfriends, cousins, and, last and quite least, inn guests. I worked on the continuing renovation, rebuilding bathrooms, recreating moldings, reseating windows, replacing doors, uncovering original details, building screens and trellises and fences and banisters, drinking at night, trying hard to perfect "You Always Hurt the One You Love" on the piano, writing short stories in the lovely attic room that was part of my pay, even bartending when they needed me. (My favorite customers were the weekend Buddhists from across the street, New Yorkers who came to the Awhana Bhari Institute for a spiritual weekend of silence and fasting. Every weekend a pair or so of failed inductees would turn up after their nine o'clock bedtime, order burgers and fries, drink and shout till last call.) But the writing was the important thing; it was hard to explain, so I tended to keep quiet about it, content for the moment to be seen as a carpenter, or bartender, or musician, or bum.

Slowly, I began to accept that Juliet and I were no longer a pair. I tried to date, as summer gave way to fall, but something in the alignment of the earth's magnetic forces made Berkshire women especially difficult to impress. The women I did find were good people, but far from ideal (as if I were ideal for them!). I had one friend whose estranged husband looked in the windows when she had me over for drinks (she said to ignore him), another whose dad didn't like her to be out past ten (she was *twenty-eight* years old), and yet another whose boyfriend kicked in the door while I was at her house (I hid half naked in the sweltering attic for two hours until he went away in tears).

So I was glad when Juliet called one bright October afternoon from Ann Arbor. She was a senior now, working steadily on her degree in comparative literature. She said she'd spent a pretty good summer, but didn't sound convinced. She said she was happier now. She said she'd like to see me again. Her grandfather had died, so her folks were going to fly her home. I rushed down to New York for the quick chance to be with her. She was sad about her grandfather, of course, but more important, it seemed she had missed me; all was not well with her various paramours in Michigan. Instead of taking her to the airport when the funeral was over, I drove her up to the inn. She skipped ten days of school, and our romance was rekindled. It didn't take much from my end; I was willing to forgive someone so young. I hadn't wanted to smother her, after all. As for Jules, she said she'd only been confused, but she made it clear that it wasn't time to start smothering now. Ah, Thanksgiving: I saw her in New York. Christmas: ditto. The phone calls! I drove my newly purchased 1961 Berkshires Bulgemobile to Michigan twice, once to share her spring break, next to attend her graduation.

In May, she came back east to work at Camp Ramapo, which is in Rhinebeck, New York. It's a summer camp for emotionally disturbed kids, just an hour of reckless driving from the inn. Once a week I bombed down there in that low-slung, two-ton car, grabbing Jules for a quick night off up at the inn. She didn't want me staying at camp, she said, constructing an elaborate reason having to do with the children, but she would show me around.

This was the famous cabin where she'd boffed that gorgeous lakefront counselor on the pool table. This was the field where she'd lost the famous leather jacket, making out with some other counselor stud. Over here the famous cabin where she'd met that guy, the one with the guitar she used to tell me about. There were also some memories involving her work with the children. Nine at night, I would whisk her up to the inn, telling her about the women I'd been dating. Independence (or the appearance of independence) had become important to both of us, so we feigned indifference to each other's stories of love and conquest and romance and sex, even as we thought of torturingly better tales to tell.

Six in the morning, we'd look for the wild turkeys as we crept back to my car in the employee parking lot. I'd yet to see those elusive birds, though I *believed* in them, had started to think of them as spirits of the forest. Charlie insisted he saw them as often as two or three mornings a week. I'd scan the trees and search the lawn, making comic turkey sounds; Juliet, faintly smiling, exhausted, would only yawn and stretch and brush her tumbled hair. Then, no turkeys in sight, I'd whisk her back down to Rhinebeck just in time for reveille.

In the renovation crew there was a core of four of us, and sometimes five. Ricky Davis was a relative of Charlie's, a sly, handsome boy from New York, very sharp and likable, if stormy and intense, who generally served as my helper. Then there were those three Elliott brothers. Dave Elliott was a friend from Ithaca days; he'd been the drummer in the Blues Rangers, a band Jon Zeeman had started in which I had played piano. Dave was an experienced electrician, confident and competent, who certainly didn't need my advice. Don Elliott turned up once in a while, too, a married man with two kids and four jobs. Sandy Elliott was the quintessential younger brother, a big, lovable fellow with a white Corvette. Sandy wasn't the greatest construction worker, but he would gladly do anything for anyone. After a while Charlie hired him on as the front desk person, full time, a job more suited to his nature. Sandy made the move from Albany, moved in with Ricky Davis, who'd found a nice little house down the street from the inn.

Ricky had a motorcycle; Sandy had his car. Ricky had a girlfriend, Marlene; Sandy was divorced, although he was only twenty-four. He still had a subscription to *Bride's Magazine*. Ricky and Sandy worked constantly on their vehicles and helped me with mine. Ricky fought with Marlene; Sandy perused his *Bride's*. The three of us did some world-class drinking at the bar in the inn, trying to be quiet, directly under Charlie and his wife, Marybell, drinking after the regular bartender went home, talking in front of the fire, helping ourselves to steaks from the walk-in cooler and cooking them right on the coals, comparing notes on women, giving each other advice, gabbing and arguing till three in the morning, or four: almost Turkey Time, as we had jokingly come to call the dawn. We none of us were likely to see the damn turkeys.

I asked Sandy to read the manuscript of the novel I was working on. He read diligently, night by night, for a month, eschewing his *Bride's*. When he got done he brought me the book, put it in my hands. "I'm not so sure about this," he said, trying to be of help. "It's not like *The Catcher in the Rye*." *The Catcher in the Rye,* as it turned out, was the only other book Sandy had ever read. "Also, I think you made some things up."

"It's a *novel,*" I told him. "I made it *all* up."

One night I sat up late at the bar with Marlene. She was stocky, strong and pretty, still in her waitress uniform. She and Ricky had broken up two months before, and now, she said, she was lonely. I told her in turn that I knew — I could tell — Juliet had a boyfriend at Camp Ramapo, not too serious, I didn't think, but I was kind of lonely, too.

"Is that why you drink so much?" Marlene said.

I had no answer for that.

The doors to the inn were locked, of course — it was three in the morning — so when I looked out the window and saw Ricky coming up the walk to the taproom door I just jumped up to let him in. Marlene said, "Oh-oh." I was drunk enough to ignore that subtle warning, just opened the door and watched Ricky's scarred knuckles coming at me swiftly. The fist hit my grinning mouth, which was still saying hi. Then his other fist hit me in the eye. I lay down on the floor, just got down — *you win* — which had worked in the past, but that wasn't enough for Ricky. He kicked me in the ribs and in the ear with his big motorcycle boots, then sat on my back and began to pummel my head.

I had to get back up. I was bigger than Ricky, and stronger, so it was simple: I stood up with him on my back. He choked me with one hand and slugged me with the other while I looked around the room desperately. There was Marlene, seeming proud of Ricky's prowess, which didn't seem fair. Next to Marlene was the inn's glassware hutch, an antique monster full of good wineglasses, mostly, and a few fancy plates. I lurched over to it and spun around fast, thinking I'd knock Ricky off against it. The plates rattled in there and fell; the wineglasses tinkled, smashing; Ricky leapt away.

We faced off again, Ricky holding up his fists, looking grim, not saying anything, nothing at all. "Okay, Ricky," I said, trying to stare him down, "that's enough. Stop it. There's nothing going on between Marlene and me, and you guys broke up a long time ago anyway."

Marlene shrieked, "Stop it, Ricky! Ricky, stop it!" and variations on that theme, over and over, but did nothing to interfere. I began to understand that she had set me up to show herself how much Ricky loved her. "You'll kill him!" she cried.

Kill. Rapidly I realized that I had to take a position here. Ricky was a wiry little bastard. I made a sincere face, said, "Come, on, Ricky. Let's stop it. We're friends, remember? What's the problem?" Pure empathy. Ricky leaned toward me, faked with a left, which I blocked, and smashed me once again in the face with his right. He was an experienced fighter, terrific with his hands. I pondered the situation in one of those roomy moments that arrive in times of crisis: *I have already tried going down, which didn't work at all. I have tried reason. I have tried empathy. But wait . . . I am bigger than Ricky. Perhaps it is time to fight.* I squared off, strode, and swung with a mighty right. Ricky ducked me easily; I fell into him. Now at least I could hug him. Fighting wasn't my strength; strength was my strength. I was a plumber, a carpenter, a lifter of great piles of wood, a cutter of pipe, a demolisher of walls, a setter of tile, a pounder of nails, a mixer of cement. My arms were as big and strong as a bear's. I could feel Ricky's chest crack in my hug.

Ricky stomped my stocking feet (I'd got comfortable at the bar) with his motorcycle boots. He burst out of my grip. We faced off again. I could hear Marlene hollering upstairs for Charlie and Marybell. Ricky got off a shot to my mouth. I felt my lower teeth pop through the inside of my lip, paused again to consider. I had twice before served as a punching bag, but on each of those occasions when I had gone down — *uncle!* — the fight was over. I'd never fought to the death.

I ran into the kitchen through the IN door, then out of the kitchen through the OUT door. Ricky was right behind me through the IN door, but in the parlor I was alone. Okay: I'd fooled him. It was over. I stood amidst the grand furnishings, the antique chairs, the table stacked neatly with old *Yankee* magazines and *Antiques Today* magazines and magazines about country living. I breathed, touched my

face. I felt terribly drunk and incapable of defending myself, decided simply to go upstairs and get into my bed.
Then I heard the familiar swish of the OUT door. Ricky
came into the parlor, still grim, still not speaking, holding a
big wooden pasta paddle, an implement as big and hard as
a baseball bat.

"You're going to hurt me," I said, belaboring the obvious.
Ricky stepped toward me. I looked in his eye, knowing that
to turn my back would be a disaster. "Ricky," I said. I
picked a big old steel poker out of the rack by the elegantly
restored parlor fireplace. Ricky approached coolly, deftly
knocked the poker out of my hands with the spaghetti
paddle, then bapped me on the head. In the movies, people
are easy to knock out. In real life, it's hard. I stayed wide
awake and on my feet, thinking very slowly as I made a run
for it, back into the taproom.

Then Charlie and Marybell were there, and Marlene.
Marybell, who was fifty-six years old, got Ricky around the
waist, which didn't stop him, exactly, but hindered him
enough that Charlie was able to get the paddle away from
him. Then Marybell's daughter Lois came down the big
main staircase. Lois was the pastry chef, and she was large,
an aerobics buff and weight lifter, strong as Ricky and I put
together, mean as a seven-layer honey-coconut cake. She
got ahold of Ricky from the front, hugged him, incapacitat-
ing him with her strength, but also with her love, which
was enormous. It was the love that stopped him cold. Everyone talked, then shouted — finally some noise.

Marlene, weeping with delight at all the attention, explained some of what had happened, making it sound as if
she and I had been on a date. Ricky still had not said a word.
I stepped close, as quiet as he, and reached over all of the
heads and arms to hit him, at least once, but he ducked,

experienced fighter, ducked so I only grazed his head and
infuriated him more. Now he hit Lois until she let go,
pushed Marybell out of the way, plowed past Charlie and
let me have it, six more shots before the assembled throng
could subdue him once more.

Suddenly he slumped in their arms. "I'm sorry," he said,
his first words of the night. Everyone rather gradually let
go of him, and, head down, he slunk out of the taproom,
back through the kitchen and outside, to get on his chopped
and bored-out Kawasaki 1000, a very nasty bike.

I sat alone at the bar then, drunkenly having declared myself unhurt and having convinced everyone else to go to
bed. Five minutes later, Sandy Elliott arrived in his Corvette, roaring forty miles an hour up the driveway. Marlene
had called him. He sat me down and looked in my eyes,
pulled on my lip, poked at my ribs. "In my opinion," he
said, "you're going to the hospital, right now." The phras-
ing was a joke, an imitation of the way I phrased my own
suggestions to helpers.

In the Corvette, looking out over its long nose, we spec-
ulated. Ricky had punched out a pile of china plates a couple
of months back. Forty stitches' worth, severed ligaments in
his hand. He'd been in other fights, too, hadn't he? Clearly,
beneath the likable surface he was a troubled guy, someone
to pity.

At the hospital I waited for two hours, although there
were no other emergency customers. Sandy sat loyally beside me, reading *Woman's Day*. He was trying to understand women. I could put my tongue straight through a
hole in my lower lip; my right eye was swelling closed; I
had a pretty bad headache somewhere behind the beery
haze. I pictured Juliet fussing over my wounds, holding a

cold compress to my head, feeding me soup. The admitting nurse was not impressed with my condition, didn't want to wake anybody on account of a smelly drunk who got punched out by a friend, at least not until I tried to smile at her and the blood in my mouth fell out. "Oh my," she said. In a minute a sleepy intern was stitching me up. He wanted x-rays. I didn't want to pay for x-rays. "Maybe your violent friend should pay," the intern said. He left the room, but came back in time to see Sandy and me sneaking out to the Corvette. Caught, I went back in for x-rays as the sky began to lighten in the east.

About six A.M. Sandy drove me back to the inn. We split one last beer, ate a couple of handfuls of cake from Lois's part of the walk-in. Then Sandy happened to look out the big window that faced the back hill from the kitchen. There, beneath the six cranky old apple trees, strutting and bobbing, pecking at rotted apples, looking warily about, pecking again, was a flock of twenty or so wild turkeys, deep brown and bronze and iridescent, happily inelegant. "Look at this," Sandy said. I went to the window, looking with my one eye, pleased. The turkeys at last.

Sandy started to open the door, to go out there. "Don't," I said querulously, wanting to see them. But he had started the motion and inertia carried him through, straight out onto the driveway. At the sound of the squeaking hinges, the turkeys only gobbled, but at the sight of big Sandy lumbering out the door, they took off, running, astonishingly fleet of foot, their heads thrust before them on their long necks, racing single file up the hill, straight through the parking lot, past the garden and the dump, past a big, solitary pine and back into the woods.

"I wanted to look at them," I said, anger rising finally, all the anger of the night, all the anger I couldn't muster in the midst of the fight (and all the anger of my miserable life, all my anger at Jules). "I've been waiting months to see them!"

"Sorry," Sandy said, surprised at my sudden emotion.

We stood there in the driveway for a long moment, looking after the birds. Sandy turned to me finally, shrugging. "Turkeys," he said, and that simple word seemed to say everything that needed to be said. "Turkeys," and we turned to each other and laughed, then laughed harder yet as the sun first broke the distant ridge to the east, laughed until the breakfast chef arrived, rattling up the long driveway in her rusty, ancient Cadillac.

I called Juliet late that afternoon, left a message with whoever answered the pay phone in that beer hall of a counselors' lounge down there, left a message that I'd been injured, feeling finely sorry for myself. My left eyeball was pure red where the white should have been. My right eye was closed. My head pounded. I had various bruises, the worst of which was on the bridge of my foot, where Ricky had thought to stomp me. I stayed in bed, more because of my hangover than my wounds, also hurting because Juliet didn't call back.

At dinnertime Lois came in with some beautiful soup she had made and a note from Ricky. It was a Hallmark get well card with a picture of a frog wearing a bag of ice on his head:

Dear Bill, I am sorry. You've been a good friend to me and I shouldn't be beating you up. I am going to look for help from a Shrink, like you have said before. Like you sing (so badly), you always hurt the one you love. I am sorry, let me say it again. I think I am going to go down to New York for a while, or maybe a long time, so you don't have to see my face.

Love, Ricky.

P.S. You are a terrible fighter.

After dinner the hospital called. My x-rays showed a hairline skull fracture, just in front of my ear.

After a few days, my headache started to go away and I went back to work. I wasn't allowed to drive. I must have called Camp Ramapo sixteen or twenty times, giving more and more details of my injuries to uninterested counselors who had happened by the ringing pay phone. Juliet didn't call for five whole days. "You shouldn't fight," was all she said.

"You've got a boyfriend down there?"

"Fighting only leads to trouble."

"Who is your boyfriend down there?"

"That's not important. It's not an important thing." She didn't sound convincing.

"To me it's an important thing, especially when you haven't called."

"Are you still picking me up on Friday?"

"I guess," I said. We talked a little more and hung up.

On Friday we were supposed to take a weekend and go down to Martha's Vineyard, place of our hearts, to try and find a shack to rent for August. But in the intervening days, as there were no calls from Juliet, I decided enough was enough. Infatuation had carried me through two years of her youthful inconstancy, but now it was time to be done with it. A lot of fish in the sea, and all that. So on Friday, in contravention to doctor's orders, I drove down to Rhinebeck, met Jules in the familiar parking lot in front of that decadent counselors' lounge. I hadn't wanted to break it off over the phone, wanted to see her once more. And there in the parking lot I bluntly announced it: "You've got another boyfriend, so I don't see any point in going to the Vineyard with you. You aren't there when I need you, so I don't see any point in keeping up our friendship. You're young," I said, wizened old bird of thirty years, "so I understand, but I can't put up with it anymore."

"Okay," Juliet said. "Do you think we could go out for breakfast at least? I'm starving."

At breakfast my black eyes fairly dripped with tears, and I didn't eat at all. Juliet finished her plate, then went ahead "as long as you're not hungry" and ate mine too. She let it be known the guy was good-looking, and let it be known that he was young, even younger than she. She let it be known further that she would be stranded at camp if I didn't take her away. After breakfast, steadfast in my determination to break it off, I drove her back to camp. When she got out of the car, I drove two big circles around her, then drove away.

Later, much later, she let it be known that she had been hurting, too, even as she chowed down, but didn't know how to say it.

Sandy Elliott took care of me. He wasn't too concerned about the fractured skull or the damaged eyes; those things were supposed to heal. He took great pleasure in pretending to stomp on my foot, and liked to watch me flinch at fake punches. No, Sandy's concern was for my broken heart. He made sure I had things to do at night, took me to the various bars in the county, introduced me to crazy women he knew, even showed me a place where he said they sold *Bride's*

Magazine, which had comforted him after his wife had split. On Sundays, the day I normally would go down to Ramapo, he refused to let me be alone, dragged me out for golf with his brothers, dragged me to his house to watch baseball games, drove me over to Albany for a party at his mother's house, anything but leave me to my misery.

The last weekend I spent at the inn (the very last; I've never been back; something about the fight spoiled the spirit of the place for me, though I hear business is booming, and the grounds are more beautiful than ever) and before I headed to the Vineyard with Zeeman (Jules on her way to California with her young prince), Sandy — detecting some Sunday afternoon melancholy — commanded me to take a walk with him. No way to say no when Sandy got an idea. He rousted me out from behind whatever book I was reading, lifted me out of bed, dragged me outside. Up past the gardens he marched me, past the old farmhouse dump, into the airy climax forest and to the top of the hill.

A long way back in the woods, at a clearing, we sat down in companionable silence, looked out through the thin spring foliage to the mountains beyond the Stockbridge Bowl — what should have been perfect peace. Sandy wore loafers and white socks, of all things, his uniform for work that night. We leaned against trees on opposite sides of the clearing, maybe napped a little — surely we had hangovers — lounged there in the early summer sun.

"Shit," Sandy said.

I looked where he was looking, and there they came, turkeys, fifteen or more of the chuckling, iridescent boneheads, picking and pecking their way toward us through the wood — stopping to look, picking, flicking acorns up, stopping to look some more, snapping up insects. The turkeys were uniform in size except for two particularly fat ones. The lead bird, whom the rest seemed to follow (not the biggest, or the most elegant), bore a beard that stuck from its breast and hung almost to the ground. The birds looked exactly like the cutouts we used to tape around Mrs. Lindstrom's class in second grade.

Sandy and I stayed still as stumps, watching. The birds flipped through the leaves noisily, muttering to themselves, poking one another and pecking sticks, their tailfeathers long and striped and sticking out behind.

After two short minutes of observation, I heard the ineluctable chuckle coming up in Sandy's breast. When the laugh finally erupted, though, the birds did not stir; indeed, several of them seemed to gobble in response. But when I turned my head ever so slightly toward Sandy to glare, the lead bird took notice. He took no time to consider or to decide about the level of our benignity but turned and flew, one, big, leaf-scattering flap from his standing position to take the air, then silent flight almost straight up, then over the understory trees and away. The other birds took wing instantaneously without looking up to see what the problem might be, flapping loudly at the ground, then silently escaping through the forest breezes to a big old white pine three hundred yards downhill, only partly hidden by the new leaves of the trees around it.

"Turkeys," Sandy said, shrugging, making a heroic effort not to laugh.

"Let's get a look at them," I said. We were good enough friends by then that I didn't have to say I was annoyed. We got up and walked quietly down the hill to within two hundred feet of the big pine tree, where we were able to clearly see the turkeys shifting around up there, quite aware of us. We stood still. The turkeys, silhouetted against the bright afternoon sky, might as well have been giant, stupid pinecones, one or two to a branch. Apparently it was all too much. Sandy's great chest heaved; he grinned helplessly; he snorted and giggled, then exploded in laughter. "Goddamnit," I said, not softly. And at that the turkeys took off, exactly simultaneously, up into the sky, above the trees, gaining height fast, then gliding gorgeously out of sight toward town.

Sandy patted me on the back by way of a silent apology for scaring the birds away, though he must have known it was my cursing that had done it. He tried to look sorry, too, but it didn't last; suddenly he grinned, hard, trying to hold back a big laugh, and that grin (a handsome one, full of fine white teeth) got hold of my troubles and pulled them off my chest, slowly, pulled them out into the open in the clean air between us, where we laughed in their faces, louder and louder, standing in the woods. "Turkeys," Sandy said. And we laughed harder, and harder yet, just standing there facing each other, laughed till we were choking with it, till there wasn't a trouble left within a hundred miles; laughed until we had to sit, then laughed lying in the leaves; laughed until there wasn't a laugh left in us, or a turkey in the woods.

Cross Canada

Oh! Canada. Canada, end to end! Canada, that beautiful, ambivalent country lying up there like a happy Labrador retriever. Canada, trying to do everything right and getting no credit from her big, violent, greedy, sloppy, fat and lazy sister downstairs. Canada, twelve provinces, three oceans, two seas. Canada, with her cold winds and clear air, her lakes and mountains, her rivers and plains. The northern nothing! The southern all! Canada, where the roads stop and the ice begins! Oh! Canada. Canada, end to end!

In December of 1984, when at last I'd gotten used to being single again, and when at last I'd remembered how to date and be comfortable with women whose friendship mightn't lead to romance, Juliet returned to New York. She'd left her new beau behind in California: he'd apparently shaved his head, refused to work or change his clothes, had slept with one of her friends, and had generally proved difficult to deal with (though he was as handsome as ever).

Safely at home in the Meat District, I was reluctant to give up my freedom or my happiness. I'd been burned now several times by Jules and by her youth, so regarded her (and it) warily, though with affection and a certain degree of lust. She seemed to fall right back into place, however;

after all, she knew all my friends, every corner of my room, some of the odder corners of my brain. I held on, however, stubbornly hanging out with my other women friends, giving Juliet no higher position than they had deigned to hold. I remained unvanquished until March, when she convinced me that the best thing to do with all that money from my new one-man tiling and remodeling business was to take her and only her and her steady new heart to Jamaica.

In the plane something started to click, the two of us laughing in the air above the Florida Keys, holding hands over Cuba. On the beach and the cliffs of Negril we had fun, we laughed, we kissed like new friends, made love like old pals. We snorkeled and dove and hiked; we ate well and danced hard and swam, and gradually I let our romance back into its battered place in my heart.

"Tell me you'll stop seeing D — — ," Jules kept saying. "Tell me you'll stop seeing T — — ."

After one week I promised on D — — , but T — — took the whole two weeks, and then some.

Home in New York, Jules got a job waitressing at a self-consciously haughty restaurant across from Lincoln Center, found an apartment in Soho with a new waitress friend, and we settled into our exclusive relationship again, thinking bromidically that what hadn't killed it had made it stronger. As for D — — , she had happened to meet Mr. Right during the very weeks I was away. As for T — — , breaking it off might have been harder, but she got transferred by her multinational employer to Berlin and was ready for the change.

Juliet and I also started throwing dimes and quarters and dollar bills into a sealed can, to see how much we could save for a summer trip. Somewhere in the back of my mind a plan was brewing, a plan that I'd originally brought up with T — —, a plan for a glorious camping trip, ocean to ocean across Canada. The only problem was Jon Zeeman's newly announced wedding (to one Ingelin, a very blond, very intelligent and very fiery woman he'd met in Norway); the nuptials would take place August third, smack in the middle of the summer.

I know there are those who disdain car camping; in fact, I myself disdain car camping, but you can't backpack 15,000 miles in two months, and that's how many miles Juliet and I traveled during the summer of 1985. There's a good argument (and Juliet still makes it) for the proposition that there is no point in traveling 15,000 miles in two months, especially when your adventure is capped by running out of gas on the New Jersey Turnpike twenty miles from home on the last day of the trip.

But I'm getting ahead of myself.

In June, Juliet and I cracked the seal on the money can and counted out more than $125 in nickels, dimes and quarters (in those days before I was connected to bank-card cash machines I'd picked the dollar bills out, one by one, when I'd needed money for beer) and bought a good tent. In June, too, I sold my Berkshires mobile for twice what I'd paid for it (still not much), and feeling lucky, began to look for a pickup truck, something big and bulky and trusty and true, something we could load all our junk in and *go,* something I could subsequently use for my construction business, something I could park around New York without worrying about dents and dings and the temptation of thieves. On the conventional advice of a thousand barflies ("The thing to do when you want a used car is to go down south! No rust! Used-car heaven!"), I got my dad to cosign a bank loan, borrowed my brother Doug's VW Rabbit and drove down to North Carolina, dragging Juliet along. Four days of remorse — how on earth do you answer classified ads when you're camping? What phone number do you leave? How do you find street addresses when you've never even heard of the *town*? — ended with the impulsive purchase of a solid-looking 1978 Ford F-100 pickup for $2,000 from a very slick dealer. The truck was yellow, was big, was trusty and true, and most important, *it had no rust.*

Juliet's driver's license was brand new (although she was twenty-three — New York City teens don't *need* to drive; their vehicular rite of passage has to do with taxis and late-night subway trips to Brooklyn), and her driving was understandably tentative, especially in the enormous pickup truck. At that time, too, she was unable to drive a stick shift, with which, unfortunately, Doug's Rabbit was equipped. On the way down, I'd shifted for her while she nervously worked the clutch. Once we were up to highway speed she hadn't a care in the world. On the way back north, however, we had two vehicles, and in the Rabbit she'd have to shift for herself. A classic dilemma: unwieldy truck or wicked clutch? We thought of towing the Rabbit but couldn't afford to rent a tow bar; we thought of selling the Rabbit, but it was Doug's, after all, and probably he expected it back.

In the end, extremely unhappy with me, Jules drove the truck. We made our way slowly the nine hundred miles to Enfield, New Hampshire, where my folks were staying at their summer place on Lake Mascoma (in the upper valley of the Connecticut River), and where it would be possible to register and insure the truck for one fourth of what it might cost in New York. After a few days of logistical hell, the truck was ready for Canada: registered, insured, waxed, polished, lubed, and generally fixed up. With the last of my money from the bank loan I bought a cap to enclose the bed, and finally we were ready to go. We divided up our already dwindling pile of cash so we couldn't lose it all at once, climbed in the truck, plugged Juliet's little tape deck into the cigarette lighter, waved good-bye to my parents, and were off.

I drove clear to the Maine coast, then drove some more, as Juliet refused to take over. She wanted to wait for a big road, a highway with twenty lanes to drive on. We stopped at Camden Hills State Park above Camden, got out the tent, and camped. In the morning, Juliet gritted her teeth and climbed into the driver's seat. She clutched the wheel tightly and would brook no conversation or music. She didn't like to stop for Stop signs, didn't like it when cars tried to pass, but we did make progress, steady and sure. Just outside Acadia National Park we stopped for ice cream at a drive-in snack bar. On the way out, poor Jules backed over their nine-foot-high curbside triple-decker ice cream cone. The lady who owned the place came running out, brandishing a hammer, hollering: "I've had it! Don't you *look* when you back up? Do you think we've got nothing better to do than pick up after assholes like you? Big vacation, knocking over property! I hope you drown!"

"We're good swimmers," I said lamely, meaning it as an apology.

By the time we reached Canada we were ragged. We'd spent more nights in Maine than we'd meant to, as Jules refused to get in the truck the third morning, then refused to drive on the fourth (it was hot in the truck, and loud, and *stupid*). We hadn't had a shower for days. Our hair stood out in great frightened fans, our clothes were sootstained from campfires. Juliet had been bitten in the corner of her eye and on her ear and all over her neck by black flies, and all the bites — she's allergic — were grotesquely swollen. She looked as though she'd been slugged in the head a couple of times really hard, then strangled.

At the Campobello Island customs station, at the end of the bridge from Maine, the customs lady glared at me, looked sympathetically at Jules, and made us get out of the car. She checked everything: ashtray, visors, engine compartment, seats. Piece by piece, she had us empty the back of the truck. We could only disappoint her with an extraordinarily mundane lack of contraband: paintbox, spare tire, camera, typewriter, loose books, pots and pans. She had apparently never seen golf clubs before, or a tent, or sleeping bags, or even a hibachi. She inspected my toolboxes and opened the handles of my utility knives to check the new blades stored inside for traces of drugs. She looked in our hubcaps, lay under the truck and knocked on the muffler, climbed up on top of the cap to look in the ends of the boat-rack tubing, smelled our toothpaste, broke our candles. In the end she had to let us pass, poor thing, let us pass to do our evil work on Canada.

From the beaches of Campobello we swam in the Bay of Fundy, where the water is something like zero degrees Kelvin (you know, absolute zero, −270 degrees Fahrenheit, in which cold all motion stops and all life ceases). The beach, though, was profoundly pleasing, rocky and desolate, alive with terns and sea gulls and racing pipers, strewn with driftwood. We thought to make love by a polished old tree trunk miles from nowhere, but at a crucial moment I noticed that a distant bird-watcher had his binoculars on us and seemed to have his own pants down. I actually ran after him, not sure what to do if I caught him.

On the ferry from Campobello to Deer Island we spotted whales; on the ferry from Deer Island to the mainland, New Brunswick, we saw a famed tidal bore, a whirlpool three feet across, formed by the onrush of a twenty-foot tide, rising. From New Brunswick we ferried on to Prince Edward Island.

On P.E.I. the sand was red, the rocks were red, the seaweed was red (dulse, laid out to dry on all the rockier beaches — food for the Japanese, as one fellow, raking it, explained). P.E.I. is the smallest province in Canada, onion fields and airy woods, very flat, an English countryside condensed and preserved in just a couple of thousand square miles.

At night the wind tugged at our tent, distorted it, sang through its mosquito netting, kept us awake, added to Juliet's general misery. One morning, while I tried to pacify her with promises of more pleasant camping to come, our neighbor's tent rolled past, very fast, the sleeping bags inside tumbling visibly as in an old-fashioned dryer.

From P.E.I. we headed to Nova Scotia, due south. But, to go cross Canada, as Jules pointed out, at some juncture we were going to have to head west. The thing was (as *I* pointed out), Zeeman wasn't going to be married until August third, in Vermont, and this was only July sixteenth. Jules thought it was stupid to hang around. "Hovering," she called it with disgust. "Knowing Jon, the wedding will be canceled anyway."

In Halifax, Juliet insisted on a few hours' city time. She wasn't feeling right, she said, not enough stimulation, too many damn trees, too much campfire cooking. I began to protest, but her desire was so energetic that I gave in, muttering about our budget, which was quite simple: camping was cheap, so camping was in; hotels were expensive, so hotels were out. We had no credit cards, just pockets full of cash that had to last nearly two months more.

We found a camping place twenty miles east of Halifax

at Porter's Lake Provincial Park, got set up, then headed in to the old town, Juliet driving, more cheerful than she'd been for the entire three weeks since we'd left New York for North Carolina. At a sunset-lit mom-and-pop gas station, she tried to get nice and close to the pump, and did, crashing into it at sufficient speed to stove it in and set it cockeyed on its base. When I pointed this out (in rather a loud voice, I'm sorry to say), Juliet just drove on as if nothing had happened, drove right to the exit. It was not that she meant to evade responsibility; it was just that she had no idea what to do — no one had mentioned car accidents to her in all those ridiculous driving lessons! I convinced her to stop. The gas station man came running, angry, but once he saw Juliet's stricken face he calmed down, took her name, her address. He wanted to know why the car was registered in New Hampshire if she was from New York. "I thought it was North Carolina," she said, turning to me accusingly. "It's North Carolina, isn't it?" Her Michigan license confused the gas man further. He asked, since I was the owner of the truck, to see my license, too. Connecticut. "Living cheaply," I explained, "is always complicated." In the end, he said he had insurance for these things and to go away.

Halifax is an old whaling town with a fort overlooking a modern harbor. It's a college town, too, its nightlife famous, at least in Nova Scotia. We spent the price of two full tanks of gas on dinner, then made a long visit to the waterfront shopping district, one of those hip restorations that gets rid of all the bars and the bums and puts paint and French windows on buildings that never saw a frilly curtain in four hundred years. We looked at beautiful dresses and floppy sun hats and hundred-dollar bras. College-boy maître d's beckoned from restaurants owned by enormous chains. Juliet began to cheer up. Maybe she'd go to graduate school here! The simple sight of an ice cream parlor without a hazard-strewn parking lot filled her with giddy good spirits. Pity was, there would be no more restaurants this trip. Our budget wouldn't have it. At two in the morning we crawled back to our campsite, I at the wheel, Jules asleep and dreaming of hors d'oeuvres and waiters and fancy, expensive desserts.

Next night we bought a whole salmon for five Canadian dollars from a fisherman in Port Hastings, built a fire on the side of a mountain in Whycocomagh Provincial Park, Cape Breton Island, and cooked the fish, along with four big P.E.I. potatoes and a couple of zucchinis. We drank Canadian beer, watched the sunset, discussed the nature of the universe: "I just don't think it's worth hanging around for Jon Zeeman's wedding," Juliet said. She wanted to get out west. "Why couldn't he have it in the spring like any other person? Why are we *hovering*?"

"The best man needs to make an appearance," I said, impassioned, as I fished from the fire four incinerated potatoes, charcoal black except for one perfect and exalted and very small bite at the center of each.

The Cape Breton Highlands were a revelation, the first of the magnificent natural wonders I'd promised Juliet, and an irrefutable counter to her charge of hovering. Though I'd had no idea of the Highlands' grandeur, I tried to take some credit for it: a highly forested plateau rising nearly two thousand feet straight out of a sea full of spouting whales. Ingonish, a little fishing town, was Scots down to the accents of its inhabitants, who were not quite friendly, tired, by July, of tourists. Here the Gulf Stream, having missed the reticent Gulf of Maine and Bay of Fundy, was back in charge of the water temperature. We swam at a small beach that was divided by a sun-heated salmon creek. Jules was more pleased than she'd been even in Halifax.

I was pleased, too. The idea of the trip wasn't to torture anyone, after all. The idea of the trip was to share my one greatest love with the other, and here in the Highlands something like that was beginning to happen. Jules looked out over the ocean, trying to spot whales. She sat with me at the edge of a pond, watching fish rise, and listened to what I remembered of my childhood fishing days. She suggested a hike along the ocean, found a trail that took us through curiously carved volcanic escarpments covered in fragrant juniper. From the foundations of a ruined house we watched whales and sailboats and surf plumes and clouds.

"I wish we could just stay here," she said.

"Newfoundland's nicer yet!"

"But Newfoundland is *east*."

True. I wanted to go on to Newfoundland, not just to see that miraculous place but to have the opportunity to set my watch ahead one half hour. Also, we had to kill another week before Jon's nuptials. To appease Juliet, who had the bizarre notion that something might have gone wrong with the wedding plans, I called Jon.

"I guess you got the message from your father," he said, first thing.

"No," I said, keeping it simple.

"Well, put it this way: the wall of the hallway across from my room is caved in, and Ingelin's back in Norway."

Westward! We took a ferry back to the mainland, then drove on, up and over Maine through New Brunswick (a kind of Old World Maryland), then down along the St. Lawrence Seaway into Quebec, watching the ships at work,

acamping and afighting. Juliet was smug about her predic-
tion in the matter of Jon's wedding, and that, of course, was
annoying. I kept telling her she was having a good time
if only she'd realize it, which statement, of course, infuriated her. We continually forgot the two golden rules of
argument-free road tripping: eat when hungry; nap when
tired.

Juliet demanded the wheel when she felt like driving,
refused to drive when she didn't. She coursed all over the
road, ignored Yield signs, parked on sidewalks, honked
when she was in the wrong. She let me know she felt she'd
been forced out on this trip. I remembered aloud that my
original plans for Canada had been made with T — — ;
Juliet remembered that T — — had big ears. I thought
maybe a trip with old Shave-Head would have been more
fun for Jules; she agreed, heartily — at least he had a trust
fund, and they could have stayed in motels! The fight, at
bottom, had nothing to do with us. The fight, at bottom,
was between each of us and any form of commitment,
between each of us and adulthood, between each of us and
a feeling of trapped dependence that was heightened and
illustrated by the confines of the truck's big cab. Also, I
think, both of us were still angry about the previous summer's breakup. Both of us threatened to get out and hitch-
hike at least twice, but both of us stayed on. We racked up
the miles.

I tried to slip past Montreal one bright morning, but
Juliet was reading the signs, too. By midafternoon we were
at La Ronde in the old World's Fair site, absorbing amuse-
ment park culture. We watched water-skiing practice, for
that was free. We went to the aquarium and watched pen-
guins flying underwater around a circular tank. Joy! We
watched people spinning and flying and plummeting on
rides that were too expensive for us, and too nauseating in

any case. We drove out at closing time, deep in the night, dead from exhaustion, drove out of the city to the Paul Sauvé Provincial Park on the Ottawa River, where we dragged out the tent, set it up, and camped.

In Ontario we drove. The land was on the flat side, all woods and water. "Too many trees!" Juliet said. "I'm sick of trees!" She had a point. There were a lot of damn trees — hemlocks, spruces, firs — and they were pretty similar, nine hundred miles of them. Ontario goes on forever: Ottawa, Arnprior, Renfrew, Pembroke, Petawawa, Deep River, Stonecliff, Mattawa, Northbay, Sturgeon Falls, Markstay, Sudbury, Lively, Nairn, Espanola, Massey, Spanish, Algoma Mills, Blind River, Iron Bridge, Bruce Mines, Echo Bay, Sault Sainte Marie. As we climbed over Lake Superior it might have been the same miles of road repeated over and over. We were hamsters in a treadmill. Wawa was lost in fog. Marathon was hardly Spartan enough a name. Terrace Bay, Schrieber, Nipigon, Red Rock.

The top side of Lake Superior was surprisingly clean, the water all but frozen, however. We took another day off, made a detour to see some Indian paintings. We hiked back into the deep forest, hiked along the wild shore of the lake. The paintings were astonishing, etched a thousand years ago into lakeside cliffs by mystics standing on ladders in canoes. "This beats La Ronde," I said.

"Nothing beats La Ronde," Juliet said.

"Well, it's better than Halifax."

"There's nothing here but trees. In Halifax, there's trees *and* a town."

In Manitoba, Juliet's mood took a turn for the worse. My Venus in Blue Jeans wore a paper Burger King crown and sang nonstop as we rolled past the cornfields. She whipped up an imitation of Cher that was just as painful as the real thing, repeatedly singing "Gypsies, Tramps and Thieves," well pleased, for a hundred miles, until lunch. That afternoon, she sang extraordinarily loud selections from *The Sound of Music,* her head thrown back, arms spread, eyes glazed. I was afraid to ask her to drive.

Before Canada, before Juliet, I had thought of cities as places to avoid on road trips. I did whatever I could to drive around them, but Jules insisted we see them all. We missed Winnipeg, Manitoba, only because it turned up early in the morning while she was sleeping. But in Saskatoon, Saskatchewan, she coaxed me off the highway. In that handsome frontier town (childhood home of Joni Mitchell!) we found ourselves staring: ranchers, schoolmarms, Indians, boys playing hoop. We felt as if we'd stepped into a *Star Trek* version of a Wild West town. We took a walk, ate further ice cream, talked to folks for the first time in days.

In Edmonton, Alberta, after a hard night of camping in the rain near Vermilion, we slogged around under thunderheads. I sputtered and fumed, worried that we'd never find a decent place to camp; Juliet made it clear I should keep quiet — if she wanted a nature boy, she'd go find John Denver. I retorted with some arch wisdom about city girls, but in the end Juliet's fearsome silence did me in.

We read menus at the best restaurants in Edmonton. We tried on shoes. We rode the escalators in two different upscale department stores. We asked a group of sullen teens where the movie theater was. *Back to the Future,* brand new that summer, owned the advantage of having nothing whatsoever to do with our little war. We laughed; we cried; we watched uncritically, sitting just as we sat in the truck, side by side, facing forward. When we came out of the theater, roused and cheered, the storm had passed. The sky was clear blue and beckoned us west into the mountains whose presence we could already feel. We camped after a short two hours more in the truck, joyfully pulling the tent out from under the other junk and setting it up in the woods.

The next morning we drove on, ever westward, over the high dry plains. For entertainment Juliet told me the plots of Broadway musicals, sang me the songs in their original-cast-album order, every word, every note, imitating the instruments where necessary, setting the scenes for me magically. She knew an extra-human range of obscure shows from a childhood of weekly theater attendance (her mother had had a successful acting career in the fifties, had retired when Juliet was born). Juliet sang from familiar shows, oh, *Fiddler on the Roof*, sure, and *Oliver*, but also from *Damn Yankees, By Jupiter, Bedknobs and Broomsticks* and *The Flatulist* (not even a musical, this last one, but she sang, she sang!).

In Edson, Alberta, the Rocky Mountains came into view, joyous snowy peaks, a long blue line of anticipation, looming up from the very curve of the earth. With our arms out the windows of the broiling truck, we sang "There's No Business Like Show Business" and sped onward, onward, into the sky. Our enforced encapsulation together was making us more like each other every day.

In downtown Jasper, dusk, we saw a black bear cross the street. Thrilled, we watched it enter a backyard. It sniffed at some garbage, then went to the kitchen door of a well-lit house. Through a big picture window we could see a little girl practicing ballet in her tutu. Heroes, we raced to a nearby motel to summon the Mounties. The desk person barely understood what we were saying. It was as if in New York we'd raced into a hotel to report a pigeon on the sidewalk. "A black bear's a normal sight here 'round," the desk lady said blandly. "Nothing more than a big raccoon, eh? Such a nuisance, such a nuisance . . ." Jules and I shrugged, pleased. We'd made a mistake together for a change and could laugh as the dark came down, and laugh as we looked for a place to camp.

At Whistlers Campground in Jasper National Park, we hugged and kissed and cooed and contrived to make love in the front of the truck, then set up for a long stay. A harem of female elk wandered past our site at dusk, squeaking to each other like rusty hinges. The buck came through an hour later, threatening cars in his path, hunching up his shoulders, pulling back his head, thrashing bushes with his great antlers. The snowfields on the tall peaks around us caught the light of a late sunset. People coughed in the campsites around us. Day-Glo-colored lichens hung from the limbs of the lodgepole pines. Thunder in the distance. Thunder closer. The temperature dropped. We set up Big Blue, our enormous K mart tarp (which Juliet hated for the noise it made in the wind) and built a fire as the rain came on.

Not much later, I dug two big cans of Dinty Moore beef stew out of the back of our glorious, rustfree truck, opened them both with a knife and balanced them on a very smoky fire in the rain. When the stew was hot I ate happily straight from the can, to Juliet's shivering disgust, watched as she climbed behind the wheel of the truck, threatening to find a good restaurant on her own. What a noise the driver's door made, caving in, as she hit the stout marker post for our campsite!

From Jasper we headed south down the Glacier Highway, enjoying the cheerful new rush of wind through the thoroughly caved-in driver's door of the truck. The Maligne

Mountains were rugged and benign, couching icefields that bred the Athabasca River. The Athabasca flows weirdly north, milky from glacial algaes, falling down the slope of the Arctic Divide, down which all rivers flow to the Arctic Ocean. We hadn't paused to pack tightly; Big Blue was stuffed wet in the back along with our blankets and cooler, pillows and dishes, interesting rocks and unused golf clubs.

We camped on Honeymoon Lake. Again the sun shone, again life was beautiful. Honeymoon Lake is one of a series of small lakes that sits beneath a line of sharply carved mountain peaks that stretch south, marching in glorious perspective, covered with landslides and loose rock, so steep that nothing can grow on them, not even glaciers. After we'd set up the tent and had cooked good chicken, Juliet presented me — happy birthday — with a fishing rod I'd admired in an expensive flyrodding store in Jasper. I'd be thirty-two the next day. The rod came in four pieces, so it was portable, but best of all it could be converted to take a fly reel. It was yellow. It was long. I put it together, broke it down, put it together again. I hadn't fished since I was a kid!

The next morning, the man who had disappeared from the next campsite in the middle of the night drove up in his Winnebago. "You must have been scared silly!" he said.

I shook my head bravely. "Scared of what?"

"You didn't hear him? There was a bear last night. Looking in your truck, snuffing at your tent. He stank! He was noisy! You weren't scared?"

We'd slept through this visit, apparently. "A big raccoon," I said slowly. "Nothing more than a big raccoon. Such a nuisance."

On the back window of the pickup were several distinct pawprints (about the size of my own hand) and, more pleasing, several distinct noseprints, nostrils and all, where the beast had peeked in. He'd rolled the rocks of our fire pit around, given our picnic table a good licking and left. I took the bear's unseen presence as a birthday omen — for luck and love and a happy life.

I went fishing. The new pole stayed a virgin, despite two days of fishing it in the midst of wildly feeding trout. I'd been taken back to my childhood of dawn fishing, however, had remembered things I hadn't thought of in years (the gravel-pit pond, the mornings before school spent fishing, the kids I'd played with, the little dog across the gravel-pit stream whom I'd caught in the hair with a lure and had no way to free), and most important, had given Juliet some time alone. She made watercolors, wrote in her fat journal, complained to her friends in long letters.

Exactly at noon, I caught a fish. Bang. I breathed hard, reeled him in, got him to shore, practically lay down on top of him as he flopped there, not wanting to lose him and not quite remembering how to handle him. A few minutes later I caught another, slightly bigger. In memory these fish are the size of legs of lamb, but in a photograph they appear to be perhaps a foot long, big enough, certainly, to make my day, as if the bear already hadn't.

That night we ate trout and drank beer and were treated to the northern lights, hours of green curtains and red fountains backed by the Milky Way in the blackness of the wilderness sky.

In British Columbia we camped in a valley through which the night trains roared, caught sight of yet another black bear as it raced across the winding road. Always we drove too far, at my insistence; always we went on when we should have been eating; we fought. The subjects of our fights are immaterial; the object of our fights, I think, was an extended form of request: Can you accept me with all my anger, and all my reluctance to be intimate, and all my other troubles, none of them the least fault of yours? We affected silences, we pouted, we sniffed, we railed, we barked, we cried, we shouted, we pinched. Then we looked at each other and shrugged, and gave up, said *sorry* and rode in silence, all our damage showing as if the other were to blame.

At Lillooet, not far from Kamloops, I chose a hundred-mile dirt road to make the pass over the Lillooet range to Pemberton. The earth was well watered here by the melt of snowfields, and in the scruffy, five-year-old clear-cuts the wildflowers grew in luxuriant profusion, great meadows of red, whole hillsides of delicate purples, long roadside sashes in Chantilly white. All the neat rows of little trees the logging companies had planted were dead, an autumnal rust.

On bridges, on felled trees, on disturbed boulders and on the back of an abandoned logging camp bus we saw graffiti: THIS IS INDIAN LAND, and THIS LAND STOLEN, and HONKY GO HOME, fine sentiments all, but being a honky (I still admire the borrowed epithet) and being alone, I felt distinctly threatened. When distinctly threatened I grow gruff and grumpy and look for a close friend to blame.

At lunchtime, Juliet was driving. She pulled into a camping area that had been trashed — huge trees felled purposefully into the picnic tables, information kiosk uprooted, fire rings dismantled.

"Not here," I said.

"Yes here," Jules said, slamming the transmission into park while we were still moving.

I put my head in my hands, a gesture guaranteed to provoke.

"Right *exactly* here," Jules said.

We were alone. All the sounds were peaceful: birds, a little river whose waters would enter the Fraser River and pass through Vancouver in a couple of days; zephyr in the trees. Around us in the parking area we saw six piles of broken and beaded safety glass, which I took as evidence of vandalism and violence.

I moderated my tone: "Let's keep going."

Juliet opened her door, hopped out, dropped her pants, peeled off her underpants, threw her shirt on the hood of the truck and marched to the river. She stumbled over the rocks and sat down in the flying, icy water. I climbed out of the truck and sat next to a pile of empty purple shotgun shells, wanting very much to bathe, but by now too angry and frightened to move. I rehearsed a major diatribe about my role as her protector and about her willful disregard for our safety and her lack of concern in the face of danger and how did she think she could do this and what would she do if I left her on the street in Pemberton, or Kamloops? Take her clothes off and sit down? Such, I admit, were my thoughts in the very few minutes of her shivering, beautiful bath in the bright water.

Soon, I heard a truck coming. No muffler. It came into view at the curve just below us, chugged up the hill, stopped over Jules on the bridge. In the cab were two Native American men, guns in a rack behind their heads. I froze, regarding them. Jules, oblivious, stood up in the river.

The driver put his head out the window, had a brief look at Jules, regarded me seriously. "Hello!" he called. "That's cold water!"

In Vancouver, another town where developers had been allowed to polish up and sterilize what had been the best part of town, Juliet and I took the only hotel room of our trip. It was not an elegant place; in the parking lot young men in leather jackets fought all night, using baseball bats to brain each other. We found an Irish restaurant that had a special Irish meal, all you could eat and drink — complete with an Irish band and an Irish comedian — for seven Canadian dollars per person. We splurged. In the end we drank enough beer that Juliet decided the time had come to go off on her own forever. She sneered at me, rose up from the table, lurched out of the place and into the night.

When she didn't come back in five minutes, I began to worry. After ten minutes, I was scared. After twenty, I grew philosophical: Jules would do what Jules would do. She knew how to take care of herself. The city, any city, was her playground. At the very worst, she'd leave forever. At best, she'd find the hotel. I ordered another beer.

Pretty soon, though, she was back, still furious, reeling. "Joni Mitchell on beer," the comedian said. The crowd roared, but Juliet had no idea they were laughing at her.

"I found a place to dance," she said. "But they won't let me in 'cause I'm drunk."

At Pacific Rim Park, at the very edge of Vancouver Island, at the very edge of Canada, at the far edge of the continent, we put our toes in the water, five thousand odometer miles from Ingonish, Nova Scotia, the last place we had touched the sea. The water was freezing. The single campground at Pacific Rim National Park was full. Twilight was upon us.

The park police rousted us from the first place we tried to improvise a camp. A fog deep as Wawa's crept up from the sea. We ended up in an expensive private campground at midnight, their last site, a bit of hard earth next to a cesspool bog, which miserable place seemed at that low moment an emblem of our trip, our guttering fire the fitting crown, the end of love, the last sighs of a foul romance. There were a lot of fish in the sea, and if we ever got home, Juliet and I both meant to dive for them.

The Pacific Ocean didn't cost anything, at least. The beaches were long and flat, with great boulders standing out in the unreachable surf. In the morning, Juliet and I had foot races, splashing contests, stone-skipping derbies — everything but a boxing match, which would have been more to the point. And what talks we had, lying under our towels out of the sun. We didn't think we'd stay together after this trip. We were through. This decision made us more tender with each other — it was sad, after all — but, come on! The grotesque deficiencies of our relationship! The wretchedness of our hours together! Misery! Blame! Why, any other couple would be fine after six weeks cramped in the front of a pickup truck with no radio and a caved-in driver's door, mile after mile, setting up a tent at twilight while the fire went out, making dinner as night crashed down around them, sleeping on rocks and sticks and roots and bones.

We took a long walk on the beach, then climbed reluctantly back into the great, dented, thoroughly rustfree yellow beast. We had no choice but to leave; the camping here cost too much. We were down to a budget of $4.29 per day apiece. We headed for Victoria late in the afternoon, headed for Victoria and the ferry to the Olympic Peninsula, State of Washington. Canada, land of sundered dreams! We didn't stop for lunch when we were hungry but pressed on, trying to make the five o'clock boat.

At three we pulled into Qualicum Provincial Park, snarling, sweating, salty from the sea. We ate in a hurry off the tailgate, facing different directions. A family walked by in bathing suits, entered the deep woods on a slight path. A young couple, a group of kids. Okay. We would swim a minute, then drive like hell, make the ferry, be camping in the States by dark. We marched down the path, not side by side, both with dreams of our exquisitely separate apartments in New York, just two short weeks and a few thousand miles away. The trees around us were enormous, the canopy above us so thick that it allowed no sunshine, no understory growth. Silence primeval.

We heard the Qualicum River before we saw it. From a high footbridge it came into view, blasting redolent and benign through its own miniature canyon, pausing in deep, black pools. Three suntanned children laughed and splashed at a shallow beach formed behind a logjam; teenagers tried to outdo one another diving off the cliffs; young boys threw rounded quartz stones that glowed like life in the dark pools, then dove for them; people took turns being swept by the current down a polished stone slide.

Juliet and I made our way down, climbing between two stone spires into the laughter of families. We found a flat rock of our own in the sun in the middle of the current. Children floated past, some flopping onto and off of our rock like visiting frogs, giggling. When the sun warmed us enough we leapt in, let the water scoot us downstream, swam hard back upcurrent, the first warm swim we'd had since Nova Scotia. We stayed two hours, then three, then four, swimming, exploring, napping like seals, even diving from the high rocks in braver and braver attempts. The sun arced through the ribbon of sky above us in line with our little canyon, kept it blessedly hot. Juliet looked at me and shrugged, letting go all the troubles of the trip. I shrugged too, something of an apology, and also letting go. When the kids weren't looking we kissed, then kissed again, hard.

Oh! Canada! Canada end to end!

Volcano

The first time I saw Mount Saint Helens was with Atalanta Lincoln on the summer solstice, 1978. The mountain was whole and benign, a quiet little sister to Mount Rainier, a calendar-perfect Fuji stand-in, the Kilimanjaro of the Northwest (as the boosters in their guidebooks proclaimed). Broadly conical, perfectly snow-capped, she rose dramatically from low foothills, was visible in glimpses in the cut of the Toutle River, then dominant, framed always by the boughs of fragrant conifers, an angel, a goddess, a peaceful old friend, the serene and transformed maiden of Klickitat legend.

In Seattle, Atalanta and I worked together in the basement disco at Sunday's, a big tourist-oriented restaurant near the Space Needle. Down there I wore a tux and splashed drinks together, ten a minute, till two in the morning six nights a week. Atalanta was my waitress, as the language of the place put it, and I was her bartender; we made a fortune in tips together. Atalanta was the sort of big-hearted, big-busted, croak-voiced, people-loving, once-ran-for-Miss-Washington-and-nearly-won woman I'd never had any luck with. She was a talented actress (I believe this, though I never saw her act), had a way of being exceptionally warm without flirting, of smiling and joking and touching my arm without the slightest romantic message being transmitted, a miraculous way of hugging, even, that made nothing of the intervening presence of that goodly bust and accentuated the fact that she was an inch taller than I. We had a riotous friendship as coworkers, and that was plenty, straight through the mild Seattle winter.

On the first day of summer, as I lounged with several crapulous roommates on our porch, Atalanta pulled up in her 1967 turtle of a Porsche, the top off, tooted three times (her signature), then popped out of the car. "Rainier's out," she called, as if Rainier were the sun, meaning that from her house you could see that distant mountain, the whole of it looming at the horizon like a ghost, a rare treat in the drizzly Northwest. "Want to take a drive?" She had her hiking boots on and a red skirt, all ready for the woods, as irresistibly bubbly as your favorite cousin. We had never seen each other outside of work and rides home from work, and though I was surprised (and my roommates agape), I dropped my writing plans for the day, grabbed a sweater, and we were off, scooting down Interstate 5 in the sunshine, cheering at glimpses of Rainier, comparing notes on our love lives (our chief topic of conversation), she first. Sex with Robert was *super-duper,* but he had no ambition, no sense of adventure. She couldn't imagine him dropping everything to come out for a drive, for example. Then again, he could bench press 350 pounds and was six-foot-six. "It's hard to find a man who's handsome and in good shape and also tall as me," she said. "And do you know what? He's thirty, the perfect age, old enough to know better."

"Better than what?" I said: I was twenty-five.

"He's not the brightest guy in Seattle, but, my-my, he makes love." She talked about sex as easily as most people talk about food, in great detail, describing every olive and carrot stick, every course, all the utensils, the table itself, and ending always with dessert, something elaborate, something dense, with lots of chocolate and Chantilly.

As for me, not so much as a snack for two months.

Atalanta laughed and gave me dumb advice — pickup lines, smooth moves, suggestions for sartorial improvement. (She'd have had me cruising art museums, popping champagne for movie dates, and wearing silken ties.)

Atalanta zipped into Mount Rainier National Park as the sun climbed higher, sped around corners, talking about our secondary subject — customers and tips and old jobs and work stories — never stopping so we might get out of the car, but gazing at that colossal, stolid mountain, driving, driving, bad-mouthing our boss. Her long brown legs pumped at the clutch and the brake and the gas pedal, her skirt and Sunday's Disco T-shirt fluttering in the convertible wind. Quickly, we shot over Cayuse Pass, tearing through the switchbacks. We stopped for lunch at a turnout over a cliff near the Ohanapecosh River, Mount Rainier taking up most of the western part of the sky.

Under the hood of the sporty car Atalanta had two Indian blankets and a basket and a little cooler. She'd made a salad and guacamole and spicy chicken wings and cake, produced a bottle of wine from a *case* of fancy Burgundy that was stowed behind the seats. We spread the blankets double over the grass. "And don't think I'm doing this for you," she said seriously. "Robert was supposed to come, the prick." We ate.

After lunch we zoomed out of the park through Packwood and Randle, Glenoma and Morton, heading south and west to see Saint Helens. We passed shingle yards, where men in beards and bare chests split big cedar logs chop by chop down to shingles and shakes, drove through stands of old Douglas firs, two hundred feet high and bigger around than the car. Atalanta ricocheted past every logging truck and every Winnebago, a second bottle of red wine clutched between her legs, pushing up her skirt. Out to our left Saint Helens appeared, which Atalanta said was her favorite mountain in the *universe*. In Mossyrock she stopped so I could open another bottle of wine with her Sunday's regulation jackknife-style corkscrew. We passed Salkum and Ethel, hopped onto Interstate 5 for a couple of exits south, then crossed the Cowlitz River on Route 505. The trees here were dense (where they hadn't been cut down), nearly all evergreen, huge firs and small spruces, straight-up stands of lodgepole pine, and one or two big and solitary ponderosas. The old clear-cuts looked like Christmas tree farms, young trees growing fast in the slash to fill the void (which in truth they couldn't be expected to fill properly for five or six hundred years). At Route 504 we turned left, picked up the North Fork of the Toutle River, barely noticing the many bridges as we crossed and recrossed it. The truck traffic became more regular; we passed the big Weyerhauser camps.

Saint Helens appeared in the cut of the river, not fifteen miles away, enormous, pristine, a looming glory. "Perfect," as Atalanta said, and for once that empty adjective was correct, said it all — the mountain was perfect, as perfect and perfectly unflappable as Atalanta. We stopped stream-side near a railroad bridge where she popped yet another bottle of wine and drove on. "It's our anniversary," she said. "We planned this for a month, but then the big lump of shit — pardon the dialect — decides that it's the perfect morning to head over to Spokane with his lump-of-shit brother." She smiled good-naturedly, her anger coming out in the form of high ground speed and shrieking tires as we entered the Gifford Pinchot National Forest.

At Saint Helens Lodge on Spirit Lake we looked around for a minute without leaving the car, then screeched out of the parking lot and down the road to Duck Bay, then back again and up the mountain to Timberline Viewpoint, where still she would not stop the car. A couple of miles into an unpaved road (her Porsche, she said, hated unpaved roads!) we stopped at a trailhead Atalanta knew about (she and Robert had twice climbed the mountain), parked under some big boulders at the head of a trail that would take us up to the foot of Forsyth Glacier, if we wanted, and Nelson Glacier, or even Leschi Glacier! Atalanta fairly danced with excitement. Or Loowit and Wishbone, if we wanted to go for it, or even to the top of the mountain!

I thought the glaciers a bit ambitious, the summit impossible, ridiculous, starting so late in the day, so full of wine. I protested.

"I'd like you to know it's the longest day of the year," Atalanta told me, packing two more bottles of wine (numbers four and five) in her day pack, and one of her woven blankets.

"Well, upward," I said. I was glad enough to take a walk, but I knew we'd never get near the summit.

We marched sluggishly up into the mountain. Behind us, Spirit Lake appeared, and it did look enchanted. In the dense wood there was snow still, and in the snow there was sign of mice and fox and rabbit and elk and deer and of at least one moose. I found some tracks I thought were bobcat, but Atalanta thought they were just from a dog. "Probably a poodle," she said. We hiked.

At a flat rock in a boulder-strewn meadow high over the world we stopped to admire Mount Rainier, which was imponderably large for something thirty miles distant. The wine and altitude had made us loopy. Among new wild-flowers Attie (early on she told me never to call her this, so I often did) laid out her blanket, emptied her skirt pockets onto the rock (car keys, three dimes, a diamond engagement ring, a lipstick) and with no more ado than that lay herself down and fell to snoring. I watched Rainier, then lay down beside Atalanta in the sun, carefully not touching her, propping my head to look up at Saint Helens. The glaciers above us were cracked and impossibly steep in the mountain's shade.

When I woke I had a headache, could still taste the wine. Atalanta wasn't beside me. The sun had fallen behind the high trees at the edge of the meadow and the air was chilly. Six o'clock. Rainier looked as if he had a headache, too, and Spirit Lake looked absolutely evil with magic, reflecting the steep, tree-covered slopes that surrounded it. I spied Atalanta, climbing way up the meadow in the scree below the bottom of the glacier. I rolled up the blanket and followed her.

Late, we came down, eating handfuls of snow to counteract the thirst that all the red wine and hiking had brought on. We'd got as far as the dripping bottom of a dirty glacier, and that was high enough. The empty bottles clanked in Attie's pack, but she didn't seem even slightly drunk, only melancholy and uncharacteristically quiet. Once the sun fell behind the tree-covered ridges to the west, the sky grew dark fast. I took the lead, talked and joked loudly to scare off the moose and bears and bobcats and bigfoots and poodles. Somehow, we managed to stay on the trail. Going down is faster than going up; the car surprised us when we came to it, shining there ever so slightly under the bright swath of stars the road cut revealed. We climbed

in, relieved, tired as hell, and just sat, companionably, for
five minutes, a very long time.

"Do you know what?" Atalanta said finally.

I shook my head; I did not know what.

"I left my keys up on that rock."

We sat again for a few minutes, absorbing this complex
truth. Then Attie reached back for a bottle of wine. "Also
my ring. Kind of an expensive one."

We ate what was left of the picnic (not much) and drank
the bottle of wine, number six. Only when it was empty did
we begin to discuss the night. We couldn't possibly retrieve
the keys and the dimes and the lipstick and the ring in this
black dark. Atalanta reached back for the seventh bottle
(which would be the last, ending up on the pavement still a
quarter full and still clutched in my hand). We spread the
blankets over us, tilted the seats back, stared at the vast,
clear sky, revealing itself in layers of stars. The air was cold,
but not so cold that it froze our breaths, so I didn't think
we'd die. I told Attie some ancient Greek science, that the
universe was a shell around us, stars merely pinpricks to
the great light beyond. That apples fell to the earth because
they were in love with it, that waves came to shore for love
of the beach, that rain loved the ground, that smoke loved
the sky. My seat made a noise whenever I moved.

"I'm cold," Atalanta said.

I leaned toward her and we cuddled over the gearshift,
most uncomfortably, and — wine loves the lips — I tried a
kiss. "No monkey business," she said good-naturedly, shaking her head. I sat back in my seat. "Sloshed," she said. A
while later, just when I thought she was asleep, she leaned
over and kissed me, and we kissed like that until we were
warm. "If we weren't such good friends we'd make love,"
she said dreamily. It didn't occur to me at the time to assail

her logic. She settled back in her seat and in a moment began to snore. She was a hell of a beautiful snorer.

Seven years later, I told the story of Atalanta and her keys and the rock to Juliet as we bombed down from Canada in my pickup truck. We were pleased to be heading home from our long and mostly miserable trip across that great country, and were pleased as well that we'd managed to make it without killing each other. In fact, it seemed as though we might even stay together once we got home. Juliet was an able driver now, even in the enormous truck. I had persuaded her long before that we shouldn't miss Mount Saint Helens — it wasn't *so* far out of our way — shouldn't miss the opportunity to see what a volcano could do: Mount Saint Helens had blown herself up on May eighteenth of 1980.

We got off the interstate at Route 505. "She was how tall?" Jules said, meaning not Mount Saint Helens but Atalanta Lincoln.

"Six-foot-seven," I said, trying to make a monster of her.

"And you let her kiss you?" Juliet sat up straight, all of five-foot-six, blond and slim, philosophically opposed to beauty contests, a waitperson not a barmaid, a wearer of blue jeans and T-shirts, not miniskirts and bras, the owner of my love, in no way similar to the Atalanta of my memory.

Before the mountain came into view, at the junction of 504, we stopped to make sandwiches next to a sign that warned us that Saint Helens was active and unpredictable and that there was every chance we would be maimed, killed, and carried away in a mudflow if we proceeded. After lunch we made the turn onto Route 504 anyway. The Toutle River was unrecognizable. Tree sections poked out of a crest of hardened mud. A steel railroad bridge lay green and twisted, askew, like a wrecked and abandoned toy in a sandbox. Chunks of asphalt showed here and there among the tree trunks and rocks and bits of houses. The old road was simply gone. The riverbed was gone, too, in a more complicated way, buried, everything in a jumble, great waves of mud frozen in flow, trees pushed aside, boulders atop bigger boulders atop the remains of bridge abutments. Awful in the oldest sense.

"You know she left her keys on purpose," Juliet said.

"I don't think so," I said. "We were drunk."

Around a corner on the slickly black new road: the mountain. She was gray instead of white and green, seemed furious still, overlooking the destruction she'd made — her top gone, a tilted crater there, a pale plume of smoke rising — gorgeous. We drove very slowly, rapt, wanting to get closer, as close to that roiling bosom as we could. Too soon, the road came to an abrupt end. "Is this as near as we can get?" Juliet said. At the dead end, a shack for tourists had been built. In it, slides of the eruption were shown every half hour. Displays explained the catastrophe. Indian dolls were for sale, and postcards and plastic dinosaurs. Also vials of ash, which seemed absurd, since ash was everywhere.

I spread out our old map on the warm hood of the truck. Jules threw her arm around me, looked on. The road, sure enough, should have gone on up to Spirit Lake and the Saint Helens Lodge. But, as the display explained, the lodge had been whisked away when the north side of the mountain fell into the lake at more than 150 miles per hour, sending most of the water six hundred feet up the opposite slope (good-bye Girl Scout camp, good-bye Boy Scout camp, good-bye Portland YMCA camp). The plane of altitude upon which Saint Helens Lodge had existed was now buried under two hundred feet of mud and ash. The initial eruption also melted five of the mountain's glaciers and launched what the slide show called the largest landslide in recorded history. Lubed by snowmelt and steam, this lahar flowed down the North Fork of the Toutle River, knocking out seven bridges, erasing all structures, surprising motorists, killing everything in its path, moving seventeen miles in ninety-six minutes.

The place where Atalanta and I had spent that wakeful night was not a place anymore. As for the rock where she had left her keys and her ring (which had still been there, come that chaste and gloomy dawn), it might have been anywhere, part of the gale of gases and ash and rocks and flaming tree sections that raged through the forests at very nearly the speed of sound, loving the ground, destroying even the topsoil for a good eight miles (farewell to David Johnston, the vulcanologist who sat up on the ridge, hoping to observe a major eruption up close; farewell to Harry Truman, the old fellow who refused to leave his only home, even knowing he would die), then, calming, merely knocking down and sandblasting everything in an area of about 230 square miles. "Think of all the animals," Jules said. Something over two million died, fifty-seven of them people, and not including insects.

I remembered a dirt road, one of the many that Atalanta Lincoln had refused to take, coming out of Randle, Washington. Sure enough, our map showed a road that — if it were still there — might take us to the eastern side of the volcano for a look. Jules and I stared up for five more silent minutes at the filled-in valley of the Toutle and up to the stunningly beautiful gray and black and still-steaming mountain that had thrown herself there.

Through peaceful forest we drove to Randle. From there the road to the northeastern side of the mountain was easy to find — freshly paved, freshly lined with yellow paint, and marked by big new signs befitting a road into the all-new Mount Saint Helens National Volcanic Monument. Jules and I stayed in a new campground under a grove of mighty Douglas firs, stared two hundred feet or more up the trunks, watching perspective happen. (I like to hug big trees like that, not out of love, really, but just to feel that girth, something like trying to hug a wall.) Jules and I set up the tent beside a fallen tree so big around that someone had chopped six big steps into each side of its trunk to make a stile for the path to the Cowlitz River, which flowed gray with ash, the only immediate sign that there might be an angry mountain nearby.

In the morning, Juliet and I drove up there on Forest Service Road 99 through miles of undisturbed woods, sitting close on the big bench seat of the pickup. Nineteen miles from Saint Helens we saw a whorl of Douglas firs, blown down in the last eddy of the mountain's awesome breath, looking like so many hairs in the swirled cowlick back of a little boy's crew cut. A high ridge parallel to the road had protected the other trees in that neck of the woods, and there was no further evidence of the cataclysm for two miles. But then the ridge dropped away. In open view of the mountain, a vast hillside of trees had been laid flat in rays away from the blast. There was nothing left to block the view of the mountain; from there we could see into the maw of her new crater. Smoke rose from the growing dacite dome (eventually this may resurrect the former height of the peak), which looked like an ominous loaf of pumpernickel, still in the oven, rising and cracking its crust. To the southeast Mount Hood peacefully waited, a handsome, glaciered cone, a volcano itself, no longer looking innocent and benign.

We passed a place where the Forest Service had made an exhibit of what was left of the car of some unlucky people who'd been interred by falling pumice bombs. After that, every slope that faced the mountain had been scoured clean. Around us all was gray, everything gray, except a few tiny plants, gloriously green, seed planted by the Cascade winds and shitting birds in eddies of ash, the first tiny harbingers of the new forest to come, a hundred years, two hundred, hence. High over Spirit Lake, the new road abruptly ended. The lake looked killed, its magic gone, its surface dull as the eyes of death. Thousands upon thousands of trees felled by the blast had been washed into it by the receding wave of its displaced water. The result was a colossal raft (best described in terms of acreage) built of shocked and denuded logs.

The open mountain smoldered there in the still air. Something alluring blew with the smoke coming from the lava dome, flew in that newly airy place, the absence that was the crater. "I wish we could get closer," Jules said.

I have a question for my ancient Greek scientist (whose name no one knows, whose ideas I heard in a college course and never forgot): What is it a volcano loves? The sky, and so blacken it? The earth, and so flatten it? The rivers, and so fill them with mud, and logs, and the bodies of men? I thought again of the glacier I'd reached with Atalanta, and of the road we'd parked on, and the buildings we'd seen, and the trees that had flanked the mountain. None of these existed anymore except as fragments, or mud humps, or atoms — new creation, elsewhere. Of course, a volcano is far too complicated to be explained by a motive force of love. Perhaps a volcano is love itself.

Juliet, beside me on the blown mountain, was everything

that Atalanta had not been. Where Juliet's power lay in expression, in abandon, in complexity, Atalanta's had lain in image, in careful control, in the appearance of simplicity and benignity. And like the maiden mountain, Atalanta lived large and solid and perfect in my memory, unruffled, elegant, visible in seductive glimpses, unblown, a great beauty always, cool and serene. (Think of it — our friendship can be truly wrapped up in the unchanging story of a single car trip.)

Juliet lived in my memory too, of course, our days together like so many trees blown down in mystical patterns, but love is a puzzle, a mountain that won't stay whole. Jules beside me was as mighty as the secret Saint Helens and as endlessly complicated and hard to predict. Throw rocks through the forests! Drop pumice bombs on cars! Melt massive glaciers! Choke rivers in mud! I took her hand and looked out over the devastation, the perfect, lovely devastation flecked with the green of new plants growing where their seeds had chanced to land.

Bluefishing

Juliet and I headed to Martha's Vineyard again on the last day of July, 1986. At Woods Hole we waited through the evening for each successive ferry, but the standby line barely moved. Come night, we were still twenty cars from the loading ramp to the boats. When the last ferry left at ten forty-five, we were parked on the dock, only three cars from the head of the line. Well, we'd spend the night, be third in line for the six A.M. boat. At the Lee Side Bar we drank beers till they closed, then sat at the end of the ferry dock talking in the sweet salt air, pleased to be anywhere that wasn't New York. Late, we climbed into the front of the truck — the back was full — and tossed and turned and thrashed until I was on the floor, draped over the transmission hump. Juliet slept peacefully across the big bench seat, which was plenty roomy enough for one.

At four in the morning, I woke up. Impossible to sleep. I climbed out of the truck, stretched, looked out over the water toward the Vineyard. Hell, I could sleep when we got there. I heard excited whispering out at the end of the great ferry dock, then noticed some kids fishing. Their rods were big, but not so big as the one I'd borrowed from my brother Randy, a surf rod twelve feet long, which I'd broken down into its two pieces and crammed in the back of my bashed-in truck along with towels and sleeping bags and flippers and clothing in garbage bags and my type-writer and boxes of books and three dresses on hangers and two broken bicycles and pillows and notebooks and oars and four boat cushions and a fuel hose and, finally, a six-horse Johnson motor for our boat. The boat, tied to the roof, was an aqua-painted Mirrocraft aluminum rowboat man-ufactured in 1953. I'd borrowed it from my family's house in New Hampshire with my father's permission but prob-ably against his better judgment.

In that truck, too, tangled in with the surf rod, was an old Sears fishing rod, green, diminutive, familiar, *Ted Williams approved* (with a checkmark), my childhood fishing rod, which I'd brought in place of the newer one Juliet had given me the summer before in Canada. That excellent rod I'd thrown into the lake in New Hampshire in a fit of anger. The anger had been released because I'd stopped smoking on July twentieth, just ten days previous, on the fourth anniversary of the day I'd met Juliet, and at her behest. The rod had sunk so fast I couldn't retrieve it — my secret plan back there in the blackness of my rage.

Jules and I were fresh from another year in New York, had managed to stay together after our giant Canada trip by staying apart for as much of September and October as possible, which was easy enough to do, as Juliet was very busy waitressing and absorbed with a difficult course at Pratt University, a trial outing on her eventual way to a master's in art therapy. She lived with her roommate, Tracy, in an unimaginably tiny one-bedroom apartment on Spring Street in Soho. I still lived with Jon Zeeman in our unfinished but ever more comfortable loft in the Meat Dis-trict, northwest of Greenwich Village, the locus at the time of forty gay bars and twenty sex clubs and a hundred butchers and meat packers. Sides of beef and scalded hogs swung over the sidewalks on meathooks; transvestite hookers hailed Johns from the corners.

Come spring, Juliet started in full time at Pratt. We relished our distance but remained a couple, seeing each other as little as once a week. I played music with various friends; the work was sporadic, the money very bad. I wrote stories and poems and worked on a novel, serving out an apprenticeship that brought little respect and no money at all. I'd managed to establish a well-paying if unglamorous niche for myself in tiling and minor plumbing, went from apartment building to brownstone to loft to tenement to warehouse, tearing down walls, rebuilding, replumbing, tiling, sweating pipe, seating toilets, eating food from unguarded refrigerators. The money was very good, but my spirit was very poor. Come summer, the Vineyard was a grand temptation, even if it meant blowing every cent of my meager savings.

So on the dock at Woods Hole I watched the kids fishing. I watched from an adult sort of distance, watched them carefully, almost nervously, trying to see what they did, what a person had to do to catch fish in the sea. (I don't know why I was so trepidatious about fishing in salt water. I guess it was the new secret society that had to be joined, a kids' society that at thirty-two I felt maybe I was too hopelessly old to join. The equipment was bigger, the fish were bigger and strange and even unknown, the medium so vast I didn't know where to start.) The kids had bait, which they loudly announced was menhaden when another haggard soul on standby asked. They impaled chunks of that fish on huge hooks, dipped it into the splashing dark water. They didn't cast; they didn't practice silence; they ran up and down the huge dock looking into the depths. I looked, too, but didn't see the fishes they seemed to be seeing, saw only crabs that swam beguiled like moths in the bright dock lights that shone down upon them.

I got out my childhood rod, thinking I'd approach this new program slowly, with dignity and diminution. Though I wished for some menhaden (or was it manhattan?), I thought I could use what I had, which were freshwater lures in a little blue tackle box that said DOUGIE ROORBACH in a boy's Magic Marker letters. I tied on a wormlike thing and dapped it in the water. A crab paddled over and grabbed hold, fell off when I lifted. Well, that was a start. I noodled around playing crabmaster for half an hour as the sky lightened.

One of the kids had something. His pole bent heavily. His friends hushed. "Too small," one of them said. They looked furtively about. "Striper," the catcher said. He was thirteen or so, had already had his night's sleep, was up early for a morning of fishing. After a long struggle, he yanked his striper rudely up to the dock. The fish was over two feet long, fat, heavy, the biggest I'd ever seen caught on a line. I flushed with an atavistic envy. Too *small,* they'd said. (Later I'd find out that stripers under thirty-three inches were illegal in Massachusetts, and that the law, designed to bring more fish to reproductive maturity, was strictly enforced.) The boy's friends looked nervously around while he pulled off his denim jacket, stuffed the fish into one of the sleeves, packed up his rod and hustled out of there, his friends behind him, his jacket flopping.

I wanted to catch a fish like that. I wanted to catch a fish like that so badly I could shout. Imagine a world where a two-foot fish was considered too small! I raced back to the truck to tell Jules but thought better of waking her, thought better of inviting her disdain.

*

A few days later I stood on the stone jetty that juts from East Chop into Vineyard Haven Harbor. I stood with my little brother's blue tackle box and my big brother's twelve-foot pole. (Funny how every fishing story devolves into a kind of phallic parade, a procession of penises, the bigger the better ...) Early that morning I'd gone out, hoping to be alone in my folly, but had found the head of the jetty already claimed by three ancient black men who joked and joshed loudly and who pulled in fish, one after the next, pale golden fish a mere foot long that glinted rainbows in the sun then rattled and splashed in an old joint-compound bucket filled with sea water.

I kept my distance, afraid of my ignorance. What kind of fish? How were they catching them? Randy's big surf rod felt too showy in my hands. The reel was the same shape and function as all the littler spinning reels I'd used when I was small, but it was enormous, the size of my foot and as clumsy, at once exotic and familiar, like a giant South American frog. I tied on a new lure I'd invested in at Larry's Tackle outside Oak Bluffs, a Kastmaster, it was called, the biggest spoon I'd ever seen, seven and a half inches long (including the hook and bucktail), stainless steel, *heavy.* I tied on the thick steel leader I'd been sold as defense against bluefish teeth, clipped on the lure and tried a cast. At three ounces, and off the whip of such a big rod, the lure went a hell of a long way, a football field at least, I thought, impressed with myself. I also made bad casts in which the lure fell on the jetty beside me. The old men looked. When they didn't look I made good casts in which the lure flew like a missile, farther than I'd ever cast before. I gained confidence, tried for greater and greater distances, as if it were distance I was after and not fish. Then I made a cast with the bail closed. *Snap!* The old men looked back at me. No question about what had happened. Freed of encumbering line, the lure flew hundreds of feet through the sky, flew as if it would never fall.

That lure had cost five dollars! Five entire dollars! A meal! A movie! A quarter tank of gas! In Doug's childhood tackle box I had nothing but weenie spoons and fake salamanders. I was licked. But then one of the old gentlemen called to me: "What are you fishing for?"

"Stripers," I said, remembering the kids on the dock.

"Well, you might," he said. "But stripers do not like that steel leader." The way he said this indicated that I was doing everything else wrong, too. He was gentle, but a little pompous — a retired doctor, I guessed.

"And what are *you* fishing for?"

"Porgies." He pointed to the joint-compound bucket. In it were twenty or more slim fish, deep-bodied, almost rectangular, nine and ten inches long, with dumb thug's lips in a dour cast and large brown eyes. Some lay on their sides, dead or dying. The living ones sculled with their pectoral fins, keeping upright. "You need yourself some bait. There's no blues out there at the moment. And stripers are tricky for starters." His friends turned to look at me. Businesslike, one of them offered me a teardrop-shaped lead weight with the numeral 1 stamped into it. The other gave me a long-shafted hook, much smaller than the enormous hook on the Kastmaster. The good doctor found a piece of light fishing line crudely discarded on the jetty and bit off a foot and a half of it. This he tied into my line so as to leave two ends of equal length. "We tie the sinker onto the thinner stuff," he said, doing so very carefully. A surgeon, perhaps, deft with his fingers. "The thinner stuff breaks more easily, so if we snag — which we are bound to do sooner or later — we only lose a little lead." He looked up at me to see if I was following. "Now, we tie the hook on the end of the main line. This way, you see? The fish will not feel the pull of the weight, and we on our end will feel the fish when he comes nibbling instead of the sinker."

One of his buddies jerked back subtly on his rod. "*Damn,*" he said sharply, having missed a fish. This man, overweight and composed, seemed more bored with life than the doctor, more resigned, was perhaps a retired mail carrier. The other buddy laid a small, pearly squid whole on a square of old board and cut a piece from the tentacles. "Best part," he said coldly, even angrily, willing to help, but unwilling to be friendly.

"And we hang it like this." The doctor hung the tentacle just *so* off the end of the hook, doubled it back, and hung the tip loose so that it would wave in the subtlest of currents. "The tide is going *out*. Now we cast, like this . . ." He cast my line, clearly afraid I would foul things up if allowed to do it myself. The current pulled the weight and squid out into deep water and held it there. "Just so," he said. "Just so." He handed me my enormous rod and went back to his own more delicate one.

My first fish out of the sea was a cunner, *Tautogolabrus adsperus,* as I learned later, digging through my *Peterson Guide to Atlantic Coast Fishes,* and fascinated as always by the taxonomical names. The postman had no need for Latin, called the fish a rock bass. The angry man called it a toothy bass, the doctor a bergall. They argued good-naturedly until the angry man got angry, and then they stopped, let fishing clear the air. Cunners are bait stealers, capable of stripping a hook without endangering themselves, and so slimy and ugly that they don't even risk much when they hook up. They have crooked and discolored buck teeth, the better to gnaw on barnacles or clams, their favorite foods. Their flesh is mottled, allowing them to blend into the weeds and rocks they favor.

The next fish was a sea robin, *Prionotus carolinus*. It looked prehistoric — straight from a bad dream — with a hard shell and a spiky head. Its pectoral fins were greatly overdeveloped into winglike structures with two or three free rays having grown into long, spiky feelers with which (so my books told me) it was able to crawl along the ocean floor, where it fed. When I tried to get the sea robin off the hook, it grunted like a pig and flopped, gouging me with one of the spines on its ugly head. The postman threw me a towel. "Cover him up or he'll stab you," he said.

"Kill you wit' poison," the angry fellow added, scowling. The sea robin grunted as I extricated him, slapped the water when I threw him in, then wriggled back into the seaweed. I inspected my spine wounds; they were slight, with none of the discoloration of venom poisoning and none of the pain of a sting. I worried a little, but in the end didn't die or even get sick.

The next fish I caught was a scup (*Stenotomus chrysops*), the fish my jetty mates called a porgy. Scup and porgies are pretty similar — same family, same genus, same page in the fish books — but don't let a Vineyarder hear you mix them up. Regardless of the name, now I was excited. Here was a fish a person could eat, a fish handsome as any bass from the gravel pit back in my childhood fishing days, a fish you could take home and cook and eat.

Next trip, Juliet came along. I played the expert, let her use my childhood rod, got her set up the way Doctor Pompous had shown me. She enjoyed chipping up the squid I'd bought at the fish store, enjoyed impaling pieces of tentacle on her hook. We got bites immediately. "Cunners," I said authoritatively.

"Nice name," Juliet said. She wore long pants to keep

the sun off her new sunburn — she'd gone to the beach with our roommates the day before — and a curiously broad sun hat to shade her face. Her blond ponytail swung out behind, swishing at her back, where there was a white stripe from its shade. I brandished my brother's twelve-foot rod, a foot for every inch of fish I was likely to catch, striking back at nibbles, reeling in empty hooks, firing bait back out there, communicating with a world I couldn't see or visualize.

Other folks arrived and I helped them get set up for porgies, too, sharing the wealth. Kids came and watched us, loving the fish we caught with brutal hands. Juliet got a sea robin, much better than nothing, shouted with delight, pulled it up on the rocks. She put her foot on its head almost tenderly, and demanded I get the ugly fish off her hook. The kids screamed with pleasure, sure she'd be poisoned. A tall man came down the jetty to look, seemed to admire Jules more than the fish. A little boy unhooked the thing and took his time throwing it back.

We fished. The tall man watched carefully as Juliet pulled in five slimy cunners in a row. The last, the biggest, she held up to him, face first. "Does it remind you of Jerry Lewis?" she said seriously. The tiny buck teeth gave the cunner a certain personality, it was true, but despite that, and although the Peterson book said they were edible, she threw it back, just like the others. The sea gulls didn't even go after it. "Well, there," Jules said. "If our lives had depended on it, we could have eaten."

Finally we got into a school of porgies and each of us caught one. Juliet was terribly proud of herself. She grinned and grabbed the fish wrong and screamed and threw her rod down on the jetty, fish and all. She'd never been a kid handling a bass or a sunny, had never learned to fold down the dorsal rays, which are sharp as porcupine quills. She put her hands to her face, leaving dozens of tiny scales sparkling like glitter on her pretty cheeks in the shade of her hat. The tall fellow, charmed, unhooked the fish for her.

Over the next couple of hours — our pride growing and excitement rising — we caught nine more. Porgies for the table! We'd feed our roommates! We'd feed ourselves! We were providers!

Toward the end of the day I tied on a leader and snapped a new Kastmaster in place. I stepped to the end of the jetty and fired the thing out into deep water, cast after cast, creating a blister in my line finger, aiming farther and farther out, casting for the joy of throwing, as Juliet pulled in cunners and sea robins and porgies. After a half hour I got a snag. I pulled cautiously, worried that I would lose five more dollars in all that miserable seaweed out there. Then the snag unmistakably pulled back. When I pulled in turn, the snag took off, stripping line from my reel. I'd never considered what would happen if I hooked up. My drag was set too lightly. The fish headed out to sea as I tightened the drag nut on top of my reel. Gradually I got control of the fish. Gradually, again, the fish came to the jetty, a stunning flash of silver five or six feet down in the clear green water, then a shape and a size. It was big — the biggest fish I'd ever caught, bigger even than the striper I'd seen the kids catch off the ferry dock at Woods Hole. At the rocks it bolted one more time, but that was the end of its fight. The tall man borrowed a net from one of the kids and helped me get the fish up to the rocks. "What kind is it?" he asked me.

"Isn't it a bluefish?"

"That's the biggest cunner I've ever seen," Jules said.

"That's a weakfish," the littlest kid said, but I dismissed

him. He was too tiny to know anything I didn't know! It must be a bluefish!

I didn't want to kill it, yet I had to if I meant to eat it. I struck it on the head, then slit its throat, not feeling remorse, exactly, but certainly aware of the violence I was doing. "So much for free days at sea," Jules said. The tall man grimaced, watching. The kids were pleased. Later when I cleaned it I would feel the same sort of shocked curiosity — blood, organs, not-life — that I feel at the beginning of each fishing season when it comes to killing.

Juliet and I lived that summer in a house called Lagoon's Edge, with Jon Zeeman and six other housemates and assorted friends and their lovers and various brothers and sisters who came up from time to time to help pay the rent. Everything in Lagoon's Edge was a little damp, always, from the breezes off Lagoon Pond. The place smelled faintly of mildew, of summer, of ease. It was a big old house, in poor repair and surrounded by pines, with two old boats on blocks in the scruffy yard, a locked garage, a big living room, too few bedrooms, a patio under a failing grape arbor and an enormous, screened-in porch, which was the place to hang out. The porch boasted a double-length built-in bunk and two big couches and many wicker chairs and a long, warped dining table. A weedy path led from one of the porch doors to a little shack off under the scrub oaks. This was the bunkhouse, and the bunkhouse was where Jules and I stayed: twin beds, bad art, high rent, and a bathroom.

Across a little road from the backyard was our beach, a thin strip of sand and weeds narrowly bordered by fences. Here I left my family's rowboat turtle on the grass. It looked smaller than at the lake, especially compared to all the real boats bobbing at their moorings off the beach. We loaded it up with gas tank and motor, life preservers and oars, and took it out for short cruises on the lagoon, but the weather was rough, and the little boat wobbled precariously.

One afternoon I went down to Edgartown Marine and bought letters — BIG WIGGLY — to put on its bow. Big Wiggly was also the name of the household rock-'n'-roll band, a name chosen by the drummer, Bruce Martin, after a worm he'd known. The name fit the worm, I imagine, and seemed to fit the band, but it definitely fit the boat, which was none too stable, built for rowing, built for lakes.

I didn't mean to fish from jetties all summer. So when at last we got a good evening, Jules and I and our housemate Mike loaded up the boat and took it out and around the lagoon for its first fishing cruise, timidly trolling. *Big Wiggly*'s little engine stalled repeatedly because of a leak in the gas line, which Mike and I thought we could fix. We had fun putting around, but we didn't catch fish.

"The fish are out *there,*" Mike said, nodding toward the rough water past the bridge.

"We need a bigger boat," I said grumpily, suffering from lack of cigarettes. "This one's not safe."

"It's awfully rough out there," Jules said.

"Or we could just *do* it," Mike said, a challenge in his voice. He was twenty-three — a year younger than Juliet — and a fine guitarist and singer. I'd known him since he was seventeen, a rough sort of moochy kid with long — very long — shocking red hair, a piping singing voice, and lots of handsome girlfriends. He wasn't a kid anymore, though I often forgot and treated him like one; he bridled against me the way he would against a competitive big brother, and I bridled back.

We stared at each other.

Juliet said, "Let's."

Mike shrugged.

I turned the boat tentatively toward the little buoys that marked the channel and we putted out under the closed drawbridge, motoring with the current into Vineyard Haven Harbor. We tied on lures and trolled around the inner part of the basin, past the icehouse and the Texaco tanks, past the West Chop jetty, through the moored boats outside the inner harbor, then back across to the East Chop side, circling safely distant from the rougher water of Vineyard Sound. *Big Wiggly* rocked, but the water seemed manageable. Only when the ferries came was it scary; their wakes looked mountainous, came in four great waves. If we took the series bow on, all was well. If we caught them sideways, *Big Wiggly* rolled violently, her little motor sputtering.

No bites. After two hours of ever-larger (though ever-timid) circles in the outer harbor we noticed a figure waving to us from the jetty. Pulling closer we saw it was Jon Zeeman, who'd said he might meet us. I brought the bow of the little boat up to the rocks. Jon leapt aboard. "*Dudes,*" he said, kidding around, "I told you I'd show up." He'd driven his old Mercedes to the little parking area at the jetty.

Mike set Jon up with a pole. Jon produced a big Red Devil (a lightweight stainless steel spoon meant for fresh water) from his pocket, which lure he'd purchased in light of my irritable complaints about his lack of equipment. He tied it on, cast, and we were off, trailing three lines behind us. We made one circle in the gathering evening — a gorgeous circle, birds to watch, and fine sailboats, and a high-cirrus sunset. An osprey from West Chop flew above us for several hundred yards, then made a dive at my Atom, but thought better of his plan when I yanked the lure away.

Then Jon had a fish on. His face lit up in surprise. I

stopped the boat, jealous. Jon reeled too fast, but his line didn't break; he stopped reeling to have a puff on his smoke, but the fish didn't get free on the slack; he yanked the fish over the gunwales without a net, but the fish didn't escape. In fact, the goddamn fish lay there on the bottom of the boat, the only catch of the day, fat, real, big-headed, black-skinned, a mystery — until Jon identified it: "It's a sea bass. I recognize it from Sung Chu Mei." Sung Chu Mei was our favorite Chinese restaurant in New York. Mike and I scoffed, but as it turned out (*McClane's Field Guide to Salt-water Fishes of North America*), Jon was exactly right; it was a black sea bass, *Centropristis striata.*

A few days later — four in the morning, a promising August day — Mike and Juliet and I made our way down North Road to Menemsha with *Big Wiggly* bouncing in the back of my dent-ravaged pickup. In the mist we saw deer and skunks and several raccoons, and around a bend, three escaped horses. The horses raced ahead of us, keeping on the road, a game, twenty miles an hour for two full miles. We took that misty apparition as good luck.

Menemsha! We'd heard wonderful things about the fishing there, had heard with our own ears that baitfish abounded, that bluefish came to feed around the twin jetties that protected the harbor inlet, had heard further that it was possible to catch bonito there, little *tunas*. Glory! We drove past Poole's and Larsen's fish markets on Dutcher dock, past all the fishing boats, past the Menemsha Texaco, past the luxury yachts, through the parking lot to the beach. There we dragged *Big Wiggly* over the sand and loaded up oars and motor and gas tank and fuel line and life jackets and fishing rods and hats and buckets and towels, then pushed off, dawn in the Menemsha Bight.

After a fruitless but pleasurable troll, we threw our cinderblock anchor out and floated just outside the jetties and bottom-fished, growing headachy in the morning sun. Scup, sea robins and cunners, then more scup, more sea robins, and more cunners. We threw everything back. Mike and I affected the look of weary Vineyard fishermen — long-billed caps, ripped T-shirts, cans of beer between our legs. Jules wore her wide sun hat with dark glasses, a faded yellow bikini, several silver bracelets and a scarf. Coast Guard boats chugged past, in and out of the harbor, but didn't give us a second look, which was good, because the license plate on *Big Wiggly*'s stern was from New Hampshire and ten years expired.

Juliet had a bite, grew intent, cranked her reel in her new businesslike manner, dragged up a fluke (*Paralichthys dentatus,* also known as a summer flounder), a lefty; that is, a flatfish with both eyes on the left side of its head (a rare few flatfish have their eyes on the right). The fish was smooth and soft to the touch, was oval, was mottled brown on top to match the sea bottom, was clean white beneath, was almost all muscle, its anus only a couple of inches from its mouth. We marveled at the thing for several minutes. Food! Perfectly shaped for a pan! Juliet was a trifle superior about the whole thing, sitting there in her worn bikini and sun hat, redolent of sunscreen and squid. She made a show of not grinning.

Around noon, out of nowhere, a school of big fish appeared off our stern, splashing and walloping at the surface. "Bonito!" someone yelled from another boat. Sea gulls came flapping out from shore, adding to the mayhem. Mike and I ripped the bottom-fishing rigs off our lines, clumsily tied on Kastmasters, no leaders (we'd heard that bonito shun leaders), as the school moved toward us, slapping the calm water. My chest pounded with an excitement close to panic. I sputtered, could barely cast. Mike, hurrying, threw a bad cast, then as hurriedly reclaimed his line and threw a beauty. Juliet calmly continued to bottom-fish, still pleased with her fluke.

Suddenly, Mike's big surf rod dipped into the water, then just as suddenly stood up. He reeled in nothing, not even his lure. Then I had one. The fish dove, pulling line. I pulled back as Mike frantically tried to get another lure tied on. The school still slapped around us; the sea gulls dove. Juliet demanded a lure, now keenly interested, biting the fluke rig off her line like an old pro, letting the squid fall on her feet, oblivious now of things slimy and dead. Mike got set up, cast again. Again he was on, and again the fish escaped, taking his last lure. By the time Juliet got her lure tied on, the school was gone, the water quiet. Even the sea gulls left.

But I was still hooked up to my fish, thrilled at its weight as it headed to the bottom. There it played anchor, exactly beneath *Big Wiggly*. When I shifted to starboard, the fish moved to port. When I slid down the seat to port, the fish moved back to starboard. Jules and Mike and I watched the water, hoping for a flashing glimpse. Fifteen full minutes later we got one, then a frothing run at the surface, a final sparkling leap, and that was that. The fish came to the boat. Since we had no net I yanked the fish airborne, hoping to get it in. The hook came free just then and the fish bounced on the gunwale. All of us jumped to catch it. Our equipment slid to starboard. *Big Wiggly* almost went over. But all on its own the fish bounced the right way, leapt furiously in the bottom of the boat. The rest of us scrambled around, tangled in one another's lines, wobbling, cheering, trying to keep *Big Wiggly* aright, laughing and avoiding the fish as it champed near our feet.

Slowly, things settled down. We stared at the fish. It was not like the one I'd caught off the jetty in Vineyard Haven. It was more elegant, more deeply colored, more rambunctious, more streamlined. "Bonito," we decided tentatively.

Later, when we beached the boat, a girl of about five years asked if we'd had any luck. "Bonito," I told her. Mike hefted the fish for her to see. "That's a bluefish," the kid spat with utter disdain. "That's nothing but a bluefish." At home, poring over our various fish books, Mike and I decided she was right. Bluefish, *Pomatomus saltatrix,* the only member of its family. No wonder Mike's lures had been lost; we'd used no leaders to protect our lines. I'd just been lucky. And what about that first fish I'd caught, off the jetty? It was a weakfish (*Cynoscion regalis*), just as that other wise and knowledgeable child had said.

On days we felt ambitious, we threw *Big Wiggly* into the back of my truck and made dawn raids on the Menemsha Bight. Other days, we went out into Vineyard Haven Harbor at sunset, staying later and later in the dark, getting good at finding our way home by the lights, first of the drawbridge, then of our street. Mike devised a bowlight using an old whaleboat lantern of our landlord's. It had a green window on one side, a red window on the other — starboard and port — and a hole to put a candle in. Mike stuck a candle in there, tied the lantern onto *Big Wiggly*'s bow plate with rope, and we were in business.

One fair evening, just a week before Labor Day (summer's end looming), we steamed under the drawbridge, set our lines out and trolled. After an hour in the familiar harbor, I thought, *Screw it,* and pressed out past the bobbing red nun and into Vineyard Sound for the first time, breaking the hump of a terrible rip where the meeting of currents over a shoal threw the boat sideways, then dumped it in a trough, then turned it nearly clear around. I held onto the throttle stick, steering as best I could, and we kept trolling, grimly. Just as the sun set over Cuttyhunk, Juliet hooked a fish. Her line ripped off the reel as I tried to stop the boat and turn it; the fish just sat, a snag, a stone, a sunken frigate, the earth itself, perfectly stationary. The tip of Juliet's rod bent so sharply into the water that I thought it would break. Her line ran. She pulled back against the fish, determined. Mike and I cried out advice, too much advice, envious. "You guys shut up," Juliet said. She hiked up her dress with one hand, flipped her sun hat off her head, and got down to work. The fish bolted. When it leapt, clear out of the water, we could see it was a big blue. It dove, then leapt, then dove again, gradually grew tired and came to the boat. Mike readied our new net in the gathering dusk. Clouds had rolled in from the east.

A bluefish for Jules, the biggest of the summer! Mike measured and weighed it with my De-liar scale, found it to be thirty-two inches long and eight pounds heavy. We laughed, congratulating Jules, and threw the fish into Mike's giant cooler, where it had to bend to fit. Mike put a match to the candle in the whaleboat lantern. It seemed dim, but adequate. We needed another fish if we were going to feed our big household — eleven people this week — but two fish in one trip was the record, and two fish seemed a lot to hope for with night fast approaching. We had nothing but hot dogs at home, had spent too much money on rent. Scott and Bruce did not eat hot dogs. Willy didn't like them. Jon would need a regulation hot dog bun, not bread or an English muffin. That there was corn was small consolation. Another fish would mean at least a little dinner for everyone. We pressed on.

Near the bell buoy at the harbor's mouth we got into the wake of one of the ferries, the *Vineyarder,* just as the rip had begun to turn us around. *Big Wiggly*'s stern flew up out of the water. The motor roared, biting only air, stalled when the boat hit the water again with a metallic slam. The bow fell under a wave, which splashed over us, dousing the candle and soaking Mike and his matches, the only fire onboard. No moon. I pulled the starter rope in the dark, pulled and pulled until the little motor coughed and sputtered and ran.

Okay. We breathed, finally, and headed home with our lines in the water, knowing we shouldn't troll in the dark, but obsessed. After a short tenth of a mile or so, Mike got something big on, then I had one, too. Mike strained and grinned and got his in as we drifted farther out. It was even bigger than Jules', ten pounds at least, a rogue fish in the rip. Mine kicked off at the gunwale, gone. I'd lost him after fifteen minutes of fight. I started the motor with some difficulty and we headed in again, still foolishly trolling, collectively thrilled to be bringing in something of a meal, greedy for more, just one more, a real meal for our summertime clan. I headed straight down the ferry lane toward the harbor in the night. Juliet got another one on. I cut the engine uneasily, and we drifted as she fought the fish in with her small rod. A beautiful five-pounder, twenty minutes of fight, during which time Mike managed to hook up, too. Seeing that, I cast, just once, and hooked a bluefish of my own.

When the fish were finally in, the night was black around us. I went to start the motor. Ten pulls in the dark. Twenty. Forty. Mike scuttled back when my arm was tired, pulled over and over again, adjusted the fuel mix, cleaned the spark plug's gap, checked the fuel line, pulled and pulled again.

"Ferry," Juliet said matter-of-factly. Out in the Sound we could see the *Naushon* coming, three stories tall, twenty knots through the rip, lit bright as a Ferris wheel, but still far away. We drifted, checking the tank connection in the dark, pumping the primer, pulling on the starter rope, pulling, pulling. "Ferry's turning," Juliet said. It was true: the ferry had made the bell buoy and was turning into the harbor. We'd drifted to a place that seemed exactly in the ferry's path; worse, we were drifting toward the ice-house now, staying right in the ferry lane. Mike tried to light his wet matches. I pulled on the starter rope.

"That ferry is getting close," Juliet said.

The *Naushon* was so wide that there didn't seem any chance it could miss. Mike quickly yanked out one of the oars. I got the other, clumsily pulling it from beneath the seats and giving it to Mike. The ferry blasted its foghorn, warning one and all to clear the way. "Oarlocks!" Mike cried. We hadn't brought the oarlocks! He gave me back my oar and we each of us paddled, frantically trying to beat the current, and the ferry, and doom. Then a searchlight came on, and the *Naushon*'s captain swept the harbor methodically, stopping briefly at gulls and whitecaps, sweeping on until he came to us. The huge light did a double take, came back and found us, fixed us in a brilliant beam. We could feel the admonishment as we sat there stalled in light brighter than day. The *Naushon* altered her course enough to miss us, kept us bathed in the spotlight's beam. Her passengers lined the rail, stared. As we rolled in her mighty wake, relieved, I tried another pull. The motor started.

A half hour later, wet and chilled and excited, we slopped up to the porch, Mike and I slinging the big cooler between us, trying to make it look light, Juliet carrying tackle boxes, grinningly pleased. "How'd you do?" Willy said. That was the usual question, but tonight it was pointed. Jon already had a fire going in the barbecue pit. On the grill the contingency hot dogs popped and bubbled — eight of them, more of us. Tom and Hugh and Jerry, jingling with cash, had already left to go out to a restaurant.

"Starving," Joanna said apologetically. We were late eaters, it's true, but here it was, past ten o'clock.

"Ferry almost got us," Mike said.

"We found some potatoes," Scott called from the kitchen. He had a pot boiling in there, five potatoes for nine people. "And there's plenty of corn."

"No fish?" Bruce said.

"Dogs're fine," Ted said, tired of the complaining.

"No buns," Suzy said. "No mustard."

"No ketchup," Griselle said.

"There's mayonnaise," Scott called.

"Ton of beer," Jon said, offering me one.

I tried hard to look as though we'd been skunked, shuffled around a minute looking dejected. Then Mike and Juliet leapt to the cooler and kicked it over so the ice and bent fish spilled out in a fan on the firelit patio bricks. Everything stopped. Silence. Scott came out, letting the screen door slam behind him. "Jesus. Fish," he said.

Then Bruce began to clap, then Ted and Griselle, then Joanna and Willy and Jon. Suzy started the cheering, I think, as a joke, but it became real suddenly, and we all shouted for a full minute, joyously, everyone picking up blues, dancing with them, tossing them from person to person, swinging the big fishes between us, giggling, roaring, cheering, dancing.

"Who got 'em? How?" And we told how the rods had bent, and how far we'd gone, and how the ferry had fixed us in its light in order not to ram us. We did a pantomime of each catch, and each of us claimed the biggest fish, which Willy was actually hugging, carrying the mean and handsome creature all around the yard, chanting like a troglodyte. Juliet talked tackle like an old salt, told about the waves coming in the boat, added an hour to her fish's fight in the telling, held her arms out, laughed with pleasure. Jon popped more beers for everyone. Ted admitted to a bottle of whiskey upstairs, which he ran to get. Willy did a good impersonation of an old Scottish captain, and everyone danced and sang. Jon searched up more wood and got the fire roaring while Juliet scaled the fish and Mike and I had our first go at making fillets.

While the fish cooked (wrapped up in tinfoil with mayonnaise and parsley and scallions, an old Vineyard recipe, smoky from the fire — *superb*), Mike drew a map of the harbor and the sound, to show where we'd hooked up. We told the stories again and again as we ate, altering details, getting it right. "It's good luck when I'm with you," Juliet said. I honored her with a toast.

We drank beers; we sipped whiskey; we ate every bite of all six fish, and lots of good corn, and the five potatoes and the hot dogs, too. When we were done, sated, Bruce began to drum on the table, using his knife and a wooden spoon. Griselle boomed a bass on the cooler as Jon and Mike picked up their warped beach guitars and began to improvise the Bluefish Blues. Juliet twirled round with Suzy, Joanna dipped with Scott. We shouted, we sang, we toasted; we danced in thanksgiving till the night got old and the whiskey was gone and it was time to go to bed.

Turtles

Consider the importance of setting, the necessity of place, the influence of surroundings, the woven infinity of details that make up human environments. Think of all the backyards, all the attics, all the porches, all the basements, all the lunchrooms and church steps and under-the-beds. Think of the ballfields and schoolyards, the woodlots and lawns, the jungles and deserts, the grasslands and mountains, the beaches and oceans, the clouds and the sky, the edge of the atmosphere, the moon, the sun, the void, the infinite all, the universe (that place without location). Then back — and back again — to places so small that only atoms inhabit them (the same sturdy atoms that have made and do make and will make everything, then and now and forever more, reused), then smaller yet. Now return — slowly, gradually — back up in scale to us. Without people, there is probably place (ask any Naive Realist: without people the earth spun, and without us it will continue to spin). But without place, there is only abstraction, mind; without place, there is nothing.

My first memories are of place and setting and surroundings, and they are necessarily sensual, necessarily tied to Needham, Massachusetts, necessarily obnubilated by the mists of a very short blast of decades: *a deep void in the edge of a plywood tabletop, a rectangular black hole at exactly eye level into which I could stare or stick my pinkie. And the looping black shape of the cast-iron legs that held this table up, the legs of adults beneath it. And the smell of dirt and diesel behind the bulldozers in the lot down the street and the bulldozers them- selves like dinosaurs. And the cool feel of my pillow, if I turned it over. And the murmur of music on my big brother's radio playing low all night. And the baleful hoot of mourning doves, spring evenings. And the smell of ice up close, the picture of my own blood, in drops, freezing, the taste of the ice hurting my tongue as I rose woozy onto wobbling four-bladed skates, my fingers touching the small wound in my forehead that still scars me today.* There is nothing without the world.

Mobil Oil moved my dad from Chicago to Boston to New York, and because of these accidents of corporate necessity I spent my grade school years near a pond, Mr. Catt's gravel pit, in New Canaan, Connecticut. The gravel pit was full of fish and frogs, tadpoles and turtles. The painted turtles were the best, dark and shiny black with foliage-green and yellow necks and brilliant red lines on their legs and a cheerful red and orange border along their shells. Hiding at the edges of the pond, they were nearly invisible; turned over, helpless, they were marked by brilliant red in fantas- tical designs on the twelve pale sections of their belly shells. The spotted turtles were all right, too, looked like someone had dotted them carefully with yellow paint (in those days I knew who). Both models had a tidy turtle shape, lounged in perfect turtle languor on the rocks and logs and snags and sandbars of the gravel pit. They didn't close up quite tight when you caught them and, like toads, they pissed in your hands. A minute after you stopped bothering them they'd stick out their heads, look around, then stick out their legs, and off they'd try to go. I spent whole days prowling the mucky shallows, sometimes forgetting to watch out for the evil Mr. Catt.

The gravel pit was also full of snapping turtles. My big brother Randy and I would dare each other to catch them, and we'd succeed, and very often the turtle would have CATT carved on its plastron (what I called the belly shell) and a date. Some of the carvings were more than thirty years old. Mr. Catt himself was a snapper, always hollering at me and my brother and our respective friends to get away from the pond, and rumored among us to store parts of kids' bodies in his basement for snacks to feed the turtles. That he could handle a giant snapper long enough to carve his name in its bottom did nothing to dispel these rumors:

CATT
6/15/27

One very early morning — before school, before even my dad was awake, fishing by myself, seven years old — a snapper took my Red Devil. It felt like a log or a tire at first, but then I knew it was alive. I pulled and reeled and waited and pulled, then in the clean water I could see it: a turtle, marching militantly along the bottom toward me with my lure stuck in his mouth. At the shallows his head broke the water and he stopped. He looked too big for his shell (the way snappers do, football linemen in tiny cars), was two feet long, splay-footed, ugly as a fungus, tall on his legs, clearly unhappy with me. He took a long look, then turned resolutely and marched back into the pond. My old-fashioned reel rolled backward. He took my heavy line to its end, pulled it hard against the knot my father had tied to the reel axle. The turtle tugged. I tugged back. The turtle tugged harder. I dug my heels in, pulled. The turtle pulled back, began a jerking motion. I jerked back, wishing for scissors to cut the line. The turtle pulled, and jerked, and won: I had to let go. The floating cork handle of my little rod traveled for thirty feet in a straight line into the pond, then sank and disappeared.

This story, even delivered in tears before breakfast, met with much disbelief at home. Randy hooted. My father thought it would take a lot of allowance to get a new rod and reel. My mother pointed out that I was known to give away my things in the eternal quest for friends. Dougie threw a spoon on the floor from his highchair. Only my sister Carol, a trusty five-year-old, found a way to believe me.

Years later, in Ithaca, New York — Nixon days, Ithaca College days — I knew an old box turtle, a tortoise, who used to cross Route 13A every day, from one pond to the next. (He wouldn't have lived in the water, probably haunted the woods around it.) On my way to band practice (rock 'n' roll!) late mornings I'd see him coming. In the evenings, when I was early enough, I'd see him going, a daily routine for an entire summer. Some drivers carefully avoided him; some didn't seem to notice him, went right over him, missing with their tires; some screeched to stops or swerved to spare him. He never paused, though, never blinked, never looked right or left, just continued forward, his head craned out, his mission clear. When he was lucky, traffic stopped and people hopped out of their cars to watch his slow progress. Some days he'd cover the entire distance himself, though most often a good, impatient Samaritan would pick him up and carry him to the side of the road.

But one blazing afternoon the turtle was dead, right on the yellow median line, not entirely flattened — his shell was too tough for that — but broken. He'd stayed alive long enough to get his head pulled in and to close his hinged plastron behind it. Two of his legs were pulled in. Two were not. Five cars had stopped, though not the one that hit him. Eight people stood about, sharing stories of his bad habit. More cars stopped. Lots of people knew him; the traffic jam was a sort of state funeral. A couple of teenage tough kids shrugged. A dead turtle, so what? I was somewhere between the mourners and the kids. I had an impulse to pick the turtle up, carry him reverently to the side of the road. I had the anti-impulse not to do a thing, to sneer privately at the turtle's dumbness and slowness and guaranteed bad luck. The anti-impulse won, for it didn't require action. After a while a man in dark glasses stepped forward and picked up the broken old tortoise. Its two injured legs hung.

"He might have been a hundred years old," a woman said.

"I've known him for ten," a man in a tweed jacket said. "Since they widened the road."

The man in the sunglasses walked delicately off the pavement and put the turtle down in some tall reeds next to the pond, not seeming to care that his loafers got muddy or that everyone watched.

That night, drinking in one of the hundred rollicking college-town bars, I wished it had been me who picked that turtle up and moved it, wished those damn teens hadn't been there to freeze me in my spot.

And I stayed frozen in that place for years, a very long time, not distant from nature (I lived on farms, spent days in the woods, stood hours beside rivers), but caught up in a bollixed web of youthful shalts and shalt-nots that kept me from my own nature the way a little boy's friends keep him from girls, say, or a young man's friends keep him from real mourning or ecstasy. I'm still unraveling the exact reasons for this detachment (the years of it seemed like fun, anything to keep wildly busy and slightly crazed — drinking the least of it, women the best, my life of second-rate-if-locally-glamorous rock bands and miserable odd jobs and bartending a kind of profitable penance). In those years I might have seen turtles, but I couldn't make them matter the way the snappers had mattered, the way the pond turtles had mattered. Those turtles had had the power to steal from me, to piss on my hands, to absorb me whole for hours at a time. But now my turtle sense was dead, killed like a tortoise in the road by something in me that didn't want to see anything very clearly. I'd lost track of joy, escaping hurts that remained hidden from me. I was in Ithaca; I was in Connecticut; I was in Seattle; I was in New York; I was in the Berkshires; I was in Norway; I was on the Vineyard; but I wasn't quite on Earth.

My folks bought their place on Lake Mascoma in New Hampshire when I was in college. It's a red house on a big lawn, complete with boats and lawn chairs and vinyl couches and shiny tables — completely furnished, even down to screws and bits of wire in cigar boxes in the basement: a man had died. On the lawn was a gazebo that had once been the bandstand in the town of Lebanon, and which an early owner of the place had rescued and moved. The lawn there is mossy from lack of sun; the oak trees above are thick; there are worms beneath the turf and great blocks of granite by the water.

On Juliet's twenty-fifth birthday (June 15, 1987), after another long semester for her at Pratt (a full year until graduation and her master's), we borrowed my dad's car and drove away from New York to the lake for a break and a celebration. I had just finished my first semester at Columbia's MFA program and was flush with the sense that my life was changing. Cheerily I bought Jules many little presents, ten perhaps, or fifteen, wrapped each one and kept giving them to her as the birthday night wore on — dinner in Hanover, a fire in the fireplace at home. We basked in the silence of the place, letting all the shoutings and loud music and car horns and pressures of the city overcome us in the quiet to crest in a bad argument about restaurants, of all things, the argument an unintentional but effective way to exorcise all the stress of home. Once the air was clear we drank beers and played games out of the deep game drawer, throwing dice and shuffling cards and keeping score until late in the night.

The next morning we woke and ran naked to the lake to swim, raced back to the house, made breakfast. Later we floated and anchored the big raft Randy and my dad had built, brought the old sailboat from the garage to the water and washed the spiders off its canvas deck and scrubbed its two pontoons and mounted its new striped sail and pushed off onto the empty lake for what was meant to be a short sail and a picnic before we raked the lawn. But we tacked the half mile across the lake five times and back, a score and back, eating sandwiches, taking turns as captain, sailing gradually northward into the faint breeze, four hours in the warm sun and perfect silence, a desultory trip, twenty miles of tacking to make two miles of lake. Around us on the shore stirred the deep climax forest, freshly green, climbing the hills and the mountains, an oaken canopy jazzed with sugar maples and white birches and copper beeches and spruce trees and solitary pines. Also around the lake was a broken and sometimes shabby necklace of houses. The irregular sound of a pounding hammer drifted over the water. Nothing and no one else. Jules and I stretched out on the canvas. "This lake would be a good place to have a wedding," I said. "You'd have lots of sailboats and weather like this and people would cook out."

"You think we'll get married?"

"And everyone could camp, and water ski, and we'd have big breakfasts and a great band."

"I think I'm too young," Juliet said.

We sailed past the rocky point across from the old Shaker settlement, sailed past the two islands with their secluded house each, back and forth, easy, in silence. I said, "I just mean it would be a good place."

"Well, it's pretty today." Brilliant and warm, one of the longest days of the year, nothing to call us home. We swam, lay drying on the canvas, investigated the shore, swam more, stared up at the sky, Juliet murmuring, telling me all the stuff she planned to do when she was finally done with grad school. She thought she'd try taking her art more seriously. She'd take a year off, at least, and just do art. Maybe there were better restaurants to work at. Maybe better places to live. Maybe out of New York.

Something about the two of us alone on that raft of a sailboat had the power to erase my detachment from the world, to ease my dense and unacknowledged fear of life and love, even my much acknowledged fear of harm. Juliet's work and her art and her life mattered to me, and was my work and my art and my life, too. And would be for as far ahead as I could see in the hot sun of that perfect afternoon. The only sounds were the occasional flap of the sail as the breeze faded to nothing and that insistent, irregular hammering away off down the lake. We said secret things to each other, drifting, and dove and swam, growing sunburned. The future was long. We snoozed.

A half hour, or forty-five minutes, or maybe an hour

later (who could tell?), we woke to the rustle of lily pads under the twin hulls of the old boat. We'd drifted into the north shore, a boggy, reedy, empty stretch, where railroad tracks lay rusting on an abandoned dike near the Mascoma River inlet. The Aqua Cat's sail did not so much as flap. I lay there with my chin on my hands and stared. Water lilies, in bloom. I thought of the fish under there, and the many larval insects, and the tires from old cars, and the lost lures and bait cans and bobbers and fishing rods. I thought of the hidden current of the river, and how the lake would spill over the recently restored dam to be a river once again, and flow to the Connecticut River (their confluence just behind the K Mart in West Lebanon), and then to Long Island Sound.

And on a peeled and partly submerged tree trunk I noticed a series of humps, an interesting burl, perhaps, revealed by the lack of bark. Then one of the humps moved, clambering up onto another. The hump next to that stuck its head up and looked around. Another hump turned until it was facing 180 degrees the other way. Turtles! Black and peaceful, peaceful and important.

I grew excited in a way I hadn't been excited for a long time — no shouting or singing, no dancing or drinking, no insatiable and generalized appetite — just a log at the shore and ten more turtles, the green and the yellow stripes on their necks vivid. And over on a rock that stuck up from the bog, three turtles more, one of them on top of the others, pyramid style. And on a drowned and fallen tree trunk that angled gently out of the water to starboard at least forty turtles more, lined up sweet and calm and powerful from the high end of the log all the way down to the cool and placid water.

Out of the Frying Pan

Camp-keeping in the Delta was not all beer and skittles.
The problem was water. The lagoons were saline; the river,
where we could find it, was too muddy to drink. At each
new camp we dug a new well. Most wells, however, yielded
only brine from the Gulf. We learned, the hard way, where
to dig for sweet water. When in doubt about a new well,
we lowered the dog by his hind legs. If he drank freely, it
was the signal for us to beach the canoe, kindle the fire, and
pitch the tent. . . .

I am glad I shall never be young without wild country to
be young in.

— Aldo Leopold

Today I am thinking of young Aldo and his brother and
the delta of the Colorado in 1922 and the bobcats and the
jaguars that were there and the beer and skittles and the
cranes and the many ducks and geese and deer and the dog
hung by his hind legs because I am thinking about the
Frying Pan River, which, by way of the Roaring Fork, is a
tributary of the Colorado. By the time the waters of the
Frying Pan reach the rich delta of the Colorado River
(which is in farms, now, a lot of farms; I hope one is named

El Tigre, in honor of the missing jaguar), that mighty river has passed through 1,450 miles of fabulous canyons and desolate plateaus, been ridden upon by rafters, been fished, been photographed, been used for state and national borders, been backed up by dams, been roughly suckled at by farmers and electric companies, been diverted, been polluted, been drained and rerouted, been all but murdered in its bed.

I am thinking about the Frying Pan because Juliet and I lived beside it for the month of August, 1987. We'd spent June and July working in New York, had decided to head west and find a cabin somewhere in the Rocky Mountains for August, assuming as always that all would go well. We camped across the country to Colorado, stayed in the Pike National Forest for a few days, then went looking for my sister Carol, who was living in Snowmass Village, near Aspen.

Over the Hagerman Pass we came. The Hagerman, a dirt track that crosses the Continental Divide between the Arkansas and the Colorado drainages, was once called the Arkansas–Frying Pan Pass and was the route of the Midland Railroad, which folded in 1917. The pass as Juliet and I found it was scarier than I remembered (or maybe I was smarter or less bold now: once I'd driven over the same pass in a red Chevy station wagon with two speed-and-beer-charged friends on the cross-country trip that landed me broke in Seattle). It wasn't just that the road was rutted and rocky and steep or just that there were no railings or that there was a generous selection of thousand-foot plunges; it wasn't just that several sections of the road had caved in leaving just enough space for us to pass, our car rather tilting toward the abyss as we crept along the hillside that was the opposite edge of the road; it wasn't the snowfields, really, with no one in sight to help if we got stuck. As in life, what was scary was the uncertainty about what was coming, the not knowing even if the road existed, one mile to the next. As in life what was scary was that there was no way to turn around, most of the way, which meant that any leg you ventured out on you might have to negotiate again, in reverse.

At the top, something over 10,000 feet, on an absolutely bare expanse of Miocene Age basalt, and exactly on the divide, a thunderhead pulled up and let loose upon us. There was no point in counting the seconds between flash and boom; we were inside the storm. I stopped the car and Juliet and I folded our hands and just watched, just lived there in the rocking car for five minutes, then ten, then twenty, the cloud exploding around us, lightning striking trees *below* us or ribboning across the sky with a kind of shrieking, tearing roar — shooting sideways, shooting upwards, shooting where it would. Some of the great floods of water that splashed around us would flow east down to the Arkansas River, eventually to end up in the Gulf of Mexico; some would flow west down to the Frying Pan, eventually to end up in the Gulf of California.

The storm passed, leaving blue skies behind it. Jules and I ate lunch, then followed the water that had headed for the Gulf of California. A nameless creek ran bubbling beside the road rather sweetly, then met another creek that helped raise the first creek's voice; then, almost belligerently, the two of them took to the road, *became* the road for two hundred yards. We stopped. Jules and I and the car (not my blessed pickup, whose transmission had given out just after our trip to New Hampshire, not a Land Rover, not a Jeep, not a Bronco, not even an Eagle or a Subaru, just a citified two-wheel-drive mini-van borrowed at the last minute from my parents) found ourselves at the bottom of a steep hill. The road behind us was two ruts in the light mud of a ten percent grade. There would be no backing up. The road before us was, as I have said, a creek. Having no choice, I drove into the rapids and we proceeded, up to the floorboards in water, like customers in some sort of do-it-yourself flume ride at a low-budget World's Fair. In the middle of our slow ford Jules and I began to argue, skirting the issue (which was fear) in favor of a noisy discussion of whether we'd ever find a place to live in this godforsaken strip of mountains and lousy roads and thunderstorms and general hell.

Once we left the creek behind, the road improved in increments until it was paved, and soon enough we were driving alongside the Frying Pan River. "Nice country," Jules said, fairly bubbling, all fear past, our current safety lit gloriously by the afterglow of danger. She was right: wildflowers bloomed everywhere, shapely trees reigned over meadows, grand peaks loomed before us, grand peaks receded behind. We camped by Chapman Lake in the fog of a cloud that had bumped up against the mountain we were on.

In the morning, Jules dug out an array of pencils and her pad of drawing paper and set to rendering the anomalous, red sandstone mountain that took up the sky downriver. I, meantime, hiked upstream and fished from the banks of the Frying Pan with my all-new fly rod, an inexpensive graphite number (which I still use, finding it more responsive than all the higher-class rods I've tried) made in Cortland, New York, a town I knew well, saloon by saloon, from my rock-'n'-roll band days. The rod was a veteran of a single weekend of practice at my folks' place in New Hampshire, having waved first over the lawn, then over

Lake Mascoma, and having taken a few warmwater fish — bass, sunnies and perch — and a lot of abuse, too. It had also seen a little practice on a lawn in Central Park (though this didn't get me far, being too embarrassing for extended sessions). That good rod, most of all, took me back to the fishing days of my childhood, to the pink dawns on the gravel-pit pond, and to a solitude that wasn't lonely.

Thanks to Tom Rosenbauer's book, *The Orvis Flyfishing Guide,* I knew how to make a nail knot now, and an Albright knot and a turtle knot and an improved clinch knot; I knew how to retrieve line with my left hand while keeping control of the line with my right. I could throw a decent cast, too, four times out of ten. I knew how to play a fish; I knew how to land one. All that was left was to catch a trout. At the bank of the famous Frying Pan River I flung my flies about, losing one in the grasses across the stream, one in the alders behind me. I lost two more in the river itself — one on a snag, one on a rock, neither on a fish. I tied knots; I untangled my line; I dreamed of hip waders. I was absorbed so thoroughly that I became part of the mossy bank I was standing on, part of the air around me, part of the sound of the river itself, coursing past.

Jules came and found me, *time to go,* and I packed up, wondering how on earth you were supposed to catch a trout in a river. I hadn't seen one, though my instruction books said I ought to be able to. I'd stared behind rocks, stared at the undercut of the bank, looked everywhere I'd been told. *Bad spot,* I concluded wrongly. The instruction books should have mentioned how hard it is to see trout at first, and how long it takes to develop the vision to find them.

We got ourselves loaded back into the car and continued on to Snowmass Village. Not a mile down the road from our camping place we saw a cabin up on a bluff over the road, a funky little cabin sided with slab wood, its roof multicolored from repairs. "That's the kind of cabin I'd like to have," Juliet said. I agreed, that was the sort, but how did you find a place like that for one month? There was no one around to ask, and I doubt if we would have asked even if there had been. We'd been alone in the car for so many days that even being *near* a stranger seemed gregarious.

We drove on, down along the river through Meredith (a general store, a phone booth, two cabins, several mobile homes), around the Reudi Reservoir (its dam approved by a vote of Congress the year Jules was born, 1962), past the raw shores of the lake and past its drowned ranches and past the drowned town of Reudi, past Reudi Dam and into Basalt (that charming town at the end of the Frying Pan), then upstream along the Roaring Fork River to Snowmass Village.

In the Aspen *Pennysaver* Juliet saw an ad announcing a cabin for rent. The address was given as "Biglow Ranch, twenty-six miles up the Frying Pan River." Jules made an appointment for the next day with the owner, a Mr. Looney, who lived in Basalt. So, after an evening of visiting with Carol and Mac and their roommates (all but Mac resident ceramic artists at the Andersen Ranch), and after a night of sleeping under the stuffed bison head that graced the wall of their condo (temporary housing, thank you very much, provided by the ranch), Juliet and I got up early and drove back down to Basalt, back up the Frying Pan River, past the dam, past the lake, past tiny Meredith and to the Biglow Ranch. Gary Looney met us at the gate. The cabin for rent, as it turned out, was the same cabin we'd seen on our trip down.

Up close, the cabin was shambly, with no furniture, part of a once-glorious guest ranch that was nothing now but a collection of randomly placed decrepit buildings. Gary Looney (his real name, I'm serious — a tall, soft-spoken man in cowboy boots, a rancher, a sweetheart, not loony in the slightest, intent on restoring the place, his hopeless project) said we'd find some chairs and maybe a mattress and table in one of the barns back up that way. He pointed. Back up there by the horses there, see 'em there?

The cabin stood at the front of an aspen grove, sported a rusty but ready wood stove, a former occupant's collection of *Hustlers,* and cold running water, at least most of the time, as Gary explained, not wanting to mislead us. At the front end there was a sleeping loft reached by a hand-hewn ladder. Gary sent me up there, apparently proud of the loft, having, perhaps, never been in it, all two hundred degrees of it, and that's where the *Hustler*s were, and an unfortunate mattress, and a *Helicopter Pilots' Association Handbook,* and mud enough for an adobe addition, courtesy of several hundred mud daubers, *wasps,* which buzzed as I stuck my head up through the hatch door trying not to breathe. "Nice fellow added that loft," Gary told us. "Nice place to sleep."

I hurried down the ladder. Gary took the look on my face for trouble. "Well. I admit it's a bit run down," he said, suddenly tense, about to lay out the price for a month on the exact trout stream and in the exact cabin Juliet and I had dreamed of as we sweltered through July in New York. "Now August is a busy time . . ." He knew how to draw out the dealings, to wear us down in advance. "One hundred dollars," he said suddenly.

Jules and I looked at each other.

Looney must have thought we were unhappy with that quote. "And no deposit," he said, dealing out his last ace.

I handed him a hundred-dollar bill, one of eight we had scratched together for rent.

And so, as easily as that, Juliet and I found ourselves on the Biglow Ranch, three miles from a phone, twenty-six miles from Basalt, and $700 richer than we'd thought. Our cabin was long and thin, a railroad apartment without the apartment building, one long living room with a kitchen at the far end, and behind the kitchen a bedroom — just a small shed tacked rudely on the back of the building. We thought that shack of a bedroom would save us from having to make the wasp loft habitable. From the sunlit front door you saw straight through the living room to the bedroom door, and straight through that to the shady rear door. Just outside the back door in the long grasses of the aspen grove a brook sneaked past, burbling, something to listen to in the night.

The moment Gary Looney's dust settled into the columbine and Indian paintbrush along the road, I shoved the ladder up into the attic loft and closed the hatch forever (or at least until Jules needed a hot place to dry some wildflowers). We swept out and mopped, and washed the bubbly, mismatched windows, noting with pleasure that here, unlike New York, the dirt was on the inside of the glass. I gaff-taped cardboard over the two or three broken panes, and we were done, ready for furniture.

The peaks of fifteen mountains rose around us, the short ones covered with trees, the taller ones — reaching twelve thousand feet and more — stony bald. One peak was made of a luminous red sandstone, the others of basalt, a rich blue-gray. High-tension wires on big steel towers swooped through our valley, power on its way from the dam. (I cursed those big towers, had been reading about the health hazards of the magnetic fields the wires produce, and yet I can still hear myself asking Looney over the phone if the place had electricity so we could plug in our writing machine.) The wires were quiet at least, not even a faint hum in the night.

Otherwise it was elk and ponderosa pine and alpine flowers and the river softly passing; it was escaped horses stepping past, staring, and cows in the night, bumping their big heads on the cabin wall, intent on grazing the delicious weeds growing hard against our house. It was stars as close and hard bright as I've ever seen stars, away from cities and agriculture, industry and dust. It was Juliet painting good pictures and working on her writing. It was the two of us cooking on a ring of stones, washing in a communal bathhouse, meeting the five other residents of the ranch, one woman and four men. (We never met the woman, but the four men turned out to be slightly cracked Vietnam vets hiding from the world, shy, reticent, alone. This didn't surprise us: Juliet and I have lived briefly in a lot of desolate places, back in the woods and on islands and at the top of high mountains; when we get settled, and feel the solitude, and understand that we are alone, and safe, we always meet a Vietnam vet. I have lots of easy theories about Vietnam vets and their need for solitude. The question is, why am *I* there? And the 'Nam vets always ask.) It was mourning doves and gray jays and owls and hawks and Stellar's jays, deep blue. It was Juliet and it was I, happily distant from New York City, where life was busy and hot and expensive, and where there were no wild rivers and no trout anywhere, no trout at all.

There are several stories about how the Frying Pan River got its name. Two have to do with the Ute Indians (who doubtless called the river something less prosaic than Frying Pan). The first story has the Utes attacking a party of trappers, leaving all but two dead, and one of these severely wounded. The healthy survivor is supposed to have hidden his wounded comrade in a cave and hung a frying pan from a spruce bough to mark the spot while he went for help.

In the second story, a party of prospectors in the valley are said to have found signs of Indians, whereupon they decided to steal back over the mountain to Aspen. But, at the top of the ridge, they found themselves looking down on the encampment of a Ute war party. "Out of the frying pan and into the fire," one of them whispered, apparently unable to coin a new phrase for the occasion. He and the others decided to go back into the frying pan, so to speak, and the name stuck.

Or this one, which ignores the Utes: two early gold prospectors fell into the river while fording it, lost all their mining equipment and ended up using a frying pan to look for gold.

Then there was this: a very old fellow who came out of his cabin to chat one day while I was fishing told me that romantics might make up any number of stories, but that the Frying Pan's name had come about simply because the river had always supported huge populations of trout. He made a pragmatic, frying-pan-full-of-trout-over-the-fire motion with one withered hand, brandished an imaginary spatula with the other. I said something like: "Leave it to Europeans to name a river after the frying pan instead of after the meal! How about Trout River? Or Rainbow River?"

"Romantic," he said, branding me. "The pan was useful at least! And permanent! Just like the river. The fish are nothing but a bunch of fish. They come and go."

"So where's the frying pan?"

"It went! But not so fast as the fish."

The Frying Pan River, etymology aside, was full of trout, lots of trout, mostly browns and rainbows, though I heard two rather dubious reports of brook trout. I also heard of people catching cutthroats but didn't believe it. Cutthroats are known for being stupid about hooks, known for being easy to catch, and now they are sometimes hard to come by; being easy to catch makes it difficult to survive. In the Frying Pan and the Roaring Fork and the Colorado, for example, the native cutthroats are gone.

The browns in the Frying Pan are descendants of English fish planted a hundred years ago and gone wild over generations. To me the brown is the most beautiful trout (vying with the brookie), a rich purply brown on the back and covered with bright spots in startling colors: red, blue, green, yellow, even orange, sometimes, and each spot circled with another color, or white. Browns are particular and intelligent, known for growing large, known for being the hardest trout to fool, the hardest trout to catch.

Rainbows are hardy and easy to farm, so rainbows make up most of the stock fish that the hatcheries plant and therefore most of the fish that turn up in the Frying Pan River. Planted fish tend to be bland in color and seldom put up much of a fight when hooked. Rosenbauer reports finding cigarette butts in these dullards' stomachs; stocked fish mistake butts for the pellets they are fed at the hatchery. The other signs of a stockie are beat-up beaks, blunt dorsal fins, missing pectoral fins, and tattered tails from living in cramped quarters in the hatchery runs. Some hatcheries clip fins or attach tags to help identify hatches; often, too, the fish are dosed with antibiotics.

The children of a stockie, of course, learn life in the river, and, unless other conditions (such as too much fishing pressure) make them tame, succeeding generations will grow more and more wild; like the children of any immigrant, the descendants of stockies forget the old ways in favor of the new. That includes dress. A wild trout has beautiful spots — lots of spots, a darkly glistening back to blend into the river bottom, a light belly to blend into the sky, and, in the case of a rainbow, a real rainbow of pink and steel above the lateral line. A wild trout is cautious, inspects its food before it pounces, watches the sky for predators, darts away at the least sound or shadow, puts up a first-rate fight when it's hooked.

I had always fished for bass and for pike and had always fished in lakes. I'd read plenty of books — Rosenbauer's for one, and Lee Wulff's book on flies, and Vince Marinaro's beautiful book *In the Ring of the Rise,* and (at a friend's house when I was supposed to be socializing) Ray Bergman's wise old book, *Trout,* and every other book of advice and instruction and theory and trout-fishing fantasy I could get my hands on — but still I didn't know what to do with the Frying Pan.

Below Reudi Dam (which was thirteen miles from our cabin) were signs proclaiming certain sections of the river to be Gold Medal Water. Here, the signs said, conditions were ideal for the sustenance of enormous trout, trout you'd need a winch to land, trout the size of pickup trucks, trout with jaws like bobcats', trout to write home about. Flyfishing only. Barbless hooks only. Catch-and-release only. This part of the river was left unstocked, for catch-and-release fishing and ideal conditions had led to a self-sustaining and self-replenishing population of rainbows. (The Roaring Fork is amply stocked, however, and plenty of aggressive Roaring Fork fish certainly make their way to the Frying Pan and then swim, rock by rock, until they are under the Reudi Dam.)

The Reudi Dam insures a constant supply of very cold water from the bottom of the lake and a constant supply of exotic food — lake shrimps and leeches and minnows — to complement the more erratic supply of hatched and hatching insects the river provides. In the Gold Medal Water the rainbows grow weirdly deep in the belly. They also grow tattered in the mouth from constant catch-and-release pressure, and tame in a way, like pets available for repeated abuse in a kind of public aquarium.

A lot of people stood in the Gold Medal Water under the dam, always. These folks came from all over the world, had boots up to their necks and polarized fishing specs and cowboy hats and camo shirts and rods like Greek gods' lances. They wore fishing vests with a hundred pockets (to hold tippets and leaders and weights and spare spools and line cleaner and fly floatant and scissors and jackknives and four or five loaded fly boxes), wore forceps and line clippers on spring-loaded retractors. Fancy nets hung from the backs of their vests on braided cord attached to instant-release clips. And somewhere in there a camera was slung, ready to record triumphs (the river might better be called the Flash Pan River now). Equipment! Oh, equipment! I was jealous of all of it.

I found quiet places to fish where no one could watch me, wader-less, vestless, inexperienced, too proud to ask questions. And at first I didn't catch fish. One fine day early in the month, Juliet and I drove into Basalt, where I slipped into Frying Pan Tackle and bought some grasshopper imitations, which the man said were always a good bet in the summer, and some green drakes (dry and wet, two each), which the man said would be hatching for a couple of weeks. I also bought a handful of other fantastical flies that caught my eye and a nice aluminum box to put them in.

Those flies and that box seemed like a good way to break in my first credit card, which I'd been issued just before we'd left New York and which I was wary of using.

Heading up the river toward home that day, Juliet and I stopped for lunch at a turnout over the Frying Pan and well below the dam. Jules offered to make the sandwiches so I could have a moment to try my new flies. I pulled my trusty Cortland rod out of the van and stumbled down amongst the tumbled rocks of the bank to a big boulder that gave me a platform in the river (which was sixty feet across at that point and perhaps three deep, flowing hard and fast over uncountable rocks and two enormous drowned logs). Impatiently, I tied on one of the grasshopper imitations, watched the loud water. Impossible that a fish could live in that moiling madness!

I cast once and it was perfect (surprise!), my grasshopper falling *plop* on the water upstream exactly as Rosenbauer and Bergman and Wulff said it should, about the way an actual grasshopper would splash down after an errant jump. I watched the hopper float, wondering how to deal with all the slack in my line, hearing Rosenbauer's kindly voice (or at least the kindly voice he'd put on the page): *Always keep control of your line.* The fly headed around a big rock, the exact rock I'd picked, a mossy chunk of feldspar, barely submerged, breaking up the surface, the kind of rock behind which a trout could find some slack water to face upstream and hold itself in while waiting for food to come by.

As I fumbled with the tangle of my line, there was a sudden blast of green and silver in the water just under my hopper. A splash, a grab, the white of the fish's mouth. My hopper disappeared into the boiling stream; the line (no time to gather slack, no way to set the hook) moved a few feet. Then the fish let go, simply spat out the thing that was not food, all in a heart-pounding flash.

"Lunch!" Juliet called from above, having missed the excitement.

I cast hurriedly and caught weeds. I cast again and caught the rock. I cast once more — starving! — and caught the back of my shirt.

Juliet brought the sandwiches down to my boulder, delicately balancing as she stepped from rock to rock, holding our piece-of-old-lumber cutting board like a tray. "Well, you've got a hobby," she said. She helped me get the hook out of my shirt. During lunch I flipped the grasshopper out there a couple of times, but even when I hit the spot where the fish had shown, nothing came of it. Jules watched as I pulled the hopper toward me in the water. "Just what is that supposed to look like?" she said. Her hair blew in the river's wind to cover her face for a second. She sat on the rock in a pair of my gym shorts, holding her long legs.

"It's a grasshopper." I wiggled it on the surface, to show her how lifelike it could be.

"It looks like a small piece of toilet paper on a hook," she said.

"Grasshopper," I said, twitching it.

"A *lifelike* piece of toilet paper on a hook."

Later that first week I made my debut in the Gold Medal Water. I could tell I was pissing off the other flyfishers, but I stumbled into the river, wearing the vest I'd made out of a purple-dyed army surplus camouflage shirt Juliet had got for twenty cents in a thrift store. I'd sewed four khaki pockets from an old pair of pants on the breast of the thing. Wearing my pink gym shorts, I waded into the extremely cold water in sneakers, stood downstream from a fellow who seemed to be trying to believe I wasn't there. In the clear water I could see big, lazy fish finning, calmly picking off passing insects or shrimps or *something* (who could tell?). The fish were so used to human legs that they didn't shy at all when I stepped around them. Tame. I tied on a two-dollar grasshopper, thinking that it did look like a small piece of toilet paper. Nothing happened, even when I managed to float it in the fishes' faces. I tied on a dry green drake, cast, watched it float nicely, no drag. I found myself very aware of the flyfishers near me. (Did they see my fine cast? Perhaps they thought I was some kind of eccentric expert.)

Blammo! A big fish took. When he realized he was hooked, he swam rather methodically under a cut in the bank, past a root he had surely used to this purpose before, and snapped my tippet. Not only tame, but educated as well — a Ph.D. in Fly Avoidance and Contingency Escape. I got the feeling he'd taken the fly just for the fun of breaking my line. Gold Medal indeed. The man upstream spoke: "Too rough, boy. Tried to horse 'im in. These fish're wild! Caught one old boy this morning that 'ad two flies stuck right in his lip!"

What, I thought, is wild about having two flies stuck in your lip?

I stopped fishing there. Started to fish above Reudi Lake, where there was no pretending. In that part of the river there were no tackle restrictions, and one could choose whether to keep a fish or not. Stockies were stockies, put there in unnatural overabundance, meant to be caught. The state hatchery people loaded the lake with fingerlings every spring, and by August, when these fish had taken up positions in the river, they were frying pan size, some bigger. Bait fishermen filled their stringers here. Kids caught piles of fish, using worms. Even in my purple vest and with my hair on end and shivering in the river in gym shorts, I got no weird looks. I could put aside self-consciousness and learn.

The river was much smaller here, much more shallow. I could look into the water and identify the trout's holding positions, learned to see fish consistently by finding their shadows on the bottom or by interpreting subtle movements near rocks. I used nymphs, tried streamers, floated drys, experimented with wets. The water was cold as hell on my legs. I thought of my new credit card, thought of my birthday coming up, and one fine afternoon made the long drive to Basalt and bought myself a pair of tall brown hip waders.

I fished every afternoon while Juliet drew. The stocked fish weren't too impressive, but I caught lots of them and put them back, always learning. Some days when bait wouldn't work for the kids and spinners wouldn't work for their dads I'd be the only one on that stretch of river catching anything. On those days I felt like an old pro. Kids asked me what I was using. Old men asked me if flyfishing was so hard, after all. I just hoped they didn't notice when I got the line tangled around my neck, or stepped on it, or hit a fish so hard that my fly shot out of its mouth and into the branches of a tree behind me. Once in a while I would keep four fish, all identical, all faded rainbows with tattered tails, all exactly eleven inches long, for dinner.

And rarely, on the way to or back from visits with Carol and Mac, I'd try the Gold Medal Water. With my new boots and new skills I felt less conspicuous, but those big, tame fish were still hard to fool. Occasionally some lesser monsters would take, and even these showed signs of having been caught, over and over again.

*

I started appreciating the wilder water near our cabin, well north of the lake and, at 8,300 feet, well above it. Here there were no restrictions and no other fishers. The fish were small and wary. I had learned to see them as they fed, and to see what they were feeding on, and to choose flies to imitate what they were feeding on. I bought tiny midges tied on hooks the size and weight of eyelashes, the hook eyes so fine that only the thinnest tippet would go through, one- or two-pound test. The midges fooled some of the bolder stockies, those that had made their way upstream. I noticed the stronger fight and richer color of these fish.

Due to an almost absolute absence of fishing pressure, the fish in the upper river were very easy to spook. Footsteps on the bank sent them scooting for cover, stopped them from feeding for hours. I learned to stalk the river, to wade silently, to wait and watch. And I noticed how the sunlight fell through the trees, how the ladybugs fell and struggled on the water, how the white gliders from seed pods rode through the air. I was a kid again, looking.

In exchange for less monstrous quarry and less definite success, I had most of ten miles of river to myself, all the way up to the Frying Pan Lakes, three little tarns couched in a sheer curving valley of 12,000-foot peaks, miles from the end of the Frying Pan Road. No houses. No dams. No cement anywhere.

On the day before Juliet and I were to head back to New York I packed a little (books in boxes, food in boxes, clothes in boxes), then pulled on my waders and tromped out across the porch, past Juliet, who drew, just starting to experiment with pastels. She didn't look up, didn't say anything at all, absorbed completely.

I crossed the Frying Pan Road and made my way to the

river, crunched through the woods to a hidden hole where I knew a certain fish liked to feed, a mysterious fish that I'd never been able to fool, a sneaky fish that held in a difficult spot and disappeared whenever I cast to him, disappeared, spooked, for whole afternoons from the disturbance of a single poor cast. Since normally I'd tried him from downstream, I thought I'd try from upstream — dry fly or no. Close to the river I began to creep, careful not to break a stick or roll a stone under my clumsy, flopping boots. After a long stalk I stood at the head of the fish's pool, which was forty feet long and twenty feet wide, a dark sweep of deep water under spruce boughs.

I settled into the river, standing on a submerged boulder in water to the tops of my new boots, watching. At the tail of the pool, just in the spot I expected, just under a particularly low brush of spruce bough, I saw a little bit of head emerge and sink. I watched the spot for more than a minute before, sure enough, the fish appeared again, gently feeding, leaving a bubble as he took an insect from the surface of the water. The rings from the rise flowed downstream slowly, hastening as they reached the riffle. I watched for ten minutes and saw the fish eight times. He was taking something I couldn't see. I tied on a barbless midge, my smallest one, the size of a gnat on a tiny number 22 hook.

I pulled line off my reel very slowly, click by click, got ready to cast, then stood for ten more minutes. Eight more rises as regular as music. I cast once, downstream, a difficult presentation, sidearm under the boughs of the spruces with enough slack to let the fly — invisible to me — reach the fish's position just before the current pulled the line taut and just in the rhythm of his takes. Knowing the length of my favored type of leader, I could guess where the fly was, and just as I guessed it was over the fish, he proved it with a quiet take. I set the hook gently. The fish took off across the pool, paused and tugged, three times hard, then shot back across the river and under the cut bank and spruces, pulling, pulling. He was bigger than the stockies, that was sure. My light rod bent harder than it ever had above the Reudi Dam. I brought the fish in slowly, worried about my very light tippet. The battle seemed long, but I don't imagine it took more than two minutes. Near me, the fish jumped, and I was amazed at its size: four inches at most. *Tiny.*

In my hand it still struggled, full of the great wish to live, a brown — only a baby — sturdily built, deeply purple, almost black, its spots as blue as the sky, and as red, and as vast somehow, and as old. He held his mouth closed with determination. He glistened, he struggled, he twitched his eyes. I thought, That would be something for Jules to draw. Easily, gently, I slipped the barbless hook out of the fish's bottom lip, support the little champ in the water for a moment while he got his bearings and his breath, then watched him flee.

Hummingbirds

When I was thirteen I looked up the word *ubiquitous*. I'd found it long and alluring in some book and had never seen it before, looked it up and then saw it constantly — especially in *Time* magazine, but also in a book by Robert Heinlein and in Tommy Schroeder's ant report in school, and in Mr. Smith's Sunday sermons, *twice* — I mean, suddenly the word was everywhere. It was as if my knowledge of it had paved the way for others to use it: yet another thrill for the pubescent solipsist. I retain the supreme ability to ignore a word until I know it, but once I've got it in my head — surprise! — impossible and obscure though the word may be, everybody already knows it. Everybody uses it. It's everywhere.

Hummingbirds are like that. Once you start seeing them, you see them everywhere. Once you start talking about them, you find out *everyone* has seen them and has, moreover, a firm opinion about them. I think I saw one once when I was little, in my mother's garden in New Canaan. Sensed it more than saw it, and it was gone. In Ithaca, college years, an enormous bee blew by me while I was sitting stoned on a dock on Lake Cayuga, a bee whose freaky buzz (a musical thrum) I so clearly remember that I know now it was a hummingbird. But that was it, two obscure and unsubstantiated sightings, thin experience indeed, until our summer in Colorado, when the wee bastards came decisively into our lives.

Our first day on the Frying Pan River, just after Gary Looney left us, and after we'd loaded our belongings into the house, and before I could get my fly rod out of its polystyrene box and start tinkering, Juliet got hold of my arm and guided me outside: there was a little matter of furniture to take care of. On the porch, something buzzed past my ear, too musically for a bee, too swiftly for a dragonfly, too invisibly for a bird. I would have liked to have thought it was a welcoming spirit, but as for tangible things, I had no guesses.

In search of furniture, Juliet and I marched up the hill to the horse barn and patted the noses of a couple of small geldings, then looked in the barn, where we found a nice set of shelves and a miniature desk. We carried the shelves home. In the old tack room, which was now inexplicably full of refrigerators, we spied a long, homemade bench. We unburdened it of a box of rotting leather traces, two milk crates full of refrigerator parts, and a big, much-welded-and-polished steel thing, apparently someone's idea of a sculpture. We lugged the table home, stood it in the middle of the floor. "Would look nice with a chair," Juliet said.

In another barn were six festering couches. In a pump shed was a chest of drawers, collapsed. But then in an old log cabin with a new roof we hit the jackpot: A mattress, clean. A box spring, broken but serviceable. A wood frame easy chair with clean cushions. A rattan chair. A table big enough for the writing machine. A box of dishes. An enormous old frying pan.

One of the Vietnam vets who lived on the ranch watched us surreptitiously from his distant cabin porch as we struggled home with all this stuff, trip after trip across the meadow to our shack in the aspen glade. Also, something kept buzzing past me, disturbing the air near my ears, keeping near me, invisible somehow, yet always at the periphery of my vision.

The next night, I saw my first hummingbird. It came up to me on our porch, which was just a deck of slab wood nailed on the front of the house next to the garage shed, which in turn was nothing more than a leaky shelter for a defunct snowmobile and two car batteries. We'd discovered that our gas range and oven didn't work, so, good Boy Scout, I was building a fire pit, one tall rock to the wind, a couple of shorter stone arms, a shelf from one of the refrigerators in the tack room as a grill. The bird buzzed up from behind me, just past my ear, *zoop!,* a foot in front of my face, where it stopped and hovered, looking me in the eye for a full ten seconds. It had a brilliant, irregular patch of iridescence on its throat and dangled its little feet, twitched its head from side to side. Its wings were invisible except as motion. I could make out their shapes in the pauses at top and bottom of each stroke, pauses that had already happened by the time I saw them.

The bird buzzed backwards a few paces, then to the side, then shot off past me and was gone. His body was about the size of my little finger. His beak was black and pointed, the shape of a piece of pencil lead, an inch long.

I got excited, called Juliet, but there was no more bird to be seen. Jules was not excited, of course, having grown up in New York, where birds were more or less something you kicked out of the way. Nature pleased her, don't get me wrong, but until the phenomenon in question was actually there to see, she would rather be drawing. (Just a few days before, she'd spotted bighorn sheep on a ridge as we drove over the pass from Leadville. "Horn-rimmed sheep!" she'd cried.)

Next morning we propped open the windows and the doors in our shack to allow the scent of sage and pine and river and wind to mingle indoors. I sat beneath our large front window, meaning to get some writing done despite all the interference from trout and hummingbirds. My knees banged the underside of the table, but I daydreamed happily, looking out at the mountain that rose across the way and hearing the Frying Pan River, thinking of the trout I might catch that afternoon. A couple of hours into my working daydream a big, unmistakable hummingbird buzzed in the front door, flew straight through the forty feet of our house and out the back door.

Hummingbirds, Trochilidae, "flying jewels," "bird-dwarves" — built in such sweet proportions, with such cute outsize eyes and endearing work habits — are thoroughly unsociable creatures. They live unmarried (so to speak) and won't tolerate other birds in their territories; they are violent, use their sharp beaks as sabers. A hummingbird's territory is large or small in proportion to the concentration of good blossoms in an area and will always contain the same number of flowers. Square footage is not the point. Blossomage is all the little terrors care about.

But a hummingbird cannot live by nectar alone; the protein from her rich insect diet is absolutely necessary. A hummer can get along without flowers, but not without bugs. Her speed and agility make her a terrific aerial hunter. And in the bells of the flowers she favors she finds not only nectar but insects, some drowned, some feeding. She laps these up with her forked tongue (which is not, as I've always thought, a hollow sipping straw), along with the nectar, not incidentally gathering pollen on the top of her head and on her chin, as efficient a pollinator as any bee.

Hummingbirds also eat spiders, right off the web. Worse, in acts of what is called kleptoparasitism, they rob spiders of their insect hoards, plucking the neat packages one at a time from storage in the web. The thieving little birds also make off with the webs themselves at nesting time, making balls of the sticky filaments, then unrolling them like spools of twine, using the string to tie their other nesting materials (odd bits of moss, lichen, and various plant fibers, including the inner fuzz from oak galls) firmly together, and to tie their finished demitasse nests securely to thin branches. In Trinidad a kind man who knew exactly which leaves to look under in exactly what sort of tree once showed my mother hummingbird nest after hummingbird nest, two sweet eggs each, small jelly beans, flat white.

And hummingbirds play the hare's role in a sort of tortoise-and-the-hare genre of Native American legends. In the Cherokee version, Hummingbird and Heron are rivals in the suit of a village maiden. The young woman suggests a race, favoring Hummingbird for his beauty and knowing he is faster. On the appointed day she sees the two birds off. Hummingbird speeds confidently away, is miles ahead by nightfall, takes his rest. Meanwhile, Heron clumsily flops along, all day, all night, taking only the shortest rests. Each day Heron gains ground on Hummingbird until on the fifth day, the limit of the race, he is in the lead. When the maiden finds out that Heron has won, she cancels her offer, finding him hopelessly clumsy and ugly. (I've always liked the realistic twist at the end of that tale.)

In a more elemental and mythological version of the same story, the Hitchiti have the two birds racing for control of Water. Heron wins, and thereafter has hegemony over rivers and lakes and the sea, leaving the land to his little friend. In another Hitchiti tale Hummingbird is more successful: an iridescent Prometheus, he is able to steal fire from the gods. Some homeless Spider must have had the storytellers' ears; Hummingbird's thieving nature appears often in Native American lore. The Central American Bororo have Hummingbird stealing a shaman's magical rattle. The practical Cherokee are content to have him stealing tobacco.

Indigenous only to the New World, hummingbirds occur from the tip of South America clear through Central America and the United States and up into Canada and Alaska as far north as there are trees in which to nest, flowers upon which to suckle, and spiders to mug, murder, and eat.

At the hardware store in Basalt one afternoon I stopped to inspect the hummingbird feeders, wondering if I should spend the money. (If I were a hummingbird I might have stolen one.) The twenty-dollar model held a quart of nectar, had plastic flowers growing all over it in yellow and red, had a red roof and a chain for a hanger. It also had perches, which seemed unnecessary, and was engraved with hummingbird silhouettes, ditto. The fifteen-dollar model did away with the perches and silhouettes, but the plastic flowers were more garish. I bought the cheapest, which was also the best looking: a simple glass bottle with a red cap and wire on the fat end, a red stopper and glass tube at the neck end. Four dollars. It looked like a junior high school chemistry project in red.

The counter lady was pleased that I was going to feed my birds, and exhorted me to buy a box of Perky-Pet Brand Instant Nectar for Hummingbirds. On the back of the box a copywriter explains that hummingbirds eat sugar and convert it to energy. A man of 170 pounds, our writer informs us, would have to expend 155,000 calories a day to equal the ounce-per-ounce equivalent of the energy output of a typical hummingbird.

With the help of my dad and his calorie-counting book I've made some good old fifties-style factoid calculations (a factoid is something that sounds like a useful bit of information but is not): to put together 155,000 calories in a day, that 170-pound man we were talking about (me at my best!) would have to eat 586 McDonald's hamburgers (263 calories each) with a side o' fries (220 calories) and a chocolate shake (383 calories). Also an apple pie (253 calories) — what the hell. Or, for a more sensible meal, the sort I'd be more likely to eat, a good helping of rainbow trout (132 calories), a bowl of brown rice (110 calories), an ear of corn (83 calories), and 1,076 cans of Budweiser.

On the feeder packaging was a warning not to use artificial sweeteners. No one is worried that the birds will have reproductive problems or get cancer. There's no time for that; first, they'll starve to death.

I mixed up a batch of nectar and filled the feeder jar. The nectar was bright red, sweeter than bug juice, pure sugar. In my toolbox I had an old red jack handle waiting to come in handy. I jammed it into a crack in the slab wood siding of the house so that the feeder would hang in front of the window over our work table, the one place where we spent any consistent amount of time. The bottle swung there in the breeze, dripping. I watched it drain. Soon it was empty. I knew exactly what I'd done wrong, had seen the instructions about surface tension both on the Perky Pet box and on the feeder packaging, had decided that cleaning the bottle carefully was too fussy. I took it down and cleaned it.

No birds that evening, but we didn't much expect any since we had a big fire in the fire pit and were cooking trout and corn on the cob and trying to boil brown rice, and were banging around and drinking beer and otherwise being scary. In my secret, most doubting heart, I thought it would be a foolish hummer who fed at such an exposed feeder, ever.

"They'll come," Juliet said, pleasingly concerned for my project, her face dark in the gathering dusk. She grinned, showing her big white teeth.

In the morning I heard a buzzing. I leapt from bed, ran to the front window. The house shook with my steps, but I was in time to see a fleeing blur, a hummer for certain. The feeder swayed. Juliet, sleepy grouch, asked what the hell I thought I was doing.

Later our guest returned, and by noon I was growing familiar with our first regular, a sleek, medium-size hummingbird with no markings on its throat. I took it for a female, but that late in the summer it could easily have been a male who had molted out his beautiful purply royal and iridescent gorget. I hadn't a bird book at the time, but the photos Juliet took identify all but one of our visitors as broadtails, the western version of the ruby-throated hummingbird (of 319 species, the only trochiliform appearing in the eastern United States). The odd bird, a small one with a black head, was probably a black-chinned hummingbird, one of the three migrant but philopatric (that is, returning to the same area and even the same nest year after year) species who spend time in Colorado.

Our bird had a scar on her breast, which I noted in hopes of recognizing her later. She'd feed quickly, then dart off, then return. Her wings beat fast but not furiously; there was no sense of effort, a sense, in fact, of absolute ease. She extended her head quite calmly, tilted it this way and that, discovering the way around the bee guard, a little cage at the mouth of the feeding tube. She kept her dainty feet tight against her pale abdomen like tiny black badges, hovered easily, in miniature elegance. Her tongue was as long as her beak and flicked skillfully up into the tube. She drank. Occasionally a bubble rose, air displacing the tiny draught she'd consumed. At each visit she would spend two or three minutes, drinking steadily for ten seconds at a time, then changing position as if changing flowers. When she was done she'd disappear for twenty minutes or a half hour.

All that afternoon she had the feeder to herself. I watched her, and Juliet watched her, mesmerized by her littleness, her confidence, her prettily buzzing wings.

And the next morning she was back. I sat down at the table, barely worked, was distracted by each more and more frequent visit. After an hour I realized that I was observing a new bird alternately with my original friend. After another hour I began to realize that I was watching not two but four quite similar birds, one at a time. The original little visitor was marked clearly by her breast scar. The next visitor was marked by her plainness, a lack of identifying characteristics. The next bird, exactly the same size as the first two — about three inches long — had a twisted foot, damaged in some way that left it dangling slightly and askew. The fourth bird, again identical in markings (rather plain, with pale breast, some speckling, no gorget, and the ever-iridescent green head and back) was markedly smaller than the others and more furtive as she fed.

Juliet made herself coffee, firing up a sooty blaze on our faulty Coleman stove out on the deck. That, for the nonce, stopped the visits from our birds. I got myself back to work.

Hummingbirds were not exactly the center of our lives that August. They did, however, decorate the periphery of each day and the periphery of a lot of my thinking. Jules and I paid visits to Carol and Mac in Snowmass Village, and there I saw hummingbird feeders on every porch and in every tourist shop. There were hummingbird necklaces carved by local craftspeople in imitation of old Native American designs. There were twenty kinds of hummingbird T-shirts. We even saw a place named the Hummingbird Diner, defunct, in a little town called Swan Lake, which we passed through on our way to Boulder. A young busker in Boulder had a little teeny Hummingbird brand amplifier for his guitar. Seals and Crofts played "Hummingbird Don't Fly Away" on the radio every time we got in the car, I swear. I heard B. B. King's "Hummingbird Blues" on the jukebox at a bar. At the Echo Lake Lodge, where we bought breakfast after a cold night's camping, we watched an enormously fat hummer guarding his food source, a twenty-dollar feeder if I ever saw one, full to the top with Perky Pet, bright red. And as I stood in the Frying Pan trying to fool trout with fake mayflies and lousy presentations, hummingbirds picked off real mayflies at the many corners of the eccentric dodecahedrons the darting birds described in the chilly air over the river.

A potter at the Anderson Ranch told me she could tell the species of a hummingbird by the pitch and musicality of the buzz of its wings. A dictionary yielded up the fact that the taxonomical name, Trochilidae, was assembled from the ancient Greek for wheel: hummingbird body as hub, hummingbird wings as spokes and rim, so speedy and deep in their beats that the human eye sees a circle, complete.

One day a smaller specimen zipped in our front door, veered, and crashed into a bright window pane, shot away and crashed into another. He fell to the floor, dazed for the barest moment, then flew again, more cautiously, only to bang his beak once more on the window. I got a big coffee cup and caught him under it against the glass the way I catch bees, slipped a piece of stiff paper under the cup, then carried him outside and let him go.

Gary Looney, who came around on weekends, wouldn't have been impressed by my rescue. "Little peckers," he called the hummingbirds, with no rancor, but no affection, either. Our nearest cabin neighbor, Truck, with his spooneristic speech impediment, called my little friends *bummingherds,* and disdained them as a sort of insect.

Gradually, the bird with the scar at her breast assumed dominance over my feeder. She took to lighting on the red jack handle, extending her tiny feet and resting, which surprised me: I'd had the unarticulated (and therefore untested) idea that hummingbirds never stop. She never walked, but used her feet (three toes forward, one toe back) only to perch. Usually in flight she kept them tucked tight against her, but on hot days she let them dangle, showing her legs, which were only a quarter of an inch long, no thicker than the legs of a good spider, and fuzzed with tiny feathers at the thighs.

We began to call her the boss bird.

When another hummingbird would swoop in, the boss would attack, squealing and piping. While she was busy with the first interloper, another would take the opportunity to feed. When the boss bird noticed, she would swoop back and give the new interloper a stab in the head, and they'd face each other, flying, squeaking, pecking, sometimes moving up in the sky, sometimes falling, sometimes so preoccupied with battle that they ended up on the ground. Always another bird would take advantage of the unguarded feeder.

Within a week we had developed a reliable coterie of

seven to nine regular visitors. The boss bird was constantly in a state of defense, perched on the jack handle, her neck craned, on the lookout for birds coming from any direction. She'd take time out from her guard duties to feed, and fed again after every fight.

When the dominant bird was busy with a challenging neighbor, other birds would come to the feeder and drink peacefully, three tongues up the tube, waiting to be attacked. When they had drunk their fill, they'd take time out to fight, or to chase off still further birds who dared challenge their illegal sublease. Sometimes it would seem that all the hummingbirds in the Frying Pan Valley were fighting in the sky in front of our desk window. The nectar went quickly, about two days per half-cup filling, a three-dollar box of Perky Pet a week. The boss bird grew fat.

I took to standing on the corner of the porch, trying to see where the birds went when they left the feeder. Boss bird had no problem with my presence, but stood paranoid of competitors on the jack handle, watching the sky. I watched, too, and one by one I found the perches of the other birds. They moved so fast I could only plot a direction, then inspect the top branches of the trees I found in that area. I began to discover that the home perches of our friends were arrayed in a circle around the feeder. One in the big aspen by the wood pile. One on the beam that poked from the garage shed. One on top of the telephone pole to the northwest. One on top of the telephone pole to the southwest. One on the wire strung between. One on the crest of the neighboring shack.

Two of the smaller birds seemed always to shoot off toward the river, but I never found their trees. Our feeder had become the center of a clearly divided pizza of feeding territories, putting me in mind of the wedge-shaped farms of Vidalia, Georgia, or the wedge-shaped farms of French wine country, land having been sold so as to touch however slightly the borders of a coveted onion- or wine-producing district.

When Juliet or I came out on the porch, the boss bird left, but she didn't go far, perching either on the crest of our roof or — after a tussle — on the telephone pole to the southwest, displacing bird number five. From that perch she would deign to let others feed at her brilliantly generous flower. If I waited at the corner of the porch, she'd come back. Gradually I stepped closer and closer to the feeder. My presence didn't seem to bother her. She was as agile as a bee and need have no more fear of me than a bee might.

After a week of desensitizing her I was able to stand right by the feeder, a foot away, and look closely at her. She began often to return the attention, hovering close to inspect the creases of my blue jean jacket or to look in my ear, probably wondering what strange bank of flowers she had come across. She didn't seem to take me for a creature, and certainly not for an enemy. If I put my finger out beside the feeder, she would land on it and feed, a fat lady oblivious of all but her bonbons.

Even obese, she was barely noticeable on my finger. Her claws were sharp as she held on. If I moved away from the feeder, she would come for the ride. If I turned my hand over, she would step into my palm. Once, late in the summer, and just before all the hummingbirds disappeared south for the year, I closed my hand on her, very slowly. She stayed with me as if she were hypnotized, allowed me to hold her completely trapped in my hand. I felt her rapid heartbeat. It's not that she was tame, exactly. Perhaps she was logy from all the nectar. I cannot explain her behavior, but there she was, snug in my hand, apparently content. (O,

Spider, I held Hummingbird in my hand and didn't crush her! O, Spider, I held Hummingbird in my hand and let her go!)

On our last day in the Frying Pan Valley we slowly loaded the car (fishing rod last in case we found a fishing hole or two on the way back to New York), then stood on the porch and breathed, looking out at the mountains, ignoring the loaded car and the late hour and our deadline: the start of school, September fifth. The air was crisp, cold; the leaves of the aspens had begun to turn bright yellow. At 8,300 feet, autumn had already arrived. "The World Trade Center wouldn't even come up to that ridge there," I said, pointing to an insignificant bit of rock on the side of one of our smaller mountains. "And my building isn't even high as that tree." Pointing to a bent pine.

"Please don't talk about the city," Jules said.

Talking didn't matter. You could already feel the quickness and heat and hustle of New York. We got in the car, took a last look at our cabin. It was still the same wreck we'd first seen a month before, but now it seemed to own a soul. I started to back out along the ruts that were our driveway. "Billy, stop," Jules said. "You forgot your stupid feeder." (Suddenly, in the melancholy of leaving, the thing was mine alone.)

I looked back at the cabin and, sure enough, hanging off the old jack handle was the hummingbird feeder, drained and forlorn, bright red against the slab wood siding, reflected in the empty window of the house. Walking to retrieve it, I looked up at the abandoned stations of our birds and missed them there: just four days earlier they'd disappeared, gone as one for Mexico.

Callinectes Sapidus

On Martha's Vineyard there are two sorts of ponds. One is the normal sort — fresh water in a muddy-bottomed bowl, with bass and sunnies and a bench used for ice skating in the winter. The other is a brackish affair, with tides and an outlet to the sea and occasional vicious bluefish and constant sea gulls and terns and a sandy bottom, and dune grass surrounding it. No matter how big these salt ponds get they are never called lakes. And though they have inlets to the sea, they are too self-contained to be called bays.

Some of the tidal ponds still have their original Wampanoag Indian names: Nashaquitsa, Sengekontacket, Squibnocket, Menemsha, Paqua and Watcha. The others were named by settlers: Black Point, Chilmark, Edgartown Great, Tisbury Great, Jobs Neck and Homer. All were formed by sandbars turning into barrier beaches, closing off bodies of water. And all of the ponds serve as breeding grounds for shellfish — mussels, clams, oysters, scallops; and for fin fish — blues, herring, mackerel, and eels; and at shore, for terns and ducks and gulls; and in a complicated nest on a dead tree or at the top of a pole provided by persons, for ospreys; and most certainly for people, young and old; and for blue crabs.

We liked to eat the crabs.

In New York, early in the summer of 1988, Juliet and I tied up our complicated city lives so we could get back to the Vineyard, this time for all of July and August — hang the expense. Jules had finally been graduated from Pratt in May, then spent six weeks cater-waitering and was almost wealthy enough for the trip. I'd used up most of my savings during the year at Columbia, but I certainly didn't want to spend the summer building bathrooms in brownstones, and didn't want to stop writing just when it felt as though I was getting someplace.

Toward the end of June, Jules and I borrowed $900 to fix the transmission on my pickup (which had spent the winter in my parents' driveway, drawing complaints from the neighbors and even from the garbageman, who couldn't turn his own truck around because of it) and — straight from a transmission garage in Norwalk — we headed to the Vineyard. In Bridgeport we stopped at my brother Doug's apartment for *Big Wiggly* (where in New York was I supposed to store that noble rowboat?).

Our destination was a big house back in the woods of West Tisbury that Jules and her friend Jocelyn had scouted out that spring, and which we rented at an exorbitant rate with Jocie's sister Lauren, and Lauren's friend Louise. We also put an ad in the local paper, hoping to fill an empty downstairs room. Jules and I, being the only couple and paying two shares, got the master bedroom. We took a lot of pleasure in sharing a room again — we lived separately in New York, of course — and moved the scant furniture around until there was room to spread a tarp on the floor under the dormer so Juliet would have a place to paint. I made a desk out of scrap lumber and stood it up in front of the window, plugged in my trusty writing machine, and was in business.

To afford the house, Juliet and Louise worked as waitresses and Lauren worked in a clothing store. I used all my meager savings and also my credit card (the next year I'd be teaching — I could pay it off then). Jocelyn used my system: make money in the springtime — in the summer, go dead-and-buried broke. Tiny Alan was our wild card roommate. We'd got him through the newspaper ad and were surprised to find him under five feet tall. He worked so hard as a waiter that we seldom saw him, which was good because he was disagreeable, demanding and dour, possibly even demented (who were we to say?). He had seemed like a nice fellow over the phone from Boston.

And my sister Janet came for a rainy week with her partner Jennifer. And many friends came to stay, and friends of friends. Some slept on the extra beds, some on the couch, some in the yard in tents. All of them paid. We were forced by a season's rent of over $10,000 to be terrible hosts.

Louise was tall and thin with a taste for the heroic in daily life. One day she had the idea to go crabbing, grew very excited, trying to enlist helpers. She said the way to do it is to tie a string to a piece of fish and wait until a crab takes an interest. Then you slide the bait toward you until the crab is within reach of your net, at which point — swoop! — you collect him. "The creek at Scatter Neck is simply *full* of them!" This is typical Louise, all dramatic tones, talking very rapidly, trying to create some excitement. "*Blue* crabs! They're *delicious,* they're *famous*! Who's got string? Who would like to drive? You *guys.*" She'd done some crabbing in Maryland.

The first time they went, Juliet and Louise came home with eleven blue crabs (*Callinectes sapidus*), one of which was female and not blue at all. By Massachusetts law, one crab taken in ten may be female so long as she is eggless. I stared at the crabs in their bucket. It's the males that give the species its name. Their foreclaws are an incredible blue, the blue of the sky on the best day of summer, the blue of the water at evening, the blue of blue eyes, much brighter than the blue of blue blood, an artist's blue, Gauguin's.

Eleven crabs for dinner! Louise was very proud, and Juliet too, and they explained how they'd captured the crabs, and laughed about all the splashing they'd done, and laughed about the way the crabs seemed to run for your feet if you missed with the net. They told the story over and over as guests began to arrive. We boiled water and flung the poor crabs in.

Louise made a spicy garlic and tomato sauce and with pasta and bread we had a nice meal of it, tantalized by the single crab per plate. In the claws we found delicious meat, white and firm (*sapidus* is Latin for savory, or tasty), but not much. In the carapace, which you open by pulling the tab formed by the fold of the abdomen (something like the pop-tops on old beer cans) and under all the digestive glands and shell supports and gills (it's mostly gills in there) we found more meat, the muscles that control all those ten legs — the first two of which sport claws, the last two, paddles — pure white meat, dense and sweet and delicious, about two bites per crab.

Tiny Alan came sulking home toward the end of the festivities. "Making a mess," he muttered, sidling around us and past our pots and pans and buckets and nets and to his room.

On the next crabbing expedition Juliet and Lauren and I went alone, without Louise to guide us. We took Jocie's manly dog, Ra, a big, well-trained chocolate lab, built for the beach. We drove down the Scatter Neck road in my pickup, Ra in back barking (no more noisy than the truck), past the fields of Scatter Neck Farm, past the hidden houses of the old development, and to the gate. Lauren opened it with her family key, and we left it open in the spirit of egalitarian trespass (and knowing someone more responsible would come along to close it). It was evening already — crab time. Ours was the only car in the little lot. We took my fishing nets in hand, marched to the creek.

The access to Scatter Neck is between the Tisbury Great Pond and Scatter Neck Pond. Tisbury Great Pond is enormous, covers hundreds of acres. Scatter Neck Pond is smaller. Between them, behind the grassy dunes of the barrier beach, runs a tidal creek which runs east to fill Scatter Neck Pond at rising tide, west to drain it at ebb. The current is never violent. Because the creek blocks easy access to the dunes and the beach and the sea, the Scatter Neck Association has built a little wooden footbridge to span it. I stood on the bridge and watched the clear water of the creek. A crab shot past, heading east, kick and glide, zigzags. Another shot past, heading west. They proceeded sideways, as crabs do, but swimming, which is peculiar to the blues and rare others. (*Callinectes,* in fact, is the late carcinologist Mary Jane Rathbun's Greekism for "beautiful swimmer.")

From the bridge I could make out the bright cerulean blue of the male claws, the red and rusty orange of the female. We had invited no one to dinner. I envisioned catching another dozen and having three to myself. Another crab flashed past. Another. Tens of them, scores of them, east and west, hundreds, a highway at rush hour, none stopping, commuting between ponds. "This is more than last time," Juliet said, and, "Leave your sneakers on." She showed us a pink spot on her toe.

Lauren said, "Leonard got six stitches on his finger, so don't be cavalier handling them!"

"Who is Leonard?" Juliet said.

I put my sneakers on and waded in as the women discussed Leonard. On the bridge it had occurred to me that while Louise's technique was ingenious — she had smashed a mussel with a beer bottle, picked the meat out of the shell and tied it on a string, then dropped the mussel meat into the thoroughfare to tempt likely crabs into range — in the narrow creek there was no need for such cunning. The crabs rushed past. Tens, twenties, hundreds of them. I slashed at them with my net, laughing at my ineptitude. Ra came back and stood on the bridge by Lauren, cocked his head, raised his ears, and adopted a stony silence.

I caught a crab.

"Female," Juliet said, unimpressed, as always. "They're slower, and you'd be too."

Sure enough, there wasn't a spot of blue on my crab, and under the segmented flap of its abdomen was a dark glob of eggs. I turned the net over and the little beauty fell gracefully back into the water, scuttled directly at my feet.

Sunburned Juliet in bathing suit and sneakers joined me in the creek, which was growing muddy from all my thrashings. Ra leapt in behind her, barking with pleasure. Lauren stayed up on the bridge, lying on her side like an Ingres *odalisque* in a stylish bikini, a languid lookout. "Male!" she cried, and I slashed at the water. "Blue! Blue!" she exclaimed, and Juliet scooped up a female. "It's a boy!" and I stumbled at the shadow rushing past, darted, lunged, missed and fell to my knees in the water, only to be assaulted by the dog, who slathered me with his tongue.

After an hour we had three crabs. I thought dinner

would be slight. The crabs rested in a joint-compound bucket, one of those big, white, five-gallon plastic buckets that will never deteriorate, ever, and that are useful for many things, especially crabbing. When you netted a good crab you flipped the net over the bucket to turn the webbing inside out, then shook it and shook it to dislodge the crab, who hung on to the heavy mesh with his claws. You'd shake and shake until he'd let go with one claw, then shake some more until he let go with the other. In the bucket each new crab caused a ruckus, and all the crabs raised their claws like dangerous flamenco dancers, castanets poised.

A man wearing corduroy shorts and a polo shirt and a kind of tennis club hat — a floppy thing made of cotton with little steel grommets to let the steam out — appeared in the parking lot, looking askance at my disreputable truck. Lauren and Juliet adjusted the bras of their bathing suits. Ra only wagged his tail.

"Crabbing?" the man said. I thought next he would ask me for a permit. "You could use a better net."

Lauren stood up on the bridge and explained Louise's technique, and how we'd given up on it, in the most pedagogical tones. She rather defended my style, which I appreciated. I demonstrated where appropriate. I even succeeded in catching a good male and adding him to our cache with only seven or eight flicks of the net. Ra welcomed the newcomer to the bucket, endangering his nose.

"You might do better to stay still," the man said. "Let the crabs come to you. You know the difference between a male and a female, right?"

The question sounded proprietary; I bristled. "The males have the eggs?"

"We throw the blue ones back," Juliet said. She lunged at a speeding shadow in the water.

He seemed to agree that we were joking, then Lauren

and he discussed their Scatter Neck connections. They were both progeny, it seemed. As Lauren and the fellow walked over the dunes to the ocean with Ra, Juliet and I kept after the crabs, perfecting our technique, needing, suddenly, to be extra competent.

Splash! — you calculate the trajectory and velocity of the next crab and nab him on his route. The crabs were terrific dodgers, but, we learned, they always dodged the same way. After a while we figured out which way to swoop with the nets. The crabs came in waves, none for five minutes, then scores. Some would see our feet and, having escaped other crabbers, stop cold. By the time the sun went down, we had twenty beautiful male crabs. By the time Ra came back, we had twenty-five. By the time Lauren got back with the man (who, by the way, was named Richard), we had thirty and were loath to quit, although we were wet and cold and hungry, and night was on the way. Best of all, Lauren, who is particular, had a date.

I put the bucket of crabs in the back of the pickup, and Richard climbed in back there with Ra. Lauren and Juliet and I rode in front. Jules and I, both well experienced at being brother or sister, said nothing, waiting for old Dick to get out before we began to tease. Not far from the gate he knocked on the window. I stopped. He leapt out. Ra leapt out. Lauren spoke. Ra leapt back in. We watched Richard walk to a house. Lauren admitted that she had made a date with him, and she was so serious about it that we didn't tease but told her how nice we thought Richard was, and how tall, and handsome.

At the honor system corn pile that the Scatter Neck farmer made every evening we took some corn and left a dollar, then went home to make dinner. I boiled an enormous pot of water, then tried to get the crabs in as humanely as possible. The little devils made it difficult, holding hands, as it were, creating an unbroken chain (just like that child's toy — I saw it in the dentist's office and again at my brother's house — a bucket of plastic monkeys whose hands hook together), impossible to drop into the water. I was able to lift the entire population of the bucket in a big knot just by pulling on the first crab. Ra barked. Lauren called instructions. Our expert, Louise, was not yet home from work. I broke the chain with a couple of unmasterful shakes, which gave me six or seven crabs for the pot but added the problem of loose crabs on the kitchen floor.

Despite whatever compunction I might have had, the crabs — feisty and colorful as they may have been, eye-wiggling and claw snapping and dog-scaring as they definitely were, under-the-dishwasher-scuttling and gorgeous and alive (I grant you this) — were items of food. I got them into the pot using a thick leather glove and determination. Before long they were cooked, red as lobster, and before long again they were stacked up on the table, and we were working them over and eating corn and laughing at the bounty and laughing not to have guests.

Two weeks later Juliet and I were invited to a party. Bring some food to share, the invitation said. Juliet thought of crabs. (Beautiful swimmers, tasty!) We borrowed the key to Scatter Neck and had a time of it, three hours getting soaked and chilled into the dusk, forty crabs, our greatest night, and (I kept assuring myself) forty crabs the merest, tiniest dent in the traffic past the bridge. (Unending abundance had been assumed in Chesapeake Bay, as well, but now *Callinectes sapidus,* there known while molting as the soft-shell crab, is endangered in Maryland from overharvest and pollution.)

We drove frantically to Gay Head, twenty miles in the night, late for the party, the crabs in their bucket in the back of the pickup. At our hosts' house I boiled five gallons of water (something I had never before done at a party) and coolly dumped the now predictable concatenation of crabs into the water. The host spread newspaper on his porch, and presently the party of us dug in, crunch and butter, break and eat.

The next day I ran errands, driving perhaps fifty miles around the island in that banging, swaying truck. The day after that I went fishing in the early morning. In Menemsha, when I leaned into the back of the truck to grab my damp fish towel, I was startled to discover a crab beneath it. He must have jumped out of the bucket or been lurched out on the lousy island roads. I thought to feed him to the gulls, but when I moved to pick him up he leapt athletically, snapping his claws, then stood at the ready, his arms raised, claws open before his face, a Kung Fu master, a Black Belt, a champ. The blue of his front leg joints was stunning.

I tried to grab him, to throw him back in the bucket, but he leapt at me, brilliantly — *snap snap!* — sidled back against the tailgate — *snap snap!* — unvanquished, alone. I threw the wet towel back over him and went fishing, impressed. Imagine! A mere *snack* with that degree of an impulse toward self-preservation.

By nine I was home, fishless. Juliet and Lauren and Louise were on the porch posing for Jocelyn's camera, naked in the service of art, holding props Jocelyn had found in the West Tisbury dump: a broken old fan, a rusty bicycle wheel, a stainless steel toaster. Jocelyn was mostly naked too, presumably to make her models feel comfortable. I said hello, watched for a minute, then remembered the crab. When I pulled the towel off, he leapt at me, then leapt again, and again, though I didn't tease him. When the photo session was over and the women were dressed, I called them over. "Should we eat such a crab?" I said.

Louise spoke for him. His endurance, she said, made him a hero. Jocelyn, too, was impressed. His beauty, she said, was enough. She went to get some color film. Juliet thought we should eat the crab, just like we'd eaten the others. Our roommate Alan wasn't home, which was probably why Louise decided the crab should be named Tiny Alan. She next proposed that Alan be set free. Hooray! All plans burst, and with a minimum of preparation we went to Scatter Neck, all of us tumbled in the truck (Ra barking) — across the island, then down the bumpy road.

The people in the Scatter Neck parking lot watched as we rather ass-backwardly crabbed in the bed of an old pickup and took our quarry to the creek. Louise put Alan back. He just sat in the water, that familiar thoroughfare, paralyzed for five minutes. About the time we gave up on him, he scooted a few feet, testing his freedom, then scooted a few feet more, sideways, then scooted away, fast, toward Scatter Neck Pond. Home, after two long days away.

Mola Mola

One of my favorite books when I was eight and nine years old was called *Fishes,* a picture book with a few facts written up for kids. I loved the frogfishes and the goosefishes, the batfishes and toadfishes, creations so ugly they made me wonder what God was up to. I liked the more colorful fish in the book, too, and the more strange, such as the blunt-head puffer, or the honeycomb cowfish, or the naughty-sounding slippery dick. The deeply camouflaged angler fish had a long cartilaginous fishing rod attached to its head, from which hung a luminescent blob that bobbed in subtle currents before its owner's mouth to attract, as the text explained, smaller fish into its reach. The California sheep-head was black with a single wide vermilion stripe around its middle, something along the lines of a saddle shoe or a woolly bear caterpillar, as I thought back then. My favorite fish in the book, however, was the ocean sunfish, an enor-mous, blunt, bullet-shaped thing, seemingly cut off in the middle and wearing a ballet skirt that was its caudal fin. The caudal fin on most fish is easy to call a tail, but on the sunfish there is nothing to rightly call a tail. The fish is cut off at its tutu, with not a leg to dance on. I stared at this fish for hours, read the text over and over as I lay in bed late at night, studying illicitly and listening to my big brother snore.

Thirteen years went by. I continued to read, but had somehow lost interest in fish. During the *Jaws* era, I was at the Jersey shore with a bunch of college friends on a wild and obnoxious weekend of sleeping under the boardwalk and taunting the police and drinking beer and stealing towels from clotheslines and trespassing, none of which is germane here, except this: as my roommate Bob Meyer and I lounged on a stretch of sand across from the jail in Ocean Beach waiting for our friends X and Y to be let out, someone shouted "Shark! Shark!" and the water emptied itself of bathers in a swift and splashing display. This had been happening again and again at beaches around the world (I'd heard of a scare in Lake Ontario!) because of the movie, and we tough, hungover guys were cynical. But sure enough, sighting off the lifeguard's pointing finger we saw the fin, waving, circling slowly. It looked more rounded and weak and translucent than I would have predicted, but I was respectful. I had actually *screamed* in the movie at the part where the fish bites the boat at the very quietest moment in an intentional lull in the action.

"*Hammerhead!*" a teenager shouted, as if he knew, and his confidence was enough to send that single fearsome word up and down the beach, muttered, shouted, confidently passed along.

The lifeguard spoke excitedly on his walkie-talkie: "Shark! Shark! Hammerhead! Station six!"

Five minutes later the head lifeguard arrived, walking slowly, unexcited, professional, skeptical. A hundred fingers pointed out the fin. He snorted contemptuously. "Sunfish," he said. He bounded to the water and mounted his underling's red and white surfboard to the gasps of the crowd and paddled out to the fish, his legs dangling in the water. *"Hammerhead,"* the teenager cried, and we watched spellbound as nothing whatsoever happened. The head lifeguard circled the fin, stuck his hand in the water and seemed to pat the fish. A couple of other intrepid souls ventured out on *inner tubes,* for pete's sake, but not I. My friend Bob went so far as to leap into the water and swim out there, but not I, not I. I was willing to pull any number of pranks in the dead of night, be chased by the cops, sleep in the damp sand under a porch, bail less fleet friends out of the quaint jail, but not to swim near possible sharks on my own (or anyone else's) say-so, and there were plenty of young women around to impress, too, if that gives you any measure of my fear. "Sunfish," the inner tubers confidently cried when they reached the circling fin, and I remembered that big fat bullet of a fish in my childhood book:

> Ocean Sunfish: *Mola mola.* To ten feet in length and eleven feet in height (including dorsal and anal fins), and weighing up to 4,400 pounds.

"What's it doing in New Jersey?" someone said.
"It's been a very warm year," someone else said. "Everything's coming north with the jellyfish."

By the time of the blue crab summer on Martha's Vineyard (where, coincidentally, part of *Jaws* was filmed), another thirteen years had passed. I hadn't been chased by the police for some time, had even started to regard them as my friends. The last time I'd talked to a cop, as a matter of fact, was to report my tackle box stolen in Menemsha.

A perfectly friendly stranger, a woman with whom I had

been chatting and fishing all morning, jumped in her red Cadillac with my tackle box when I went to get lunch. An old man fishing with us off the wharf saw her take it, but he'd assumed we were friends. "Imagine a lady thief!" he said. The cop I spoke to was a woman, too, my age. I never got the box back, several hundred dollars' worth of lures and leaders and fluke rigs and reels, possibly karmic payment for the thefts of my youth.

And that was not the only bad luck I had that summer of 1988. Higher than usual water temperatures disrupted the fishing, not just for me but for the commercial fishermen and the charter operators like Captain Squid, who told me it was the worst fishing in the forty years he had been operating his boat. (All of us were quick to blame global warming — as quick as we were slow to do anything about it — but global warming works in much smaller and much more pernicious increments than the heat waves of a given summer.) The water in Menemsha Bight was too warm for bluefish or striped bass or much of anything else, and although for a period in August the bonito were running, I never had a bit of luck. One small bluefish, a couple of big stripers who got away. There were lots of porgies, sure, but porgies are for tourists, greenhorns, bonepickers. Every day I was out there, throwing lures and baitfish and flies into the hot water and waiting, quite happily, for nothing.

On days when it was not too windy I plied the wine-dark seas with *Big Wiggly* (still only a rowboat, and still powered by that ancient six-horsepower Johnson outboard motor). Even on the best of days *Big Wiggly* could be difficult — rocking wildly in light seas or stalling in the worst possible places (there's no exercise quite so aerobic as pulling on the starter rope a few hundred times as a fast-flowing channel full of rocks and snags and boats and barnacled pilings spins by). Many days the little Johnson worked well, however, and Juliet and I would take a friend or two and go fishing. Or not-fishing.

On the day I saw the second ocean sunfish of my life, Jon Zeeman was with us. (He was staying at Lagoon's Edge again, this time with the grown children of the people who owned the place.) Jon and Juliet have enormously different personalities on land, but get them out on a boat, fishing, and they are the same. Smart as they are, if there are no fish they get bored. Fishing dilettantes. An hour here, an hour there. "Drop me off on the jetty." That kind of thing. But then again, they were always the ones to catch the fish. I would fruitlessly whip the water for two weeks only to watch with some anguish the bend of Juliet's and Jon's poles as they'd catch ten of the fattest fish of the summer, all in a quick morning's work. Jon's theory was that if you fish too much, you use up your luck/hour units. He's a rock-'n'-roll musician, remember, a guitarist, which to my mind explains everything.

On the sunfish morning we pushed off in Clam Cove, a safe harbor in Nashaquitsa Pond where Jocie's folks allowed me to leave *Big Wiggly*. Jon bailed it out and we loaded it up with life preservers and fishing rods and bait and oars and gas and my new (much smaller) tackle box, and putted out past the boats moored there, past the clam-breeding floats where cormorants liked to sit and air their wings, then through a tiny channel into Menemsha Pond, which is subtly surrounded by eight or nine big handsome houses tucked into the scrubby woods and dunes. A few of the old-time fishing families — Larsen, Poole, Mayhew — still live right there, a short boat ride to Menemsha Basin.

In *Big Wiggly* it took about a half hour to putt-putt across the calm water of the pond to the red and green nuns that

mark Menemsha Creek, the channel. There we passed
three blue herons standing on one leg at the shore, as if
beside a river, and passed snowy egrets and ducks nesting.
Scandalized terns swirled shrieking over the dunes, pro-
tecting their own nesting grounds, or dove headfirst into
the water behind us, coming up with sand eels (which made
me jealous — good bait). There were plenty of sea gulls, of
course, four or five species, bothering the terns and each
other, making a racket, busy at their various jobs. As always, too, there were the two salvaged fishing boats
propped up on large beams of driftwood in the dunes across
from Pease's Point. KEEP OFF! DONT TY UP! They had been
there like that for years, someone's guilty project and duty
that someday a hurricane will end, bringing good with evil.

Past the last red nun and the rocks was the Coast Guard
Wharf, where my box had been stolen, then Dutcher Dock
and the basin, where the lobster boats and draggers and
commercial line or gillnet fishermen shared space with the
sailboaters and yachters. Summer dinks, I had heard the
former call the latter. I was sensitive to this, being myself a
summer dink, but my contempt fell always in line with that
of the fishermen. (Or almost always: once Juliet waved to a
lobsterman as we passed him in the channel; he turned and
eyed her and with no change of expression raised his man-
gled hand and gave her the finger.) In the summer there
are perhaps sixty boats of various sizes docked in the Menemsha Basin, and a few extra moored at the wide end of
the small harbor beside the Coast Guard's cutters and
speedboats.

There was always something interesting going on: people fishing for bait; a sailboat being run aground despite the
markings; an apoplectic summer dink yelling to the laconic
harbormaster that *he too pays Chilmark taxes.* "Sorry Cap,

we're full." That "Cap" spoken with a tone pushed just past the edge of respect yet never quite contemptuous. Between Squid Row (the meeting place for Captain Squid's charters) and the Harbor Master's booth was the Menemsha Texaco, where a kindly but taciturn Yankee couple sold fishing tackle and hats and Ring Dings and other indispensable items of sea and land. Wizened old salts sat on lobster pots most of the day there and talked, and watched, and spat at the feet of the summer dinks.

Jon and Juliet and I pulled up four feet below the level of the dock in tiny *Big Wiggly* and debarked inexpertly, a quick stop for gas and juice and a snack. I was wearing my long-billed fisherman's cap and a flannel shirt, but the gas station helpers made fun of me anyway, as always, telling me the bonito had been in that very morning: "Everybody caught two!" "Yep! Even this little old nun who wasn't even trying!" I teased them a bit, too, but no one laughed. I sat there pondering for the thousandth time the how and why of the fact that two oil-stained teenagers could mortify me.

Jon, oblivious, came grinning out of the store, tripped off the dock and fell into the boat. I felt my summer dinkness showing as the harbormaster began to stroll our way. *Big Wiggly* (have I mentioned this?) wasn't registered. Juliet seemed to take forever; the old salts were staring as Jon dropped an oar in the water and recovered it. The boys at the pumps shook their heads. The harbormaster ambled closer, pulling at the long brim of his hat. Not a smile in the crowd. Then here came Juliet, wearing a dress, a pink dress for Christ's sake, a sundress, and bearing a big bottle of Perrier for the ride. You can't fool anybody, except maybe a tourist or two. Summer dinks.

After an embarrassing forty pulls on the starter rope, I

got the motor going while Jon and Juliet stumbled over each other and the fishing tackle, getting us untied. We putted past the boats and out of the protection of the basin into the bay by way of an inlet framed by two massive stone jetties, sphinx feet between which the pond emptied itself furiously down to low tide and was filled by the sea with equal fury up to high. There was also calm in the channel — three or four times a day at high and low tides when everything stopped and turned around. In August there were nearly always irritable people fishing from the jetties. They were irritable because there were so many of them, and so many tourists and kids and sea gulls underfoot, and so many lures of the inexperienced flying through the air, just ahead of their dumb questions, which would be answered, wrongly or rightly, by someone with a full day's further experience. I felt for all of them, but I couldn't quite reach them; I had been both the irritable jetty fisherman and the person with the dumb questions, sometimes on the same day. I was glad to have a boat, even one so insignificant as *Big Wiggly*.

Outside the protection of the jetties was Menemsha Bight, a part of Vineyard Sound, which was in turn part of the Atlantic Ocean. (A bight is a bay that I like to think was named after its shape, like a bite out of a piece of toast, though the dictionary points to an early etymological relationship to words meaning bow.) We shot with the current like a sluggish arrow from the mouth of the creek and out across the waters of the bight, trolling. A slightly rough day with an onshore breeze, which I appreciated, because if *Big Wiggly* decided to break down we would be blown to shore instead of over to the cliffs of the Elizabeth Islands, some miles away across the sound. Before long Jon was lying down in the bow of the boat, listlessly holding his rod out over the water. Juliet had stopped fishing altogether, was checking her hair for split ends, bored and cold. Those two didn't seem to realize that fishing is more than a matter of catching fish.

After an hour of torturing them, I gave up, too. The wind had picked up and clouds had drifted in from the mainland and it *was* cold. I fished a little longer, to exercise my prerogative as grumpy captain, then headed back through the inlet, past all the summer dinks fishing, who waved, past the real fishermen, who did not, past the poison-ivy- and wild-pea-covered dunes that lined the creek, past the herons, the geese, the Coast Guard station, past an old salt pissing off the stern of his boat. And back across the pond.

The sun broke out. Ah! Warm again. Juliet asked me to stop, and after some irritable consideration of her request, I did. We drifted in the calm water, a slight breeze propelling us. It was warm again and lovely. The sea gulls wheeled. The boat rocked quietly. We lay back, each on a bench, using our life vests as cushions and thinking with quiet satisfaction of the many possibilities of this and other worlds.

"Shark!" Jon cried. He pointed. I struggled to rise. Immediately I saw the fin, a couple of hundred yards away. It was rounded, waving.

"Sunfish," I said confidently, although I wasn't so sure. It had been thirteen years, after all. "Sunfish." I pulled once on the starter cord and the motor started, always a good sign. We splashed over to a spot just upwind of the fish. I cut the motor, hoping the wind would take us close without scaring the visitor. The fin circled lazily, flopping back and forth with the demure motion of a southern belle waving her hanky. We drifted sideways directly to it with the breeze. As we drew close I saw with some pleasure that it was not a shark. "Sunfish," I said again, enjoying the sound of myself being correct. The fish was not tubular, as I had imagined for twenty-six years because of the profile drawings in *Fishes,* but flat. More a gargantuan pumpkin seed than a bullet. A pumpkin seed cut in half and wearing a tutu. Four feet long, four and a half wide (counting the dorsal and anal fins), perhaps a foot thick. We bumped it. It effortlessly sank itself a foot or two as we passed over, then reappeared and surfaced on our starboard side.

Oh, calm fish! We drifted away, silent, pleased, staring. When we thought we were far enough away I started up the little Johnson, made a wide loop around the sunfish, returned upwind and cut the motor again. We drifted back to the fish. It looked at us, supremely innocent and accepting, with an eye the size and approximate color and mobility of a cow's. It floated, waving its fin, one flat side up, looking first at Jon, then at Juliet, then at me, then back at Jon again. It had scars on its body, propeller wounds perhaps, a familiar injury to baskers such as manatees, for example, and mermaids. Its mouth was not pretty, a stained and perpetually open wound of a thing, a hard-lipped pore, an orifice, obscene looking, about the size of my own.

This time when we bumped the fish it stayed up, floated along with us, with intention, stirring its small pectoral fin to turn itself and get looks at us from various angles. Jon put a hand out tentatively and patted it. "Rough," he said. "It's like sharkskin. Sandpaper."

It was white with a ribbing of gray. We guessed it weighed as much as I did, which was as much as a heavy middleweight boxer, close to two hundred pounds. (We must have been wrong — on the light side — by half or more.) Its dorsal and anal fins were identical, keel and sail, positioned at the end of its truncated body just ahead of the caudal skirt. The top or dorsal fin, the one we saw waving, was a greenish gray, about eighteen inches high, ten inches wide at the base. The anal fin, at the bottom, was white. The total effect was of a stubby, lazy rocket. It had a male presence, which all of us felt, though there was no evidence to tell us this. He drifted with us. We patted him, we stared at him, we talked to him. He made friends of us, forgave us for the wounds he had received at similar hands. He was a thousand miles or more from home, had drifted, we conjectured, in the unusually hot Gulf Stream, had bailed out near the Vineyard, was surprised by the cold water in Vineyard Sound, swam until he found a warm current — the sun-heated pond water as it left the basin approaching low tide — and followed it into the huge brackish pond. And now he was sunning himself.

We posited the ride in the Gulf Stream because it was hard to imagine the thing swimming twenty feet, much less a thousand or more miles. Juliet wondered if he were lonely, if there were others of his kind around. Jon made a half-serious crack about putting a hook in the fish's hard mouth and reeling him in. The two of us made disrespectful jokes about lifting him into the boat and saying at home that we'd caught him for dinner.

"You leave him alone!" Juliet said.

"Joking," Jon said.

We all patted the fish. A kind of pure happiness descended on us. I was transported back to my childhood book, and a certain innocence. A rare creature, bigger than I, alive. Normally talkative Jon grew silent, stroking the fin presented to him. Juliet, chilly and unhappy an hour before, spoke baby talk: "Hey, cute little fishy. Do you need a girlfriend?"

After a while Jon suggested poking him with an oar, just to see what he'd do, to see, specifically, if he could move, for we had begun to worry that he was hurt or sick. I pulled an oar from under the seats and touched him with it, lightly. I prodded a little. He didn't move, even seemed to like it. I poked him sharply, and you have never seen anything alive move so fast. Blink! He was upright, slim, almost fishlike. Blink! His caudal fin, the tutu, twitched, and he was gone, deep and fast.

Well, we were cold, anyway, and though we missed him, and I felt guilty to have bothered him, we knew it was time to go in. We'd spent an hour with him and fairly glowed. I steered back upwind, toward the inlet at Nashaquitsa, and we all kept a sharp eye. "There!" but it was a lobster buoy. "There!" but it was a floating cormorant. "There!" and it was him, waving. We went back to him, got upwind, drifted down over him, and he stayed with us, trusting boy, stayed with us even when I poked him again, the accommodating fish having understood somehow that science was science and we wouldn't hurt him.

Just when Juliet said she was cold and maybe it was time to head in, and just as Jon was agreeing, and just as I was wondering how to get away from the fish so I could start the motor, he pumped once with his high dorsal fin and his anal fin, which shot him ten feet away, then let himself sink. We drifted over him, watched him drop into the deep green of four fathoms of water and disappear. We putted to shore, exultant.

Back at home in the woods of West Tisbury I looked in my adult fish books and finally found a reference in the *Peterson Guide to Atlantic Coast Fishes*:

Ocean Sunfishes: Family Molidae
Large to giant pelagic fishes of worldwide distribution in warm waters. They are very strong swimmers;

reports to the contrary are based on observations of sick and dying individuals. They swim by sculling with their high soft dorsal fin and anal fin.

I liked that "large to giant." And Jon remembered seeing a drawing of a sunfish in John Hersey's *Blues*. I was skeptical. Why a sunfish in a book about bluefish? We found it though, sure enough, at the head of a chapter titled "October Tenth." Hersey and his Stranger (a supposed neophyte fisherman, who serves as the narrative interlocutor) see a fin, just as we did. The Stranger yells "Shark!" and Hersey calmly steers abaft of the thing and fills the tyro in: *Mola mola*. He describes the fish as having "what I can only call a cute little face, with big teddy-bear eyes and a tiny thumb sucker's mouth." This was a bigger individual than ours, eight feet long, with three-foot dorsal and anal fins. Hersey's information gives the maximum weight as six to eight hundred pounds. He says that the only means of propulsion is a "feeble slow sculling" of the dorsal and anal fins.

An old *Webster's Dictionary* offered this: "Ocean Sunfish. A large, sluggish, oceanic fish (*Mola mola*) with a greatly truncated tail."

Sluggish! Feeble! Not our sunfish! I felt as if they'd observed Michael Jordan on vacation in Bermuda and concluded that he was fond of the sun and torpid and liked lying around on big, colorful towels.

Other books around our house and in the Chilmark library told me that *mola* is Latin for "millstone" — apt enough for such a rough, round fish — and that the big sunnies are also known as headfish. I also found quite a lot of the nonsense about sluggishness, along with the unimaginable information that they are sometimes harpooned for sport. And in an ancient edition of *The Columbia Encyclo-*

pedia there was this excellent description: "Its appearance is that of a huge head with fins attached, as its body does not taper."

Back to Peterson for feeding habits: "Ocean Sunfishes apparently feed largely on jellyfishes, the Portuguese Man-of-war, ctenophores, and other soft-bodied pelagic invertebrates and larval fishes." I could almost hear the *suck* as I imagined the meeting between a soft-bodied pelagic invertebrate and the hard open mouth of my friend, which was not to my mind a cute thumbsucker's mouth but something more along the lines of the opening at the business end of an old Electrolux.

One Tuesday a week or so after our tête-à-tête with the young headfish I was on the Coast Guard wharf in Menemsha, fishing happily for bait, enjoying the roar of the current as it came into the inlet on a rising tide. I kept my tackle box close by and eyed a woman fishing across the channel suspiciously. Safely away from the crowd that annoyed me so much, I fished the water, and the water fished me, and I stood in the sun, warm, and fished, growing slowly relaxed, and unsuspicious, and un-irritable.

"Shark!" I heard a boy call, way over on the jetty. "Yi! Yi! Shark!" Someone else. I looked up in some excitement and watched for the fin, and sure enough it was our friend — oh, it must have been him and not another so far north — and he waved his fin, basking his way into the pond, twenty miles an hour in the current, looking as if he were having fun.

"Shark!"

Everyone was yelling and throwing lures idiotically in his path and brandishing expensive gaffs. Summer dinks.

"Sunfish!" I yelled. "Sunfish! Leave him alone!" The

sunfish floated past the jetties, and past the rocky banks of the inlet, and past boats full of fishermen, and past me. I waved; I actually waved back. I could see the propeller wounds on his side. I cried "Sunfish" again, and had the satisfaction of hearing the cry "Sunfish!" go up, followed by the advice, all along the channel: "Leave him alone!" And a woman's voice — "Leave that fish alone!" — from the wharf, some distance inland. It was the lady cop, yelling at some excited boys who were throwing rocks. They ran away as she approached, giggling furiously, firing the last of their rocks ineffectually into the channel. The lady cop stopped and shook her fist, calling after them, but I saw she was smiling. When she turned and saw me watching, she threw her arm up and waved. And I waved back (waved back to a *cop*) and pointed to the sunfish, who waved his fin as he floated in the creek, waved his fin clear up past the nuns and into the pond, waved his lazy fin, floating with the current till he disappeared from view.

Fishing with Bobby

Somewhere during the summer of 1988, in between crabbing and fishing and rushing to work, Juliet decided she didn't want to go back to New York. A beach acquaintance warned me ominously that a woman who wanted to be alone on the Vineyard all winter was looking for more than independence, but I knew that wasn't it: Juliet needed time alone. She hadn't lived on her own and by her own devices ever, not really, and now that she'd finished grad school she saw that the time had come, and that the time would irretrievably go unless she did something about it. Also, as the summer wore on, the idea of New York and a serious job search became more and more distasteful, flavored always by the realization that she'd given up her apartment and would have to find a new one if she meant to live alone. The last thing she wanted to do — so young and untraveled, so fresh in the world, so jammed full of promise that her sides hurt when she smiled — was to move in with me and watch as I started in teaching. The idea that we'd be married someday had taken hold, and Jules, never one to rush to intimacy, wanted at least to be out on bail before the sentence began.

I didn't put up a fuss — I liked my freedom, too, and I liked my apartment the way it was: clean pots stacked neatly on the stove, closets full of fishing gear, plumbing tools on the kitchen table, books stacked high around the bed — I didn't put up a fuss at all; in fact, I helped Jules look for a place on the Vineyard. At the last minute, she found a woodsy house in Chilmark to rent with an artist friend, a roomy place with a grand view and a gorgeous kitchen for the off-season price of $300 a month, everything included. That would leave money for art supplies, and the art supplies were key — Jules meant to develop her talent.

I went back to New York with the Labor Day crowd. Juliet remained on the Vineyard, enjoying the clear September days, her new house a haven. I put on a tie and met my first freshman English classes at Columbia, struck by a surprising nervousness, trembling down to the laces of my new shoes. Jules kept her profitable breakfast shifts at the Black Dog Restaurant, painted afternoons at Lucy Vincent Beach and Gay Head and Menemsha. We spoke to each other nearly every night and wrote short, cheerful letters.

Jules kept my pickup truck and commuted through the fall and winter in the predawn stillness from Chilmark to Vineyard Haven, banging down there in that clattering behemoth. She felt like a scalloper or a lobsterman, a real island regular — part of a community — got to be known as the lady in the beat-up truck. One morning (her first attempt at driving in the snow, which she didn't think should be any different than driving in anything else) she zipped off the left side of a curve and into the woods, missing a small stream and many large trees, but not missing work; she simply left the truck in the woods and hitchhiked into town with the snowplow at five A.M. Not till much later, when I helped her picture the truck upside down in the stream, did she think to be worried.

By December, our letters were longer and more lugubrious. Juliet had found her independence, all right, but independence was a touch more lonely than she'd expected. Through the Black Dog and through her roommate she'd made many friends, but her friends seemed to disappear, leaving the island one by one as the days shortened down to the winter solstice. She went dancing at the Hot Tin Roof and at the bars down in Oak Bluffs, was asked out by men, of course, handled them with precarious poise: she was single, yet spoken for; attached, yet alone. She did fine, I was sure. But I didn't ask her. Those months were her own.

As for me, I'd *had* my independence, had it a good long time, and the truth was, I was weary of it. In January I went to the Vineyard and spent a fine chilly month with Jules, studying hard to know more about what I'd started teaching, and writing faithfully each morning while Jules was at work. The two of us took afternoon walks on the icy shore and found the beaches as appealing as in summer. Jules pointed out the delicate colors of the winter scenery, took me to see her subtlest winter woodscapes, her most dramatic cliffs, her oddest dune-crest views out over the hard gray sea. At Cedar Tree Neck we came upon the wreck of a fishing boat. Farther down the rocky beach we found a lobsterman's black flag and pole. I propped the flag on the wreck and it stayed there for weeks, an elegy in the sand.

By February I was back in New York, back at school. After the month of romance, I couldn't stand the winter, couldn't stand to be alone in New York. Jules suffered too: her roommate had found a boyfriend, and even life at the house was empty. Gradually the population of the island had thinned down to its slightly crazed winter nadir, leaving very few customers for the Black Dog, very few tips and shifts for Jules. The days were short and it was damn cold for painting. The beaches, she wrote, were not so good without me.

In March, Juliet came back to New York, not having failed or given up — indeed, having succeeded amply — and announced her experiment complete. We made shelves for her books in my bedroom, made space in my tiny closets, stacked her dishes on mine, chose between our respective lamps and beds and TV sets, set up a drawing table in the living room, and moved her into apartment 6E, 57 West Ninety-third Street, with me.

After three short weeks of our new arrangement — the two of us dying to skip over spring and beat our way to summer and to celebrate being together (or possibly to escape being so close together in that little apartment) — Jules and I took advantage of my spring break (ten days!), borrowed my father's little van again and, forgetting my fishing rods and her bathing suit, headed south, hoping to find someplace where it was summer, as quickly as possible. The first leg of the drive took us to Stone Mountain, Georgia, where we saw my brother Doug and his wife, Jennifer, and where we visited an active pine plantation straight from antebellum dreamland. Not hot enough. Doug and Jen sent us on to Jekyll Island, which is off the Georgia coast and overdeveloped, perhaps, but peaceful and warm. We camped in the pines, admired tall palm trees, waded in the freezing Atlantic amidst the detritus of a pulp mill, and agreed: good spring weather, wonderful spring weather, but *not hot enough.*

In Florida, after a full-blast drive to the Gulf Coast, Jules and I set up camp on an alligator stream in the Oscar Scherer State Park, the closest oceanside campground we'd found on our free tourist map of Florida. The camping cost as much as a motel might cost anywhere else, but it was pleasing terrain — jungle dense, and hot. We laid our damp sleeping bags out on our campsite picnic table, set up the tent, then raced to the beach. We'd picked the Gulf Coast in hopes of avoiding students of any description, especially students on spring break, *especially* drunken freshmen, and it worked. In quiet Osprey, we seemed to be amongst retirees and withered fisherfolk and secretaries on vacation. The only student in sight was me.

I did not want to think about my thesis, or my own students, or anybody else's. I just wanted to fish, and the afternoon was wasting. We stopped at a roadside stand and bought two dozen live shrimp for bait, drove over the drawbridge to Casey Key, a barrier island five or six miles long and very narrow, lined with rich pink cottages in stucco and stone. Jules spotted a public beach immediately, and immediately we parked and leapt out of the car, changing into swimsuits as we hopped on the hot pavement. Soon enough we were swimming in the warm water, then sunning with our feet in the mild waves — two days away from relaxing, but cheerful nonetheless.

Down the beach a preternaturally tanned old gent was fishing, shooting sour looks at the waves and the sea gulls and me. I watched him a long time before he caught something, but then he seemed to get into a school, pulled in small fish one after the next. I wandered down there and stood near him, looked in his bucket. "Pinheads," he said grumpily. He could have been talking about everyone in Congress, the way he said it, or all the kids on spring break, or even Jules and me. I didn't let him intimidate me. I stood right there and watched him, inspected his catch.

The pinheads were small, less than a pound, I guessed, six to eight inches long, and built slim. They looked like the porgies I'd caught on Martha's Vineyard — the same quill-sharp dorsal and anal spines, the same brutish profile, the same small mouth, tough and protruding lips, big eyes. The Vineyard fish were silver, however, and the pinheads were yellow, with a slimmer profile. Later, I looked in my Peterson guide. The book name is pinfish, *Lagodon rhomboides*. I preferred the local name, although there was no guarantee that the old grump was any more local than I.

After a decent interval (so he wouldn't think he'd inspired me), I went to get my new six-dollar rod and my new six-dollar tackle kit, which I'd bought at the same place Juliet bought her six-dollar bathing suit, a store called EVERYTHING SIX DOLLARS in Brunswick, Georgia. At the car, which was hot inside, I found my live shrimp dead. No matter — still good bait for bottom fishing. I put on a shirt and loaded up my gear, full of stratagems. I figured bottom fishing in Florida would be the same as bottom fishing on the Vineyard: tie a lead weight on a short length of light line so that it sits on the sand while the dead shrimp hovers provocatively in the water above. Back on the beach I stood as far away from the old man as possible. I cast. Plunk. The cheap rod seemed to work.

Juliet wandered along the beach, picking up trophies from the extraordinary concentration of small shells on the high tide line and taking pictures of the storm clouds that had suddenly appeared just inland. It was probably raining where we had camped. I thought of our tent left open at the river and our sleeping bags out on the table, felt a tension that had nothing to do with Florida or wet sleeping bags, but was left from New York. I saw my apartment, which was now *ours,* my ascetic, blank walls newly covered with photos and paintings, my clean bathroom sink full of sweaters and bras, my companionable old carpet rolled up in the hall on its way to the garbage barge, or worse.

Consciously, I switched my thoughts in an effort to relax: Unbidden came the face of each of my students in turn, especially the one who had called me an idiot and a lunatic in his best paper of the semester.

I cast again, trying another new subject: dinner. We had tiny potatoes from an inland farm, a couple of big onions from Vidalia, Georgia, four ears of corn and a fire pit to cook on; we only needed a fish, maybe one of the pinheads I'd seen the old gum gnasher catching earlier.

Juliet snapped my picture. Her hair, I thought, was a touch blonder from all the sun we'd had during the afternoon. Her legs, exposed after a long winter, looked vulnerable, were newly pink. Her bathing suit, probably meant as a leotard, was bunched up in front and drawn up in the rear and would have been comical if she didn't look so appealing. "I'm going for a walk," she said. She took my heavy red shirt right off my back and slipped into it, then ambled off, down past the old guy, who was packing up his gear and his fish, on down toward some tall palms and pines that grew in an airy green park just past a jetty.

I got a bite, tried to set the hook, failed, reeled in a shrimpless rig. On the next shrimp I succeeded, and my cheap new rod bent stiffly. I thought, Dinner, and started to reel in the fish, who wasn't much of a match for the equipment. Looking around for Jules, I caught sight of an astonishing wing span, double the span of the pelicans that cruised low across the water like bombers trying to avoid radar. An enormous bird was flying straight at me, neck tucked in, which meant it was a heron and not a crane. I watched, kept reeling absently. The heron hit the beach beside me, stumbled, pulled his wings in, looked embarrassed for a moment, then gazed steadfastly at the bend in my rod.

He was four feet tall, mostly legs and neck, and he kept

exactly four feet away from me. He had big amber eyes that protruded from the sides of his slim head. He had large, unwebbed feet with three long toes pointing forward and a slightly shorter toe pointing backward. (So: herons were responsible for the perfect peace sign footprints I'd seen in the sand at the bottom of a pond in Scherer Park.) He kept his wings tight to his body, hunched up at the shoulders. From his fuzzy head stuck a pair of plumes that lay flat when his head was in flying position in order to bridge the unaerodynamic gap formed by the S-curve of the tuck of his neck. Now, however — as he stood on the beach watching my rod and pointedly waiting for me to reel in the fish — the plumes stuck out behind him like a poorly pomaded cowlick. He looked like a dotty professor, missing arms.

I pulled in the pinhead. Confident I'd catch more, I unhooked it and tossed it to the bird. My throwing gesture startled him, and he stepped away, his body moving faster than his long neck and head could follow. The fish fell in the sand, flopping. The heron didn't care about the grit; he snapped up the fish in his long hedgeclipper bill, and again stepped away. Black-helmeted gulls began to gather as he grappled with the sandy fish. He tossed his head, tossed and clipped at the fish with his bill, not in the least a graceful operation, tossed and clipped and juggled until the fish was positioned for a headfirst ride down his throat. He pulled his neck in, then straightened it out, and the pinhead disappeared. The heron's neck distended just below his head in the exact shape of the fish. The heron shook his head and the fish moved downward; the heron danced a little and the fish moved downward; the heron pulled his neck in, shot it out, shook, wiggled, twisted, and the fish went down, its shape finally disappearing into the bird's football-size body. I saw no evidence of peristalsis; it was a gravity operation all the way.

The heron regarded me, waiting for more. He shook his head a couple of times, apparently pleased to have got the first fish down. I put another shrimp on the hook. The heron stepped closer, stood at my side as I cast. I let the sinker go to the bottom, forty feet out, and waited. The heron shifted his weight from foot to foot. I took a step toward him. He took a step away. I took a step back. He took a step toward me, looked out to where my weight had splashed. He didn't want to dance. He wanted to eat fish. The sun had reached the horizon.

I pretended I had a bite by pulling back hard on the pole. The heron drooped his neck forward with interest, watched the rod tip intently. When I relaxed, he relaxed. After ten minutes he seemed bored, stepped away, walked along the water, had a drink. But each time I got a bite he trotted back.

Juliet surprised us when she reappeared. "Who's your friend?" she said. She took his picture. "Put your arm around him."

We showed her our dance. I got another fish on, reeled it in. "Here's our dinner," I said.

"Oh, give it to him."

"I already gave him one."

"Well, give him another one. I want to see him eat."

"I want to eat."

"There's more."

She was right. I threw the fish. The heron, not concerned for his image, ducked away, making no attempt to catch the pinhead in the air. He wasn't some silly golden retriever. He snapped the fish up quickly to save it from the gulls that had begun to gather. He went through his comic swallowing routine for Juliet, shaking and twisting and shuddering as the preposterous lump proceeded down his gullet. I thought of eating a pinhead like that. It would be a one-way operation, since the dorsal and anal spines — very sharp — would prevent the fish from moving backward in a fleshy tube.

The heron eyed me, waiting for more. Juliet took pictures, though the sun had now gone down. "Put your wing around Bill," she said. The heron stepped gawkily to the water for a drink. He came back and stood closer to me. I could have reached out and patted his head except that when I tried, he stepped away. If I extended my arm slowly, he stayed in place, but moved his head away on that long, long neck. He put up with my experiments; I was, after all, the agent that transferred fish from the sea to his sandy table, saving him a lot of boring labor. He began to eye my rod and step from foot to foot.

I cast.

Two groups started to gather: laughing gulls, aptly named, and people, hungry for further spectacle after the spectacular sunset.

"What sort of bird is that?" an older woman asked.

"It's a great blue heron," I said.

"It's a pet," Juliet said. "Three years old."

"What's its name?"

"Bobby," Juliet said. "He's like a son to us. Put your arm around him, I'll get a picture."

I cast a new shrimp. Bobby was intent on my every move. More people gathered, stood at a safe distance from my casts, commented on the bird. I began to feel tense again. A young boy threw some sand. His sister shrieked. A youth (with the distinct air of a college freshman) said the bird was a crane. "The fisherman said it's a heron," the older lady said.

My heron stepped closer to me. "You might as well split, Bobby, my boy," I said quietly. "The next fish is for me."

He watched my rod, poised himself when it bent. I reeled in another little pinhead. I thought it would look nice delicately blackened on a tin plate with a roast onion and potatoes and corn. The heron leaned toward me. The kids grew silent. The older woman raised her camera.

"He's eaten too much," I said. "How many can he hold? He's got two pinheads in there already. Three's a crowd."

Everyone watched, waiting anyway.

"Go ahead," Jules said.

I threw the bird the pinhead. The heron shook my fish down his neck to applause. He went to the water for a drink. A toddling boy lurched after him. No one showed concern for the child; it was clear that the heron was more threatened. He stepped sprightly around the boy and came back to my side, closer yet.

"Put your arm around him," Juliet said.

"His pet," the lady said, amazed.

I began to pack up my rod. The heron turned his head from side to side, assessing the situation. I bit the hook and weight off the line and tossed them at my tackle box, disgusted: the heron had got my dinner. I asked Jules for my shirt back, threw the shrimp out onto the beach. The gulls descended, roaring with laughter, but the heron tripped into the midst of them, snapping up shrimp. Then the toddler waddled into the melee, arms outstretched. The heron stepped nimbly away from him and began to trot — five feet, ten feet, fifteen feet, fast, faster — stretched his wings, beat them and flew, big strokes, neck tucked back, suddenly graceful. He was full of fish, and shrimp, and gone.

Canyonlands

Mrs. Grippi was one of my art history teachers in college, and I took her courses semester after semester because she had *passion.* A lot of other kids thought she was just weird, moaning over yet another Jesus on a cross, but she wasn't weird — she was *obsessed.* One time she got Courbet's conceited self-portrait as a peasant up on the screen in front of us and became speechless, rapt, just dropped her pointer and stared for ten minutes while the goof-offs giggled behind her (Jack Tetlebaum used to leave class at moments like this, and she never caught him). At last she seemed to remember where she was. "Isn't he *beautiful,*" she cried, clicking the projector. Another slide, another few minutes to compose herself, and the lecture resumed.

Even if she was a little weird, Professor Grippi filled me with ideas about art and gave me tools with which to evaluate artists — not just lists of dates and hoary old judgments. I remember lots of paintings because of her, but one is a surprise, because it is a painting I disdained at the time (in a brash paper) as melodramatic and absurd: van Eyck's "The Four Ages of Man." It was painted in four panels — deep Renaissance tones, much light and shadow, and big on the wild, soaring clouds. The first panel showed a baby in a boat recently pushed from the shore onto calm waters — just starting life, as Professor Grippi pointed out — all innocence on a pleasant, bluebird day. The next panel showed a young man, his chest thrust out against the possibility of difficulties, his staff held high, his chin atilt, more than enough iron in his bearing and bones to take any blows that might befall him (and more than enough hubris showing in his face to sink him *and* his boat). Professor Grippi directed our attention to the huge storm coming on the horizon, and groaned with fright because the young man didn't seem to see it.

Up to that point I was with the painter: you stood up to trouble, and you either won or got some help (usually in the form of a check from your dad). No big deal. The next panel was where I thought the painting went bogus. There the same character was in the midst or near aftermath of a storm, looked as though he'd been through a hundred of them, all bent and bowed and cowed and contrite, his shirt torn, his boat a shambles. Most of all he was exhausted, and it didn't look as if he was going to make it.

Professor Grippi stopped and looked at this panel a good long time before she turned and addressed us, nearly swooning: "*What* do think has *happened* to this man?"

None of us could figure it out (and Jack Tetlebaum was long gone in the gaping span of silence that passed before class resumed). Finally, Mrs. Grippi clicked the projector, leaving her question in the air, where it would stay for many years.

The last panel of the painting showed the man in old age, sailing into a glorious sunset, erect with wisdom instead of bravado, bowed with humility instead of fear, leaning on a cane that was once his staff. I ask you: hackneyed, or what?

In New York — spring of 1989 — the new storms of responsibility were wearing me down, though I still sailed with my chin far forward and my chest thrust out. If sometimes I coughed and dropped my staff, well, I didn't think those were harbingers of a personal panel three in a quadripartite life. I taught my classes; I codirected the Riverside Writers Group; I helped edit the Columbia literary magazine; I lived through graduate courses in writing and English and philosophy; I was roommate and helpmeet to Juliet, son to my parents, brother to my siblings, companion to my friends — and all that looked easy in comparison to what I could see coming: kids and houses and jobs, illnesses and accidents, aging parents, dying pals, and things I didn't even know about yet, inconceivable. "The Four Ages of Man" kept coming to mind. I finally had the answer to Mrs. Grippi's question, and I didn't like it, as I eyed the endless line of storms before me.

Juliet and I got along pretty well in our little apartment after some adjustments: my bookcase moved to make more work space, my clothes to the foyer closet, my tools behind the couch. She painted in the living room and I wrote in the bedroom; or she napped in the bedroom and I read in the living room; or the two of us sat together in one room or the other: there wasn't a lot of domestic variety. We had a potluck dinner party one night and found that when all the food was laid out around the place the people didn't fit.

After our trip to Florida, Juliet got down to work, took a painting class at the Art Students League and cater-waitered for two big companies, cater-waitered straight through the spring and into the frenetic wedding season, making a (very) small fortune. She worked on pastels at home, creating in the process piles of fine, colorful dust on the living room floor. In late April I was routinely offered another year of teaching at Columbia. Juliet and I conferred. We both thought we wanted to get out of New York, but neither of us wanted to get out quite yet. Besides, if I were done with school, what would come next? As for Jules, a year of full-time life drawing and oil painting classes at the League might lift her out of the hobbyist's realm. So I signed up for one more year of teaching, happily postponing the due date of my thesis in the process. In mid-May I finished the spring semester, then went to work tiling and plumbing, feeling more and more lucky that graduate school (and therefore my income and my very sense of self) was going to be extended by an extra year.

It struck us in that warm June that if we put our money together we might be able to go someplace, struck us further that we could probably come out ahead if we left town for cheaper pastures than New York. (Zeeman and friends were headed for the Vineyard, but that was very expensive, as bad as the city; Juliet and I declined a share in their house.) My sister Carol had moved to Montana. That gave us a Rocky Mountain destination. A cater-waiter friend of Jules' needed a place to stay for two months. That gave us a subletter. So, when my father put his little van up for sale (pointing out that 25,000 of the 60,000 miles on its odometer had been put there by Juliet and me), we bought it ($1,000 down, the rest on credit), our first big purchase as a team. My brother Randy then did me the favor of selling my pickup truck (175 big bucks, minus the cost of an ad) to a man who needed something for trips to the Stamford dump.

Two days before we headed west, Juliet and I took a subway ride down to Canal Street, where she wanted to buy art supplies. Walking back uptown, carrying paper and tubes of good water colors and boxes of pastels and packs of erasers, we happened past her old apartment on Spring Street in Soho. Juliet pointed up and shrugged. Someone else lived there now. Directly across the street we stepped into Spring Street Books for *my* supplies — lots of books from the remainders' table and a couple of good new paperbacks.

Walking up West Broadway we passed the first building I'd lived in when I came to New York, looked into the now-familiar hair salon on street level, $200 haircuts in what had been a screw warehouse. On Prince Street Juliet stopped at the window of a fancy jewelry store (once a shoe repair place); she surprised me, ducking inside. I wasn't used to going into Soho shops — I had boycotted them all as they replaced our diner and hardware store and newspaper stand and deli and bar — but, bygones being bygones, I stepped in behind her. The jewelry store was very small and severe, all white inside, with no more than forty items for sale — and no cash register — just glass cases and a workbench with two stools. The proprietress looked up slowly, and seeing no weapons in our hands, returned to her work, carefully filing a chunk of bright metal. Juliet looked into a case that held a pink-gold ring set with a purplish sapphire. "This'd make a nice engagement ring," she said.

I nodded, again surprised, although twice since Florida Juliet had kiddingly asked me to marry her, the joke in the question so subtle the second time that we'd looked at each other a long while before we'd laughed.

The jeweler took us seriously, anyway. As soon as she heard *engagement* she stood up and came over, her face seeming to say: *These days you can't tell who's got money!* With her blackened and calloused hands she unlocked the case and quickly put a series of large rings on Juliet's small fingers, excitedly quoting impossible, five-figure prices for custom work, the cheapest ring (at $15,000) ten times what we'd saved for our trip. I kept a poker face, nodding at each new ring. Juliet admired them all, settled on one, got my agreement, then said we'd be back.

"Take my card," the woman said. You could tell she had had a lot of experience and knew we wouldn't be back. She tried not to show disappointment as she gave Juliet a three-by-five postcard picturing a much-magnified stack of seven hand-wrought and bejeweled gold rings.

On July first, Juliet and I got in our new car (the same old mini-van) and left the city. In my notebook, buried in my briefcase, I'd hidden the postcard of rings. At each stop on our long route through West Virginia and Kentucky I checked on it and thought of new ways to present it to Juliet, thought what I might say when the time came.

On the Fourth of July we stopped at the Oddfellows Home in Liberty, Missouri, and saw my grandmom, who was almost ninety, as chipper and active as ever despite her strokes and still surprised to find herself living with so many old people. We took her for a ride (though she was fearful) and she showed us where her husband had died and where my father had grown up and where their cow had been pastured. Back at the Oddfellows Home we met her hundred-year-old friends and made the same jokes about what odd fellows they all were. I played the piano for everyone to spotty applause from wheelchairs. Then quite bluntly the nurse came. Time to leave.

That night we camped on a lake near Osage City, Kansas, drove back into that fine town to watch the fireworks and the school band. We camped next in the tip of the panhandle of Oklahoma, then in New Mexico, enjoying the dry heat, enjoying the car and the open landscape, enjoying ourselves. We knew how to do road trips now, kept out of fights, kept fed and rested and out of each other's hair. I wished at times for a real ring to spring upon Jules with the proposal, but it was a matter of the trip or a grand gesture, not both, and something about the postcard seemed richer than any budget ring I might be able to afford at a department store.

After a week of calm travel we found ourselves in Utah. Jules and I stood at the edge of the Canyonlands and looked out over five hundred square miles of unimaginable spires and arches and carvings: the handiwork of two rivers at their juncture. The Green River undulated in from the north (O, truly green, a serpent way down there on the dusty canyon floor) and met the smaller, southwest-bound Colorado in our sight, swelling the smaller river, giving itself up.

A high cirrus veil moved in toward the end of the day, then lower clouds, long clouds moving quickly, which made the sunset more glorious. I had the card of rings in my hip pocket, but the hour was late. If I were to pull it out now, how long would my proposal take? How long the answer? How were we supposed to set up camp in the night? I verged on various gestures without making any or saying anything until the sky was almost dark. Not another soul around. That afternoon in Moab it had been 107 degrees in the shade, and now the cooling sent up a breeze that turned to wind and nearly to gale, rising balmy from the deep and complex excision the ancient rivers had made.

"My stomach hurts," Juliet said.

I patted the card in my pocket. Patience. There would be other grand vistas and plenty of perfect moments. Right now it was time to make camp and get dinner. We had passed a deserted campground earlier, so I drove back that way and we stopped. Out of the car, out of the canyon's wind, the air was cold. A coyote called from the bluff over us. Very far away another coyote answered. There was no wind at all here, just a kind of permeating vastness, and the two of us, and our little van. I pulled a bunch of sticks from our collection in the car (not much wood in this corner of Utah), dropped them in a ring of charred stones that was already there and lit them.

"Stomach *hurts*," Juliet said.

We went to work in the firelight setting up our wrinkled and ragged old tent, a familiar ritual. When it was half up, an igloo of nylon, Juliet walked away and lay down on the picnic table. "Killing me," she said.

"I'm sorry," I said. I always apologize like a parent in the face of illness. We were a long way from anywhere, didn't have any stomach medicine. In our old cooler I found a can of orange pop. Juliet said she didn't want it, then drank it, grimacing.

I made dinner, proceeding as if we were both going to eat, hoping that suddenly she'd be better, or that food would solve the problem. I chopped up two onions, two garlic drupelets, two scallions. Juliet watched me unhappily, then jumped up and ran to the outhouse, three hundred yards away.

Just then the sound of a car took over the silence. I heard it a long time coming over the miles, coming toward us on the dirt road. I walked over to the outhouse, which was a pretty nice one, as outhouses go. "Okay?" I said.

"Not so good," Jules said. "I have bad cramps and it's dark in here."

"Well, get it all out," I said. What kind of advice can you give? "I'm sorry."

"You didn't do anything."

Back at the site I kept making dinner, kind of trimming down the size of things, knowing that Jules wouldn't be eating. The car was still coming, unquestionably coming here, and I just hoped it wasn't someone bad, like the carload of skinheads we had seen in Blanding, earlier. But that hope turned into an imagined certainty that it *was* the skin-heads, five of them, big guys with homemade tattoos on their temples and their fingers. They'd been harassing a waitress at an A&W when I saw them, and now they were coming here.

I had my hunting knife in hand as the car turned into the campground. It was a little station wagon, not the skin-heads' car, which had been bigger and older. The car drove through the loop of the campground very slowly — proba-bly people picking a campsite — paused as it passed me. I stood my ground, holding my knife. The station wagon had tinted windows; I couldn't see in. What if the skinheads had changed cars? It would be nothing for them to steal a little Japanese station wagon and go molesting campers.

The skinheads parked as far away as they could get from me within the campground. Now instead of the pure silence there were murmurings, one low voice, then another voice, higher and more musical, with a timbre of complaint. They banged tent pegs; they made a fire; they played their radio, the news. I didn't think skinheads would listen to the news or that skinhead women would be so querulous. And de-spite the emptiness of my stereotypes I relaxed.

Juliet came back. "Who's with the radio?" she said.

"Skinheads," I said. "They always listen to news radio. No one knows why. There's five of them with tattoos on their heads."

"Oh, shut up." Jules lay back on the picnic table, with her feet near the chopped onions and garlic and scallions. "Not going to eat," she said. "Sick."

I went back to work, chopped up some zucchini, chopped up some carrots, chopped up some potatoes, stuck it all in aluminum foil. "One day I'm going to get Alzheimer's from all this aluminum," I said.

"I've got it now," Jules said. "Could you ask those people if they have any stomach stuff?"

"They are skinheads. Skinheads don't *use* stomach stuff. They *like* diarrhea."

I stuck the vegetables in the coals and flames of the fire and looked over toward the skinheads' campsite. Jules groaned on the picnic table. I said, "Something you ate?" We tried to think if she'd eaten anything different than I'd eaten all day, but she hadn't, except a different flavor ice cream cone at a Frostee Freeze.

Jules said, "How do you know they're skinheads?"

I smiled in a way designed to let her know I was just joking about the skinheads but that really I'd been scared for a minute and that I wasn't yet completely relaxed about the identity of our neighbors. I said, "They have no hair on their heads."

Jules leapt up again. "Ow," she groaned, then sprinted to the outhouse.

While she was in there (a good long time) I dug my vegetables out of the fire and ate right from the foil. The food was fairly bland, which I thought was good, since probably I'd be sick by morning, too.

"Hello," someone said with such a friendly modulation that I didn't start, but simply turned around to face him. He was tall and thin, wearing glasses and blue jeans, with a full head of unshaven white hair. "Thought I better see who the neighbors were," he said.

"Well, hello."

"Camping alone?"

I told him about Juliet's plight, pointing to the outhouse. "Do you have any Pepto or anything?"

He was pretty sure he had some Alka-Seltzer, and invited me to walk back with him to his site to get it. I looked at the outhouse, then got up to go with him. On the way he told me he was a retired geologist who lived in Massachusetts now, teaching the occasional course at MIT. In his salad days, the best days of his life, he'd lived near here, searching the area for uranium, and finding it often as not. He stopped, stood ten feet away from me with his hands in his pockets and told me about the big, defunct mines and the mile-deep shafts and the heavy equipment and the vigilant guards. "Why, today I drove up past what had been three security gates and right into the mineyard. The trailers are all still there, exactly as they were. I could almost hear the voices." He grew wistful. "Mr. Drinnell, my boss. Big, loud character. And Sylvianne. A French lady who kept the books."

The way he said it, I knew instantly that he'd had a romance with this French lady.

"And most of all the mines. I spent my days driving and looking and flying and sporting around with a Geiger counter, looking and finding, that was the thing, finding the stuff. The war was on. A wonderful time of my life."

We walked. As we got close to his campsite I could see his tent, glowing with light from within. A lady spoke from the tent: "They all right? Should we clear out?"

"He is named Bill and he is right here."

"Hello," I said. I was chagrined to hear they'd been afraid of me, too, but noted that the geologist's strategy was more effective than mine: he'd come over straightaway to my campsite, facing me and whatever fear he'd had at the same time.

He said, "His girlfriend has diarrhea, is all. He wondered if we had something for it." That was wise; if the woman had any worries left at all, talk of something so human as diarrhea should dissipate them.

The lady came out of the tent, hidden behind the bright beam of her flashlight. "Oh, diarrhea," she said pityingly. "I'm well stocked." I was disappointed to note that she didn't have a French accent. She went to their car and rummaged around in an enormous purse, came up with a vial of pills and a bottle of Pepto, brought them over. She was tall and thin as the geologist and a lot younger than he, which at least pointed to an interesting romantic life for him after Sylvianne.

The geologist, meanwhile, had opened up a big leather suitcase and found some Alka-Seltzer. He handed the little packet to me. "Be prepared," he said wryly.

"*Merci, au revoir,*" I said, wanting to call up a little of the French lady for him. I felt safer with him there.

I hiked back to our site.

Juliet was lying on the picnic table again, not interested in the vegetables I'd saved for her. "Where have you been?" she said, pointing at her stomach. "Hurts." I showed her the pills and the Pepto and the Alka-Seltzer; she chose the Alka-Seltzer.

I went to the pump over by the outhouse to get a cup of water. Back at the site, just as I was about to open the tailgate of the little van, my heart stopped at the unmistakable buzz of a rattlesnake. I cried out, jumped backward three feet, froze and stared. I had never before seen a rattlesnake, or heard one, but my reaction was sure and instantaneous, purely automatic. The snake had its head raised high, ready to strike. I'd nearly stepped on him. I took another step backward. The snake relaxed a little. It had a big, flat head and a thick body, coiled. I took a small step toward it. It tensed again. It seemed to have the distance of danger gauged pretty accurately. If there had been any sticks around I might have tried to induce a strike, for the sake of science, but this was near desert, and there were no sticks. I took a step back. The snake relaxed. Another step back and the snake sped off astonishingly quickly, curling himself sideways, and hid in a tuft of sage.

I followed him, carrying the cup of water in one hand and the Alka-Seltzer packet in the other, peered into the sage at a safe distance, found the snake's eyes upon me. At eight feet he did not threaten, just bunched himself up against the stalks of the plant. I took another step and he reared up, ready to strike, gently rocking his head, looking not quite in my direction. I took another, smaller step and he pulled his neck back a little farther, cocking his gun. I was three feet away from a two-foot snake.

"What are you doing?" Jules cried, exasperated. She hadn't heard the snake, had only seen me come back with the water, then step mysteriously into the brush.

"There's a rattlesnake," I said.

"Oh, great. Skinheads and rattlesnakes."

"There're no skinheads."

I abandoned the snake and went to her side at the picnic table. "I feel a little better," she said. She had eaten all the vegetables I'd left in the tinfoil, and was munching a piece of bread. She drank the Alka-Seltzer. I went into the tent and made up our bed, three blankets as padding with our one sleeping bag zipped open on top.

When Jules was safely inside and covered up, I went out looking for the snake. He wasn't in the sage anymore. I got the flashlight out and stepped into the darkness, ten steps, twenty, but got spooked suddenly and turned around. *Buzz!* Another snake, the same type except much fatter and a little longer. I stood still, fixing the new snake in the beam of my light.

The outhouse door slammed. Footsteps on the campground road. It was the geologist. The snake suddenly bolted, quickly rolled out of my sight into the dark. I picked my way carefully out to the road, stood in the geologist's path. "I've just seen two rattlesnakes," I said.

"What kind?"

"I'm not sure."

"What color?"

"Just dusty."

"Well, that would be one of your western rattlesnakes," he said authoritatively. "In this area it would almost have to be a midget faded rattlesnake."

"Do they ever get into tents?"

"Not if you zip up. Sometimes they might go *under* a tent, but I wouldn't worry. They're more scared of you than you are of them. And a midget faded rattler — that's not a bad bite. I got one on my ankle once, right through my workboots. They were old; the leather had got thin. All by myself about twenty miles from here one afternoon. I swear I thought I was done for, one fang broken off in the leather there. I just sat down, pulled my boot off and stared at those holes, two very tidy holes, tiny, and got out my knife and sliced 'em, you know, big slits — doctor said they were way too big — and sat there like a monkey with my ankle in my mouth, sucking half the blood out of my body."

"What happened?"

"Well, nothing. I sucked a long time, then tied my leg off with my belt — my next bad move — but nothing happened whatsoever. Turns out that a rattlesnake can withhold venom if it wants, or just inject a little, or maybe he'd just used it up on something else, or maybe I just wasn't sensitive. But nothing happened. Nothing whatsoever. Just my leg turned bluish from the tourniquet, which was much too tight. Could have lost this fine leg for nothing." He patted his right leg affectionately. "Anyway, that's what happened. I ran out of there, two miles or more to my car, then drove clear to the camp. Then the bookkeeper, Sylvie, drove me to the colonel's house — there weren't and still aren't any doctors anywhere near here — and he took me into Moab, three hours from the bite, mind you, and that Mormon doctor just lectured me on the tourniquet."

He had got in the mood to talk, stood with his hands in his pockets the way he must have stood in front of his classes at MIT, rocking on the balls of his feet, five feet away from me on the road, having commandeered more space for himself than most people do. "Good country here. Lot of snakes."

I was in the mood to talk, too, with Juliet sick in the tent and rattlers crawling around everywhere. I asked if he were scared of the snakes, and let him know that I was by the way I said I wasn't.

"It's like anything. You can either be paralyzed or continue along as best you can. After that experience I don't worry much about rattlesnakes. I lived through it, after all, and it gave me a story I like to tell. When I hear that rattle though, wham! I can jump like a New York Knick. Though now they are scarce. The snakes, not the Knicks. We had hunts on Saturdays sometimes, in the spring. The ranchers would all catch snakes and bring 'em into town, to Traveling Stan the Reptile Man, kind of a one-man circus. One year Stan got 2,194 pounds of rattlesnakes in a single collection down in Arizona. I remember that figure clearly, for some reason, 2,194 pounds of snakes. Spring, they come out of their dens, you know, after hibernation, a hundred, two hundred to a den, down in the crevices of the rocks, or down in old prairie dog holes. They don't stray more than three miles from that den all summer, then come the cold weather, back they go. You watch out on bare rock in the springtime, I'll tell you that, because the rattlesnakes'll be out there sunning themselves."

The geologist looked vaguely over toward his campsite, which was dark. He cleared his throat as if he meant to wrap up the conversation. But I wanted to hear more, as each little fact seemed to take away some of the snakes' power to frighten me. I reached for a question, asked at last what the midget faded rattlesnakes ate.

"They eat mice," he said, still looking away. "And other warm creatures I guess, mostly rodents, so they are very beneficial." Then he turned to me and got animated: "But like anything that can hurt a person or especially anything that can hurt livestock, or be perceived to be a danger to livestock, they are killed indiscriminately. I mean, there's a real chance of endangering some of the species — probably even midgets — with the human population absolutely exploding, wrecking habitat and food sources. And don't forget there are plenty of people actively fighting to see the population increase! But I used to kill them — I mean the snakes, of course, not the people."

I asked how he killed them, thinking of film I'd seen of people like Traveling Stan the Reptile Man grabbing snakes by the rattles and snapping them like whips.

"Oh, jeez. I got myself a little .22 pistol after that bite experience and must have fired it a hundred times, a hundred snakes. Also bought a new pair of boots. Did your midget give you a good rattle?"

"Good enough, I guess." He had indeed; he'd scared me right into this conversation. "And I knew just what it was, too."

The geologist crossed his arms over his chest and grew almost misty: "That rattle is just a bit of horny skin that doesn't shed when the snake sheds — they'll get, oh, ten, fifteen sections long, as a record. I think the longest I ever saw was fifteen. After that they break off, you know. My father — who is still alive, by the way, ninety-seven years old — used to tell me you could tell the age by counting rattle sections, but that's not true; all you'd be counting is the sheddings of the snake's life, a variable number — four a year when they're young, sometimes — and no way of knowing how many sections may have got knocked off. The rattle, I guess, represents high evolution. It's there as a warning device. But did you know that if the rattle gets wet it won't rattle anymore?"

I shook my head, smiled at the landslide of information.

"So watch where you step in the rain!"

The geologist looked into the sky, admiring the stars (brilliant, the Milky Way a pulsing slash in the deep blue of the night), his patient voice, his quiet knowledge, still alive in the air between us. Something rustled in the desert litter just at the side of the road. I stepped closer to my interlocutor; he subtly moved away. I didn't want him to start in on stars; stars didn't scare me. I asked about the rattlesnake's natural enemies.

The geologist seemed to have trouble pulling himself back from the sky. "Well, civilization," he said at length. "Always number one. And deer, surprisingly. Did you know that deer will kill rattlesnakes? I mean, I've seen it twenty times out here, a mule deer will run past a rattlesnake, do a double take, stop and go back and stomp the daylights out of it, sort of as a matter of principle. And antelope, too. They just dance on the snake with their hooves, cut the thing into ribbons. Sweet little antelopes, right? And buffalo were a natural enemy, just being so heavy. And raptors. But that's about it, except man, as I said, who's always formidable. And their own appetites: once I came upon a rattler dead, he'd eaten a prairie dog too big for him and just split wide open. How about that?"

I loved hearing that the snakes were vulnerable, too. I nodded him on.

"Now, do you know how the venom works?"

I imagined the feeling of fangs shooting suddenly through my thin socks and into my ankle. I'd left my cowboy boots in New York, unworn since my days in country-and-western bands. I ventured a guess: "Paralysis?"

"Well, that might be a symptom, later. First it breaks down your blood. Enzymatically. That's the hemotoxic type, which is your midget. Neurotoxic venom attacks the nerves, that's your cobra, and that's sudden death. Some rattlers have a little of that, too; in fact, more and more the herpetologists seem to be abandoning these rigid classifications. Then there's cardiotoxic, you can guess what that does." He pounded at his chest, to illustrate a cardiotoxic effect. "The fangs are hollow, like syringes, like needles, with the opening just off the tip so that the victim's tissue won't block the flow of venom, which comes from a sac up under the teeth. The snakes have got a choice, as I said, of hitting you with a little venom, or a lot, or none, I think, and also have a choice as to how hard they bite, how far the fangs go in, how long they hang on, how many bites they give. So try to stay on your midget's good side! He's only attacking out of fear. A snake will never chase you, for example."

I found that reassuring and said so, described my feeling at the sight of the coiled snake, the urge to run away, fast and far.

"Do you know how the snake finds its prey?"

"Smell?" Another guess, but one I was rather sure of.

"Well, no, though you're not alone in that belief. Rattlers like your midget are pit vipers. I used to believe that meant they lived in pits, but that's not it. Actually, the name refers to two little facial organs, something along the lines of acne scars under the eyes, pits that the herpetologists used to think were ears (snakes are deaf; did you know that?), or vibration sensors or what-have-you, lots of bad theory. So a bunch of fellows made a study, took a pit viper and covered its eyes, put it on a table on rubber that kept out all vibration, snipped off its tongue (pity, of course, but all in the name of knowledge. The tongue is the smelling organ in snakes. Did you know that? They lick it out to smell what prey's in the area). So they blocked all of this pit viper's senses, and still he reacted to a person entering the room, and would strike at a person who got too close. In the end they figured out that the pits sense *heat,* minute variations in the ambient temperature, so our friend the pit viper can crawl down into a prairie dog hole or what-have-you, which is going to be full of prairie dog molecules whether it's occupied or not. Smell is just confusing in that situation — total blackness. So, with the heat sensing of the facial pits, our snake crawls into a hole, feels a slight rise in the heat and follows it, like the game: *Getting warm. Warmer. Hot. Hotter.* When he's within striking distance he starts turning his head from side to side, and the evenness of the heat tells him, *Strike.* Which he does."

I asked what the symptoms of a rattlesnake bite might be like.

"A good deal of pain. Swelling, edema, discoloration, thirst, nausea, diarrhea. Jeez, how's your wife — girl-friend?"

Juliet was asleep, I told him, and better.

"Sometimes some numbness, shock certainly. In a bad bite you're going to get internal bleeding, sphering of red blood cells. You mentioned paralysis, but that's extreme. In a *very* bad bite, coma. Even death. But that's rare, especially with the snakes around here. Are you sensitive?"

I said I'd never been bitten by a snake and didn't know.

The geologist picked up my train of thought, somehow: "Knowledge conquers fear, as the Bible says. Fear only begets panic. I think panic is the most dangerous symptom; anyway, it's how I almost lost this leg, forty years ago. With your midget, probably you would have felt bad for a few hours. I don't imagine he'd have killed you, though you never know. Friend of mine — oil geologist — reached into a crevice way deep in the outback down in Australia and got bitten on the forefinger by a *death adder*. Neurotoxic venom, of course, the world's most deadly snake. He protested — quite violently, as he tells it — but one of the fellows with him just pulled out his Bowie knife the second after the bite and cut the darn finger off. How about that? Doctor later said it saved my friend's life. Now he points with his pinkie.

"The rules are, don't stick your hands anywhere you can't see. Don't set your foot anywhere you can't see. Don't step over a log without looking. Don't walk around after dark. The snakes like the night, it's cooler. Wear big shoes. Don't sneak around. And carry a knife."

The geologist looked at me closely then, reached his hand out over the gulf between us for a shake. "Well, I've bored you plenty, I guess. Good night," he said. The lecture was over, and the geologist was not one for small talk.

"Just one question," I said.

The geologist raised his eyebrows in anticipation.

"What ever happened to Sylvianne?"

He smiled, appreciating my memory, and the nosy quality of my question. "Sylvianne?" he said wryly. "You needn't worry. Sylvianne was never bitten." Then he said good night again and walked briskly away in the dark.

"Watch out for snakes," I called after him.

"The snakes had better watch out for me," he called back.

I got my toothbrush and followed the beam of my flashlight warily to the water pump near the outhouse, brushed my teeth. Coming back, I poked in the bushes a little bit, thinking of all the geologist had said, then got spooked and rushed to the tent, leapt in, zipped the flap tight and lay myself down by Jules, who protested all my noise in her sleep. I dropped my arm over her and tried to conk out, but it didn't work. I heard rustling outside. I turned slowly around to face the noise, but now it seemed to be behind me. I turned. Jules protested again, closer to wakefulness. I quietly pummeled the floor of the tent through our blankets, but didn't think I felt any snakes beneath us.

After a half hour I got back up, found the flashlight, inspected the area in front of the tent for snakes, then opened the flap and followed the flashlight's beam, walking (naked except for sneakers) to the car. I checked under the van, then quickly got my notebook out of my briefcase. Back in the tent, unbitten, I pressed my butt against Juliet's and propped myself in writing position amidst the blankets and sleeping bag, holding the flashlight against my ear with my shoulder.

What I wrote, as it turned out, was something along the lines of an exercise I'd given my students: *Please recreate a complicated conversation.* I tried to get every word the geologist had said, amazed at how easy it was to remember (and amazed, too, at how much the geologist started to sound like me), and terrorizing myself in the process, thinking of snakes, pausing to listen to noises — none of which was as loud as a rattle, but all as scary in the night. "It's like anything," I wrote, quoting the geologist: "you can either be paralyzed or get along the best you can." And I wrote, and thought of Sylvianne, and this old guy's life and all the trials he must have been through, and how kindly he'd come out of it.

About ten minutes into the project I turned the page and came to the postcard from the jewelry store. The rings glittered in the flashlight's beam, beautifully made, beautifully photographed. I felt Juliet at my back, thought about her for a moment, thought about how I would show her the card, thought about what I would say, then got spooked on that account and began to write again. I wrote and got it all down, and by the time I was done I'd forgotten all about the snakes that must have been operating around our tent. I fell into a half sleep, a half-dreaming meditation on fear, and in the midst of it "The Four Ages of Man" came full color into my consciousness, especially that awful third panel, that poor beaten man in his tattered clothes and ruined boat.

I woke back up. Just lay there in the perfect desert silence. Eventually I began again to fall asleep to the thought that there were storms worth facing. I felt Juliet's fanny against mine, thought of that ridiculous postcard, thought of all the money I didn't have — money to buy a ring, for one — thought of snakes and storms, thought that even the most vicious snakes must miss the strike sometimes and the worst typhoons pass harmlessly, put my hand back to touch Jules, thought, Here is the woman I will marry (if she'll have me), thought, Here is the woman I will wed, making a kind of lullaby of it, and finally falling to sleep, cringing under thunderheads, ready to chop my fingers off for death adders, no end of the tempest in sight, a hundred ranchers with snakes on sticks, a thousand wild storms coming at me, fangs through thin socks to my ankles, fierce winds shredding the sails of my suddenly pitching boat.

Water

In Montana, Juliet and I lived enamored by water and mesmerized by the spirits of water: Undines and Dracs, Sirens and Nixies, Nickurs and Kelpies, Naiads and Nereids, who'd swum up great rivers from the sea. There were mortal spirits, too: beavers and muskrats and cows; ospreys and herons and pelicans; kingfishers and cliff swallows and insects; trout and crayfish and snakes; eagles and hawks and even children, sometimes, flocks of human children on inner tubes, the local kids, dropped off upstream for a screaming ride home in the wild.

I promised my few neighbors I wouldn't give them away — it's a kind of Eden they live in, though sometimes dangerous and too dry for fruit trees — so I'll be coy about the name of our river except to say that it was named in 1805 by Meriwether Lewis (as if it had never been there before his expedition with William Clark) for the secretary of war who held office from 1801 to 1809. No one I asked knew what the original inhabitants called the river, or exactly who the original inhabitants may have been, though they were probably the ancestors of the Blackfeet or Flathead or Crow. I'd like to imagine they called it the River of Promise, and so I have overruled Mr. Lewis. Why not?

The River of Promise is short, as rivers go, sixty-five

miles from its headwaters on the dry side of the Continental Divide to its confluence with the Missouri River at a bend beneath a railroad bridge. Juliet and I lived 4.5 miles upriver; our address, therefore, was 4.50 River of Promise. Our landlord, Theodore Opalowski, was one of the adult ceramics students at the Archie Bray Foundation in Helena, an artists' enclave of which my sister Carol is the director.

Jules and I had made our way up from Utah into Idaho across the Sawtooth Range (where I got sick with Juliet's one-night diarrhea bug), then crossed into Montana on the Lost Trail Pass from Salmon on July 11. From there we drove up to Missoula, then over to Carol's place on the outskirts of Helena. The Archie Bray Foundation (affectionately known as the Bray) is a defunct brick factory — beehive kilns, ancient extruders, drying rooms, fantastical boilers, and piles upon weedy piles of rejected bricks in fifty varieties. Archie Bray himself was a brick manufacturer and a patron of the arts; he invited potters to use his plant, then funded the foundation, which is now a modern if somewhat decrepit ceramics paradise, with wood, gas, and electric kilns, many studios, and most of all artists: sculptors and potters from all over the world, gathered in one place for year-round residencies during which they have a chance to confer with one another and to focus their lives on clay. They also teach people from the community of Helena, and this is where our landlord came into the picture.

Juliet and I met Theodore Opalowski on the third night of our visit at the Bray, when my sister dragged him out of his class and into her house (which is a former chicken coop behind a fence near the wood kilns and the firewood shed). She'd overheard him saying he had an empty cabin. Theodore was a distracted sort, vague but friendly, a youngish leftover from the sixties with his long hair and Mexican peasant blouse. Carol said he was known as a sometime construction worker and part-time artist. Juliet and I talked with him and arranged a chance to look at his cabin the next day. If we liked it, he said, we should go ahead and get set up and stay. We could pay him, oh, two hundred dollars (for six weeks' rent!) next time we saw him. No rush: golly, sometimes when he himself went up there it was hard as heck to leave.

Along with a shotgun and a five-gallon water jug Theodore gave us a map, carefully and proudly rendered in pencil. At the top, in heavy lines, he'd drawn and labeled *The Interstate,* then the beginning of *The River of Promise Road.* The first landmark he labeled as *Hill Number One (very steep),* followed by *Broken Windmill, Broncoe's Place, Blue Trailer,* and *Pointed Rock.* Next there was a crude drawing of four horses, and finally the cabin, a sweet little drawing just down the road from *Hill Number Two (goe very slow).* At the bottom of the page was this important information: *Comboe of gate lock is 14–3-31.* Through the map snaked the seductive line of the River of Promise, drawn by Theodore in an innocent blue.

The next afternoon we put the map to the test, drove up the interstate past Buffalo Jump, turned off at the Promise exit. Just past the Promise Inn we found the road (we were pretty sure) and drove in the dust up a terribly steep hill past ten No Trespassing signs, one as big as a billboard. The windmill turned up just as Juliet and I began to think we were lost (breathless on the shoulderless, dirt and rock, dry riverbed of a shitty road). The four horses were in their appointed place a mile later, then the second big hill, and exactly 4.5 miles from the head of the road we found the barbed-wire gate to Theodore's cabin. The combination worked on the padlock, which I took as proof we were in the right place. Juliet climbed out of the car and opened the gate, then we drove down past a wrecked pickup to a home-made bridge and across a dry creek and into the cabin's lower yard, where we parked beside an old Saab with four flat tires. From there we could see the River of Promise, just a hundred yards down the hill. We got out and had a look.

The cabin seemed to be knocked together with at least some proficiency: a tin roof, walls of commercial siding, several expensive but mismatched windows (probably lifted from construction sites). Inside, once we got the door key to work, we found a big, single room with a kitchen in the left front corner. On the right-hand wall, a pair of salvaged sliding doors opened into a Plexiglas sunroom. Directly in the center of the place a large and solemn old wood stove held court. On a landing below the ladder to a spacious loft and next to a window was a stack of mattresses made up as a bed; it looked cozy, and would command a pleasing view once I got the shutters down.

Outside, a picnic table stood amongst wildflowers. Chunks of construction granite and bales of wire and two old gas refrigerators lay about the yard. Thick-boled ponderosa pines shaded the house on the south. An outhouse was hidden behind a cedar tree. Across the river to the left a steep, scruffy, stone-strewn hill rose, forming cliffy heights above the river. Directly across the water was a meadow, at the back of which were two eccentric rock spires, one sporting a finger at its top, pointing skyward. No sound but the River of Promise and a peeping bird and a small breeze in the tops of the pines. Jules and I never made a decision about staying. We just stayed.

And so water became the center of our lives. Our first evening on the river we saw a chain of nine ducks come around the bend riding the hard current, a perfect line, bumping one by one over the standing waves and adjusting their faces identically to miss the splash of white water, speeding along with the confidence of Eskimo kayakers, no need for flight, a curious commute all the way along our quarter-mile stretch of river and out of sight. In the ice-clear water we saw a muskrat beating home against the current, swimming hard, keeping to the rock. He came up for a breath and saw us, or smelled us, and dove, sped through a crack on the clean bottom, four feet deep. We saw him all the way to his den in some rubble under the bank.

In the morning before Juliet awoke I went to work trying to restore Theodore's water system. He'd explained it in hopeful terms, but now I knew he was dissembling — not so much to fool us, but to spare us displeasure until it was truly necessary to be displeased. He'd mentioned that we ought to bring drinking water, just in case, and that the neighbor, Jim, had a manual pump on a deep, sweet well.

Theodore had a well, too, on the hill next to his old pickup, but it looked to me as if it had been capped by the drillers. It may never have produced water at all. Heavy black polyvinylchloride tubing ran hidden in the high needle and thread grass from the hopeless well to the yard, ending uselessly in the weeds. On further investigation I found the real water system: another length of pipe led from the house almost to the river, where it should have been connected to a pump. The pump was the missing link between the pipe from the house and a final piece of PVC — which I found in the weeds — a tube of wider diameter with a wire mesh leaf-and-muck-encrusted cage on the river end.

Up at the cabin I found a nipple of white PVC pipe protruding from the outside wall above the kitchen area. I crept inside so as not to wake Jules, who was sleeping with one arm out the open bedside window. She looked content, with her other fist at her cheek, and dreaming: no car alarms, no sirens, no music but her own. I stepped over her and climbed the crude ladder up to the loft, discovered that the white PVC ran into an elevated fifty-five-gallon drum next to an eagle's-claw bathtub. A hose came out of the bottom of the drum. One branch led to the tub, the other downstairs and into the kitchen. It wasn't hard to figure out: stick a length of the black PVC into the river, connect it to the gasoline-powered pump Theodore had mentioned, connect the pump's outflow to the next length of PVC, stick that into the white nipple at the house, fill the drum, turn off the pump, and presto — a fifty-five-gallon, gravity-fed cistern system for bathing, dishwashing and cooking.

But not drinking. There are no streams in the West (or probably anywhere anymore), no matter how clear, that have not been touched by the threat of what Theodore called beaver fever, giardiasis, caused by *Giardia lamblia,* a protozoan microbe that causes violent gastrointestinal upset. A lot of my friends and acquaintances scoff at *Giardia,* play a sort of thirsty Russian roulette on every hike and boat ride, but on a river like the Promise, which passes through ranch lands, the threat is very real, almost inescapable. *Giardia* is carried by beavers, it's true, and other rodents and people and most other mammals. Five minutes of boiling, I thought, or walk to the neighbor's house, once I figured out where it was; all we needed was a couple of gallons of drinking water a day. No big deal.

I found the portable gasoline pump, also known as a ranch pump, where Theodore had said it would be, under a heap of flooring scraps and collapsed inner tubes in the winter sunroom, where the temperature was already ninety or so, and rising. Theodore had allowed as how the impeller housing on the pump might be cracked, and perhaps he was correct, but I couldn't tell — the impeller housing was missing altogether. The carburetor, too, was missing, as was the spark plug. A piece of stick had been threaded into the spark plug socket. The pump, bless its heart, and Theodore's, too, was little more than an iron weight painted yellow.

I quit. Went fishing. O, to fish in a river! The sun had just made the distant rocks at the headwaters of Epistle Creek, and glinted almost painfully from every wave crest and every gurgling bulge in the rocky stretch of the River of Promise just below our house. And O! to stand in the River of Promise for the first time and feel the thigh-high current hurrying me as I stepped downstream in my hip boots. I flycast a tiny nymph into the current, a fly I'd tied in New York. A mule deer grazed her way along the crest of the rocky hill above me. Hawks at work. Butterflies. Then *bang,* and *splash,* a small brown on my barbless hook, undamaged, spotted brilliantly in red and pink and shades of blue, a tough little fighter, anxious to live. I put him back educated and forever wary (I hope) about the color of brass in the shape of a hook. I slowly waded a quarter mile downstream, studying mayflies and goldfinches and a possible bluebird, and fishing.

As I made the bend in the river I stopped. There was a deep green-and-blue pool ahead, placid under a sheer rock. Chipmunks made their warning — a distinct high *chip* — at my presence (*chipmunk,* an onomatopoetic Native American naming word). There were two small cabins visible ahead. One would be Jim's, the neighbor with the manual pump and the sweet, deep well. He lived in Helena, would be here only infrequently. As for the other neighbor, Theodore had said there were some grumpies about, and I didn't yet know that Montana trespass law allows access to the entire length of every river, as long as you don't cross private land to reach the water. The theory is that a person can own the riverbed but not the water that flows everchanging through it and over it. And the theory sounds pretty reasonable until you consider the old Native American way of looking at the world — river and riverbed owned only by themselves, the concept of individual human ownership of waters unthinkable, akin to the ownership of sky, or stars, or night, and stewardship a holy privilege, all decisions made with the seventh generation to come in mind.

Well, not knowing Montana trespass law as yet, and not having been raised to eschew property relationships, and further, wary having been provided by my landlord with a shotgun for unstated purposes, I paused awhile, then figured out that I could wade into the pool and be out of sight of the cabins. I stood at the head of the very deep pool and fished into its mystery, and, as always, the water fished me, and I fished the water, and the water felt me, and I it, and the birds flew by, and I flew, and felt the water and fished, one tiny beat closer to satori, believing for just that sparkling moment that enlightenment was not a long way off.

The sun rose higher. The sky grew hot. If you think it is always cold in Montana, go stand in the River of Promise when the sun is high. I stripped out of my vest and my shirt, tossed them to the rocks of the bank. Hotter yet, and the fish had stopped biting. I stepped to the shore and looked in the direction of the cabins and listened for ten minutes. Cicadas. Swallows. A bit of a breeze in the ponderosas. A pinecone falling branch to branch through its tree. Wing-beats of a lone duck. A hummingbird buzzing past, then two more. The river, of course, sloughing by in the deep. And nothing whatsoever else. I took off my hip boots and my pants and my socks and baptized myself naked in my new river, quite pleased with my morning and my new life. I floated downstream faster than I could walk, then swam hard against the flow in the pool, thinking of the fish resting below me. At a full crawl I could just keep ahead of the current. When I relaxed, puffing, I shot downstream. The water was surprisingly warm, too warm for good trout.

Later I'd figure out that the River of Promise flowed across a treeless section of plains before reentering the mountains. That sun-heated water passed our cabin twenty-four hours later. Twenty-four hours after a hot day the river would be warm. After a rainy day, it would be cool. The current weather at 4.50 didn't matter; the River of Promise was a time machine. After two rainy days, its waters would be cold, the cold of the mountains, the head-waters, the melt off of glaciers, the chill water of springs. After three days of rain, big trout from the Missouri would come upstream, following the precious chill.

I dressed and walked overland to our cabin, a little worried that I'd be seen by some unknown neighbor. Home, I found Juliet on the porch, drawing a bouquet she'd gathered of purple asters and butter 'n' eggs and columbine. She was beginning to be skillful, even impressive, with her pastels. Her hair was getting long again, and very blond from all the sun. She drew intently, more serious in the morning than she would be later in the day, when I could count on her to grow boisterous and funny.

In the house I was surprised to find that it was ten o'clock. Jules had a little pot of water on the stove, boiling it on a tidy gas flame that was fed by a tank of propane outside. I made coffee for her and brought it out on the deck next to the sunroom, a good way to get her to talk to me when she's working.

She said, "Did you get the water figured out?"

"Yes," I said. "It doesn't work."

Juliet drank her coffee. "Well, it's beautiful here," she said, apparently satisfied. "Now what about the water?"

The path to the river went straight from our door a hundred yards, then took a right and ran another two hundred yards along a high rocky ledge, then ducked to the water at a dead end formed by a twenty-foot-high cliff of old volcanic stone. Hidden from the house, I crouched on the flat, jutting rock where we'd seen the muskrat and the ducks, and pushed the big plastic water jug under. It blooped, filling.

As it filled I watched the current upstream. A log appeared. It floated toward me and stopped. It stared at me. It was brown, did not seem happy to see me. Its eyes were subtle, all brown, everything brown. The jug got full. The log stared at me just as long as it pleased, then quietly sank and disappeared. Later I figured out it was a beaver.

Water weighs about eight pounds per gallon. My plastic vessel therefore now weighed forty pounds. Forty pounds didn't seem too heavy, even in bare feet, at least not at first. I made it up the steep path to the ledge, rather waddling with the unbalanced weight. Still several hundred yards to go. Forty pounds at the end of one arm gets uncomfortable quickly. I rested. I walked. I rested. Each stretch of walking was shorter than the last. My shoulder grew tired. My elbow felt disconnected. I pictured a cartoon arm, stretching. I made the last leg of the path in one speedy stumbling tack, hoping to impress Juliet, though by then we'd been together seven years and she wasn't likely to impress too easily. I *oomph*ed the water up onto the wooden deck not far from her. She looked at me briefly, went back to her pastels.

I humped the water into the kitchen, poured two of the five gallons into a picnic jug that had a spout and the name JIM written on it in Magic Marker. Placed next to the sink, it would make a weak approximation of a faucet. I washed a glass Theodore had left there, using a sponge he had also left and some Dr. Bronner's dish soap, which Juliet and I had in our box of camping food and blackened pots. I pushed the button on the jug. The water flowed, rinsing the glass. I grinned, climbed to the table we'd set up in the loft and went to work — mostly daydreaming, which is the best way to write. In my notebook was the postcard of rings. I inspected it often, knowing I'd found the right place and hoping that later on in our stay I'd find the right time. Pretty soon Juliet came in, sat at her table downstairs, and got to work, writing about the abused and frightened tough kids who'd been the objects of her art therapy internships back in New York. I peeked at the card, gradually forgot it, and wrote.

After lunch, at three, Juliet and I blinked out of our different worlds, went to swim in the deep pool I'd discovered that morning. We were alone. The water was warm. We took off our clothes, thinking of the possible unfriendlys in the cabin we could not connect to an owner. The sand between the rocks made a beach. We heard laughter then, the sweet maniacal laughter of children, and I thought of all my European water spirits, the ones I'd brought with me. The laughter echoed off the rocks, was answered by higher laughter yet, and louder. We jumped into our clothes just as five children made the corner on their inner tubes. The oldest child was a pubescent girl, shepherding her baby sister with a lot of scorn. A boy got caught in a whirlpool and whined, spinning. Two little girls held hands, floated daintily by. Slowly the family passed, looking at us as if *we* were the water sprites, spirits to treat politely, spirits who were not necessarily malevolent, but not spirits to trust at first meeting. We couldn't even say hello, we were so surprised. Then their dad came around the bend, floating low, bumping his butt on submerged rocks and grimacing. He gave us a surly nod, floated past. Later we'd figure out he lived at 1.44 River of Promise, a long ride home.

When they were well away we stripped again and bathed, using weird Dr. Bronner's soap. His label says that the soap is biodegradable. His label also says *One World God Love Religion Makes One And All Brothers In Skin And Spirit,* and many other things spirited and idealistic and capitalized and slightly unbalanced. His soap burned my eyes, and my ass, and a good many things on Juliet, but we used it, in deference to the river, used it hoping that *biodegradable* meant it was harmless, but not knowing, not really. As Juliet said, "How could something that burns my butt like that be okay for the fish?"

In the evening a thunderstorm came, violent, spectacular, and ours alone. We lay in our new bed and watched it come, and watched it stay, and watched it go. The sky returned to its everyday perfect dry blue. I fished and got two good rainbows for dinner — a good thing, because we'd brought little fresh food with us. Juliet made some spaghetti. I built a fire outside and cooked up the fish. We read till it was too dark, then went to sleep, listening to the River of Promise.

In the days that followed we bounced out on the dusty road to Buffalo Jump and bought ice and canned soup and some lousy bread at a barren food-gas-and-fishing store. The couple there had a pay phone, too, so we'd call my

sister to arrange our weekly visits, and call New York to
grow distressed: our subletter never seemed to answer the
phone. What if there were a leak in the bathroom? What if
the fish in the tank were all dead?

At home in the cabin we put three big blocks of ice into
Theodore's ice fridge, which was nothing more than a ver-
tical cooler manufactured to look like a refrigerator, upright, so that every time we opened the door the cold fell
out and splashed to the floor at our feet. The ice trips
became a ritual as important as bathing. And we were good
about it: we kept one jar of mayonnaise alive the whole
summer. The need for ice was the only need strong enough
to budge us some days. We forgot entirely about news-
papers and showers and telephone calls.

We began to explore. I figured out that the land directly
across the river was a peninsula, and that the river curved
hard around it, passing just behind the large rocks that
pointed toward heaven. There was a big, deep pool back
there, a sandy beach at the inside of the bend formed where
the sheer black wall of the rocks had kept the river from
going straight toward our house. The river narrowed before the bend, narrowed into one lane of high, standing
waves. How it roared! Later I described the place to our
landlord. He said, "Oh golly yeah. That's a regular tourist
attraction there."

One afternoon when our work was done for the day we
carried a couple of Theodore's big inner tubes across the
meadow of the peninsula and back to the river to the Tourist Attraction (as we had come to call it), a quarter mile or
so, no more. We swam and we sunned and we kissed, and
read, and thought about the world with pleasure or dismay,
depending on the subject in mind. We tried a tube ride
through the chute of water as it entered the pool. Fast and

splashing, get your feet forward, fight the spin, fend the rocks off with your toes, whoosh through the chute into the cliff, bounce and float, repeat, over and over, a hundred times, laughing. At four, the sun fell behind the rocks. We got cold, so we floated away from there on our tubes, back into the sun, then home, a half mile as the river flowed. Along the way I saw the beaver again. He looked at me with the same disdain he'd shown the first time, his eyes and nostrils barely above the water. He dunked himself before Jules could see him.

And every evening we had a thunderstorm, fabulous rain. In a normal year there is lots of lightning, little rain, the stuff of forest fires. We had rain every night, but still the ground was dry and very thirsty. And every evening the sky broke to blue and we ate on Theodore's picnic table under the sunset. The river would grow slightly silty, by sunrise be clear. And every morning I went down to our rock and filled our vessel, brought home water with easier and easier steps. I was losing weight. I was getting strong. I'd pour two gallons into the JIM jug, and boil one gallon for silverware washing. Juliet would pour a quart or two for her bouquets. The sound of splashing filled our house.

I fished farther and farther downstream, had good days and bad, kept a very few fish for eating, inspected the cabins along the way. At the first bend past Jim's, maybe a mile from our place, there was a big log cabin, the Gunnarsons' place, as Theodore had told me. They were often home but never looked at me, choosing to believe I wasn't there. At the second bend down, there was an abandoned homestead, seven rude buildings, someone's life work. A high, dilapidated footbridge made of cable and boards spanned the river across the rocky gorge there, unusable. I passed under the bridge imagining the homesteader's children swinging it as they shouted with laughter, alone in the world. I continued downstream. At quarter-mile intervals there were cabins, for the most part unoccupied, owned by weekenders, as Theodore called them, people escaping the bustle of the capital: Helena, population 23,938.

I had spent two high school summers in Helena visiting my uncle Bill, who was a minister there. I remembered the place vaguely but fondly, kept having blasts of recognition as Juliet and I went about our weekly business — shopping for real groceries, mailing letters off at the post office, checking in at the fly goods store and the bookstores, picking up art supplies. Most important, we visited Carol and Mac and the many superb potters in residence at the Bray that summer. There we had a social life and some conflicts to consider, even if they were not our own. We went to minor league ball games and museums and stores. We did the water things we weren't willing to do in our river — washed our car and did laundry in the laundromat. But living on the river had made us wonder doubly where the bubbling waste went to. We bought biodegradable soap, but worried still about the burning anuses of all those fish who had to swim in human detritus. (So many of us people, and so many more coming.)

Juliet and I couldn't stay away from water, swam twice or three times every visit at Spring Meadow Lake, an old quarry near the Bray. We took hot showers, too, with decreasing urgency as the summer wore on. The bathtub in its stall — all dark and tiled and curtained — no longer appealed to us: no chance of seeing a muskrat there, or a heron, or a pelican on high.

Mostly we stayed home. We had several spots to swim, chose one each day after work and spent an hour or two. Once, as I flailed against the current, laughing, getting exercise, I noticed that a snake swam with me. I didn't stop to identify him by species, but gasped and flailed harder and beat my way out of the river and stood breathing at the shore, unwilling to tell Juliet what I'd seen. He was pale and he was quick and he'd sped past me.

"What's wrong?" Jules said.

"Snake," I said simply.

She didn't mind. She went on with her swimming. Her theory was that he'd been there all along, avoiding us just fine, the way the beaver did, and the pelicans, and the trout and the crayfish and all the birds. I stayed onshore and thought Boy Scout thoughts: make two cuts in the shape of an X one quarter inch deep on each fang mark suck the blood and venom and spit it out keep sucking and spitting on your way to the nearest doctor. The nearest doctor ... an hour? I thought of the geologist we'd met in Utah, thought of him treating his own rattlesnake wound, and wished I had him there to explain water snakes, good and bad.

The evenings grew cooler. In Montana, autumn starts in August. Juliet mentioned hot baths more than they might normally come up in our conversation. I began to invent. The sunroom was a porch, really, nothing more than a deck with a Plexiglas roof and walls. Theodore had built it to have a warm, bright place in the killing winters. By noon it must have been a hundred degrees in there. By two, one hundred twenty. It smelled like the squirrel nests it contained. I don't know why it took me three weeks to think of it, but I finally put our water vessel in there one morning after I had gotten in shape enough to make a second trip to the river. I found that the top of a certain jar of Theodore's Folgers Crystals screwed nicely onto the spout of the jug. I spent my fishing time drilling holes in the cap with a hand drill, didn't say a word to Juliet.

In the chill just after that day's thunderstorm Juliet went for a wildflower walk. I checked the water. It was not just lukewarm; it was hot, uncomfortably hot, nearly scalding. I poured some into the pot for the silverware, then added cold water from the JIM jug. I could barely contain my excitement. I wanted to surprise Juliet, but when she was back I could think of no way to trick her into taking off all her clothes and standing at the bottom of the stairs under the deck, which was just the proper seven feet above the pine needle carpet below. I had to tell her. She stood naked and shivering, hugging herself, while I screwed the drilled Folgers cap onto our vessel, then sighed as I dumped hot river water over her head in a perfect shower. Two and a half gallons lasted only about two and a half minutes, but that was sufficient.

Juliet dried happily and dressed, grinning, as I stripped and shivered. Then she gave me my shower. I was proud of myself. I stood in the hot splash and pine needle puddle and was proud as hell. We were clean. We were warm. Showers became a new daily ritual; the sound of splashing filled our yard.

Toward the middle of August it rained. It rained all day, all night, without thunder, just rain. We watched out the windows at the rain, and worked, or read, or talked. We had a visitor, a deer who lay down in our yard under a small ponderosa tree. He lay there for hours, just watching. The air grew cold. I went to the river and got a vessel full of water, easily, even carrying the JIM jug full in the other hand. Our sunroom was without its source of power, so we used the propane stove to boil two gallons in the steam pot, two gallons in the silverware pot. We poured from vessel to vessel. We had our hot showers in the rain, feeling only slightly sullied to have used propane instead of the sun.

In Helena we visited my sister, saw a movie, ate at a restaurant, felt awkward standing in the bathtub for showers — felt greedy using all that water. From Theodore we got another five-gallon vessel, filled it with clear water, and went home. The rain stopped, but the river had turned brown with silt.

Juliet and I walked to Jim's house every day then, a quarter mile overland, pumped his red pump until our arms were sore, bringing clear water up from the earth. (When we finally met Jim, he thanked us for using his pump, keeping it primed and clear, before we could thank him for letting us.) Juliet strapped a couple of gallon jugs to her belt, carried two more in her hands. I carried one five-gallon vessel and the jug named Jim, full, for a total of eleven gallons of water. I grew stronger yet, and thinner, watched Juliet march home ahead of me. Were we staying longer, I thought, I'd make a yoke, I'd carry a hundred gallons a day; after a while I'd look like Li'l Abner, and be as simple, and good.

We had a week of no rain at all and the River of Promise began to clear. On the morning of August 18, which happened to be my birthday, number thirty-six, I climbed the hill next to the rocks that pointed toward heaven, climbed quickly, in good shape from water, climbed up a game path along brittle rock to the top. From there I could see the peaks of all of the small mountains we lived in. From there I could see the distant, high-mountain home of the headwaters of the River of Promise. I could almost see the Missouri through our river's slotted canyon.

From up there on top of everything I looked down on the River of Promise road. I looked down on our little cabin half hidden in the grove of ponderosas. Juliet was in there, still sleeping, and safe on my desk in my notebook was the card of rings. Behind the hill and well below me I picked out an old homestead cabin that I'd failed to spy before, then picked out its road, which led to a shallow place in the water. I watched the river go by, looked down on its progress, saw the place from whence it came, saw the place to which it would go, saw many miles of its work, saw the Gunnarsons' house and the ruined footbridge of the bigger homestead downstream. I saw the place I lived, entire, uncomplicated, sublime, and thought for one pixilated minute that it was possible to live simply in the world.

Visitors

When I lived in Soho, one of the graffiti artists started a series of street silhouettes — shadow figures lurking or making threatening gestures from alleyway walls or from the walls beside vacant lots all over New York — absolutely harmless, of course, but menacing, menacing enough to get me hurrying some nights, hurrying anyplace there were people, or running all the way home. At home there was safety (if no one came through the skylight; a long story, but the folks in the next loft — actors — had spent a quiet winter's night bound and gagged like stars in a movie while robbers emptied everything out of their place and into a big, new truck). In New York, when things were too quiet, when no one was about, when the breeze picked up a newspaper whose rattle was the only sound — that was when I was most wary. The silence itself was dangerous. If you were the only one around, then you were the only target around, and the only witness, too.

For Juliet and me on the River of Promise — our paradise of waters — it was *always* quiet. Breeze in the grass, the river shushing by, mice in the eaves, the tinking of our cabin's tin roof, the sudden slam of the window shutters, crows, sometimes a bleating hawk, and every so often the weird horn of a heron. Otherwise nothing, quiet. Some nights you could feel rocks rolling by in the river, a subaudible rumble. Owl wings whushed in the dark, and the owls spoke eerie questions. The neighbors across the road never, ever came, their cabin empty and forlorn. The three neighbors downriver were seldom there, except the Gunnarsons, a full mile away, whom we never heard and who ignored us.

Juliet and I didn't have a phone; phone service was not available. We didn't have a short-wave radio. Our only means of communication was our little van, and though it is odd to think of a van as a form of communication, that's what it was: our only link to the outside world, our only way to reach a doctor, say, or mail a letter, or fetch an ambulance, find a phone. It didn't take long for me to figure out that if someone bad were to come in the driveway and park behind the car we would be trapped. We didn't even have shells for the shotgun that our landlord had given us.

So enchantment wasn't my only reaction to living on the river. Life (my life, anyway) is more complicated than that. My other response was a low-level fear. What was I scared of? Why was I worried about evil people in the midst of paradise? Listen to this: my cousin (whom I hadn't seen since she was a sassy seven-year-old making fun of the size of my nose) a few years before had been dragged out of her quiet house in a quiet Montana town by a man who'd pretended to want to buy the place. He beat her and threw her in his car and drove her to the wilderness, where he raped her, then stabbed her *twenty-seven* times and left her for dead. My pretty cousin, not yet thirty years old, read the labels on his shoes and studied the litter on the floor of his car (candy wrappers, mostly) and memorized his ring and everything else she could see and hear and smell about him. In the woods after he left her for dead she read the stars and made her way out to the road, stopping to rest, crawling, stopping to rest, kept alive by her outdoors skill and a red flannel Christmas nightie that saved her warmth and retained her blood. They got the guy because his boss read my cousin's description of him in the newspaper (especially the ring and the Reese's Peanut Butter Cups).

And this: a father-and-son team of Montana mountain men had recently intercepted a world-class athlete as she ran past their backwoods house, kept her captive, raped her, chained her, beat her, shot at her husband and a friend when these two heroes, unarmed, tried to rescue her. The friend was killed. When the police came in commando-style to liberate the woman, the mountain men put their hands up and came out. The dad had only wanted a wife for his son, as he told it in court. He got life in prison. His son got ten years.

The River of Promise was peaceful, all right, and our water tasks absorbed us, but I meant to look out for rapists and fugitives and marriage-minded mountain men. I wasn't worried about bears and coyotes and earthquakes and floods; I was from New York: my worry was people. I kept my thoughts to myself, not wanting to scare Jules, and knowing she'd say I was crazy anyway, or say that I was only punishing myself for being on vacation. (But if it were just paranoia, why had Theodore given us his shotgun?)

Such were my thoughts on our first evening out there. I put a stout beaver stick by the door, and Jules and I made a late dinner. Afterward we cleaned up a little, poked around the cabin looking at Theodore's odd art and his collection of antlers and feathers and rocks as the world got dark. We got into bed at ten-thirty — early for us — and read by candlelight. Pretty soon Jules dropped her book (something by Alice Miller), said good night and rolled away from me and the bugs that had fallen in love with the sputtering candle. Pretty soon again I blew the candle out and snuffed the wick, put my book (*Blind Corral*) down on the window-sill and looked out. No one coming. Perfect silence. I stared at the stars from bed, saw Cassiopeia up there, saw a satellite passing (no wilderness possible anymore), saw the gravely placid ponderosa pines of our yard silhouetted by the Milky Way. The sky positively glowed with stars. At midnight I was still awake: no refrigerator motor, no clocks ticking, no sirens, no car alarms, no argument down the street. A cluster of pine needles sweetly falling. Then nothing. Juliet's smooth breathing in sleep. The mattress rather crunching as I moved. Those staring stars. And silence.

I began to wonder why the bed wasn't up in the sleeping loft where it ought to be. Was it warmer here at the foot of the ladder? From bed I could see some of the road as it came over the hill, could see our driveway as far as the little plank bridge over Epistle Creek. I could also see just a little bit of one of the posts of the barbed-wire gate at the end of the drive. Suddenly I figured it out: Theodore had put the bed in this strange corner not for comfort or heat or convenience but for surveillance.

Engine. Airplane? Car? No, a truck, rattling like that. Definitely a pickup. No muffler, the roaring a sound I associated from high school days with trouble. I stiffened in bed and listened to the progress of the noise toward us, loud over the ridge, past the unexplained sign by the curve there: *3 so far don't U B 4.* I could feel the quietness being pushed aside by the bow wake of the truck's big noise as it came down into our valley, gradually closer, louder, banging over rocks, then quieter — hidden momentarily behind the crest of our hill — then very loud as it came over, its headlights sweeping the tops of our ponderosa pines, flashing once in my eyes, then darkness. Splash in the puddle just past our gate, then no sound. Had he parked? (I pictured a man, an ugly son of a bitch, big and bearded, Bluto.) I held my breath to listen better, to hear if a car door would close. Where were my pants? I didn't want to face him bare-dick naked. Then a sweeping slash of light, and the roaring engine, very close, almost in the loft upstairs, then fading upriver, echoing, fainter, fainter, and gone.

Eventually I fell asleep but woke twice, three times in the night, startled by the silence.

Next day, I went out and walked the road, tracking the course of the loud truck that had passed. Here the big hill that came down past our driveway, here the puddle where Bluto must have avoided the Epistle Creek bridge (Epistle Creek being dry at the moment, and the bridge being quite narrow and bumpy with loose boards, which I would have heard). And here the curve of the road through the gulch, the steep bank of which had blocked the sound of the truck. So that was why I thought he'd stopped. At the top of the bank of the gulch the road was practically in our front yard; in fact, Theodore had installed a makeshift gate in the barbed wire up there that could be opened if someone wanted to drive down to the front of the house. And here the further path of the truck, down a long grade to the river and along the echoing cliff at its banks.

In the afternoon while I worked at a folding table up in the loft (where a normal house would have had a bed), I listened to the four cars and pickups that passed, listened carefully to get used to the pattern of the sound. The fifth car did not splash in the puddle. I stood up and looked out the tall and narrow window. A door slammed. At the end of our driveway I could make out just a hint of white pickup truck through the undergrowth. A big man in a flannel shirt walked into sight. He looked tentative, wore a beard, stopped at the bridge in our driveway and looked around. I bounded down the ladder and past Jules (who was drawing at her desk, oblivious of the intruder), down the steps into the yard, stood safely between our car and Theodore's dilapidated Saab and said "Hello!"

He didn't smile. "Theodore Opalowski?"

I said, "No," clearly, and told him who I was. "Who are you?"

He smiled now, just a little. "I'm the outhouse inspector. Or, more formally, the Lewis and Clark County sanitation officer. There's been a complaint."

"From whom?"

"Not allowed to say. May I come on up?"

"We don't actually have water," I said.

"Ah," he said.

In the house I introduced him to Jules, who barely looked up from her drawing, as if he were the superintendent of our building in New York, or some knucklehead friend of mine. He came in, commented on the bed as he climbed over it to the ladder and into the loft, where he checked out the bathtub and cistern. As there was no water, the bathtub and cistern didn't work, and if they didn't work, they didn't concern him. He stopped for a long look at my pile of books, and we talked about writers for half an hour, just standing there. He was a reader, someone who'd grown up and then grown middle-aged without TV. He knew every obscure little title I could come up with and had a dozen of his own.

Downstairs he had an obligatory look at the kitchen sink, then outside he tried to figure out where the drain led to, giving Theodore the benefit of the doubt at every juncture. We talked more about books — he didn't think much of Don DeLillo, for instance, and neither did I — then we walked down to the outhouse. I helped him measure its distance from the dry creekbed, and then he stuck a ruler in to get the depth of the hole from ground level to the top of the shit (he claimed that this was the technical term), which, as it turned out, was over six feet. "All legal," he said. "Long as you're not using that sink. And listen, don't worry about this. Sometimes these complaints are real petty. People have feuds, you understand; I think you might have stepped into a bit of an altercation here. The complainant drew us a map and everything." He pulled a folded piece of paper out of his pocket, unfolded it. It was carefully drawn and labeled: *Pipe from sink. Illegal outhouse.* Etc. "And he's obviously been trespassing. This guy writes my office, your guy'll call the cattle inspector on him, back and forth. Some of them go on for years."

Next day a fellow in jogging duds ran right up to Juliet as she sat on the porch drawing and said hi, asked if Theodore was home. Before she could get straight what he wanted, I came out. "Theodore!" he said. "Good to see you! I'm staying over in Jim's cabin a couple days. We'll have to play cards."

"I'm not actually Theodore," I said.

He looked at me as though he thought I were joshing him. Then he peered at me more closely. "Oh, jeez, you're not. Well, I'm sorry. We got to know Theodore a little last summer. Jeez, if you don't look like him. Mustache and everything."

"I think he's a little taller than I am," I said, understating our differences, which to me were vast.

"He's a nut," the jogger said affectionately, and jogged away.

✱

The third night I slept fine. The third morning Jules and I ate breakfast on the picnic table in front of the house, soaking up the early morning sun. A brown cow appeared in Theodore's thirty acres of scrubby grass and cacti across the river, what he called his meadow. In an hour, two more cows appeared, one black, one black and white. Quickly, then, a herd materialized, walking in from the alder underbrush, munching, a motley group, stunted cows and nearly grown calves, thirty-one animals in all, including a single sheep. Juliet set up to draw them, but they moved too much for her, ambling along, knocking down alders, chewing.

They crossed the river when it pleased them, just stepping in wherever they were. At the riffle they crossed knee high. In the pool above it, one calf walked in until he was up to his face in the water, then stood there, perplexed, for fifteen minutes. When the herd moved on downriver, he bellowed four good ones, then made a bad step and fell in. The current carried him benignly to the riffle, where he kneeled and stood and leapt out of there like a rodeo calf, bucking and kicking.

By late afternoon the cows had made it halfway down the quarter mile of river we could see from our yard. Upstairs I wrote, listening as pickups approached, gauging their distances, memorizing the downshift patterns and the sequences of the echoes off the hills and the timing of the silent spots so I'd know it was all right in the night. What feud? Who? Which of the handful of neighbors I'd seen might it be?

The fifth passing vehicle, the fifth in an entire afternoon, stopped. Again I could see a hint of color down by the gate, and again I heard doors slamming, but this time, as I stood in the narrow window waiting to see who would appear, I realized that whoever it was was taking down the gate, which meant he or she knew the combination or had broken the padlock. Before I got downstairs the big truck was in the driveway, coming over Theodore's homemade bridge, clattering the boards. Instead of parking in the yard there, the truck took a sudden crazy left and crashed brazenly through the bed of Epistle Creek, knocking down small cedars, tumbling rocks. The truck was clean and white, had big, jungle-stomper tires, had a white, thousand-gallon tank on its back. On foot I chased it out into the lower field, caught up when it stopped. "What are you doing?" I shouted, at distance enough to escape if necessary.

"Hey, Theodore," a big fellow said, climbing out. Two other young men climbed out after him. They all walked toward me cheerfully, stood around me, a circle of white uniforms. "We're just here to spray your knapweed."

"I'm not Theodore," I said.

"No, you're not," the big fellow said. He appeared to be the foreman of the crew. "Well, we're just here to spray the knapweed."

"What do you spray it with?"

"Juice," one of the crew members said. "Knocks it right out." He was proud of this juice, didn't catch my disapproval.

"What juice?"

"Perfectly safe," the foreman said. He knew when to patronize. That's why he was foreman. The other young men nodded enthusiastically.

"Well, don't spray near the house," I said.

"Got to get that weed. It's evil. Spreads faster than wildfire, displaces crops and grasses, poisons the soil in perpetuity." He sounded like a chemical company pamphlet written by John Wayne. He pointed to a bumper sticker on the truck: *War on Knapweed,* as if that should answer any objections I might have. His assistants — no masks, no gloves, no protective gear whatsoever — climbed into the truck without him, drove wildly around the field, stopping at each of the twelve or fifteen two-foot-high knapweed plants in that five acres and spraying prodigiously.

"Doesn't that stuff get in the river?" I said.

"Not in dry country like this," the foreman said.

"It rains every day up here."

"But that's unusual."

I glowered. I was the picture of a crank. My hair was dirty and standing on end; I hadn't shaved for two days; my pants were ripped; I'd raced out to yell at them. Well, if I was going to be a crank, I might as well be a crank: "What exactly is this so-called juice you're spraying with?"

"A mixture. It only kills knapweed. A selective mixture of chemicals."

"Nonsense," I said, trying to make it sound conversational. "Selective? Impossible. A mixture of what? *Selective?* It'll kill you, too. Doesn't your boss give you protective gear?"

"I just hold my breath," he said, joking.

I could smell the chemical, whatever it was, all over him. "I'm not sure I want this land sprayed," I said.

"Opalowski's got a contract."

"There's only ten plants out here. I'll pull them up by hand."

"You'd miss all the seeds. A thousand seeds per plant. We've got to protect the environment around here, don't we?"

"These plants are in flower. Seeds come later. Three young guys like you could pick all the weeds in this valley in half the time it takes to spray and without driving over every goddamn thing in that truck."

He shook his head, condescending to my ignorance. He was doing Great Things, after all. Saving the environment from its own ill nature. I was hopelessly uninformed. Would the sweet, fatherly giants of the petrochemical industry spend millions on advertising against knapweed if it weren't evil? If spraying weren't the best way? ("There's no such thing as a toxin, only *toxic amounts*!")

I had a hunch that the next thing out of my mouth would not be conversational, so I walked off, his satisfied grin at my back. When his crew was done, they came raging back across the field, ignoring the rutted Jeep trail, bouncing wildly over rocks. They collected their foreman, then drove straight through the riverside alders to a shallow riffle in the River of Promise. In the center of the river they quite purposefully took on a boulder, no doubt pretending it was a Volvo beneath their great tires. The truck tilted, then tilted more. I saw the little hatch on top of the tank open. Twenty gallons or more of "juice" came pouring out, straight into my river, straight into my fish, straight into the birds that ate the fish, straight into me, straight into all of us, and into the lives of our great grandchildren.

"Hey," I shouted. "Hey, you wretched myrmidons!" They couldn't hear me over the river, of course, only laughed as the truck bounced down off the boulder.

Next night Juliet and I went to the river for a sunset bath and swim. We used Dr. Bronner's soap sparingly, not convinced it was degradable in any useful way. A great snowy owl, greeting the night, came swooping past, a big, judgmental face attached to wings. A muskrat swam by. Jules was beautiful to watch, standing on a rock, leaning over the river, squeezing the water out of her hair. "I could stay like this forever," she said.

I thought of the postcard of rings. Would this be a decent moment, naked as our ancestors? I thought of yet another variation around the theme of proposal, thought the basic *Will you marry me?* seemed too old-fashioned, almost rococo.

Then I thought I heard an engine. Next I thought I heard a slamming car door up by our house, the sound so faint that I didn't believe in it, but again my ease was interrupted. Juliet was naked, after all. I was naked. I dressed quickly, marched up the path along the river, came around the escarpment that hid the cabin in time to see an intense and bullish man coming out our front door. He was pale, built short and thick with wild long hair.

"Oh, ha, ha, ho." He laughed like that, very deliberately when he saw me. "Theodore. Old shit!" He had a sixteen-ounce can of beer in his hand, raised it up in toast, showing the homemade skull tattoos on his forearm. "We are drunk as six peckers!"

"I'm not Theodore," I said. He had said *we,* so I looked down to where his car was blocking ours, and sure enough there was another man, very tall, waiting down there, hovering back, either uncomfortable with his friend's trespassing, or nervous about what they were going to do. The short man didn't seem to have stolen anything.

"Oh, ha, ha, ho." He laughed again. He was missing several teeth to the left of his one remaining front tooth, and someone had given him a good gash down the cheek, and recently, too. The wound — no childhood lawn mower accident — had healed poorly and the scar was thick and gruesome, especially near his mouth, where it pulled at his lip.

"All right," I said, trying to find a balance between firmness and friendliness, not wanting to provoke anything, but not wanting him to feel comfortable enough to stay. "How did you get in here?"

"You're not Theodore," he said. This observation seemed to anger him. He stepped toward me, suspicious, tried to get a better look.

By way of strategy I went all jocular, good old beer-drinker-buddy Bill. "Are you-all friends of his?"

"We're his cousins. What happened to him?"

The other man came up the stone steps from the lower yard, also holding a beer. He was quiet, still seemed slightly anxious. "Ho," he said in greeting.

The short cousin said, "We just come down from Great Falls for Theodore. Hell of a ride, can't barely see the fuckball road."

"Nineteen beers thus far," said the tall one biblically.

"You're not Theodore," said the short one again.

"I've rented this cabin," I said, back to firmness.

"What happened to Theodore?" he said, accusing.

"He's in Helena," I said. Just then Juliet came up behind me on the path, stood still, twenty paces back, wearing a towel. Her sweet shoulders and her long legs looked awfully bare. The short guy whistled around his missing teeth. "Well, hi and hello," he said. The little fuck had been in my house. The shotgun was in there. I thought it would be a good idea to get around him so I could get to the gun. If he were just an innocent drunk, well, that was no problem. But if he wanted to make trouble, Jules and I were entirely on our own. There was no one to hear me if I shouted, nowhere to go, no way to drive past his car and out of there. "Let me go on in and get his number for you."

"*Shit!* We was going to spend the night. Theodore wouldn't mind."

I stepped past him, aware of Juliet frozen behind me,

went inside, found Theodore's number and wrote it on a bit of cardboard. I gave it to the short cousin, stood by the beaver stick, mapping a route past the easy chair to the shotgun, which I thought might scare them if they got aggressive, though I had no shells and had often heard that an unloaded gun is worse than no gun. The tall cousin was looking dully at Juliet. He had a big hunting knife in a leather holster on his belt.

"But Theodore's only in Helena," I said jovially. "He'd love to see you — you could make it before dark, easy. Shoot, he'd be bummed if he missed you. Cousins!"

"I could offer you beers," the short cousin said, gazing back at Jules. Neither of them looked a tiny particle like Theodore. Shorty walked down the river path toward Juliet, turned to the bramble there and pissed in plain sight. Juliet stepped past him, her manner almost dainty, and scurried by me into the house.

I turned to the abashed cousin, the tall one. "Helena's not far," I said. "Your cousin would like to see Theodore, and he's right in Helena."

"Norton is not my cousin."

"Seen much deer?" the short not-cousin said, coming back.

"Some." You could hear Juliet in the house, scrambling up to the loft, where she kept her clothes.

"Much cattle? Those fuckball cattle still coming around?"

"Right there." I pointed into the field, to a black shape rummaging in the alders.

"I'd shoot 'em right now," he said. "Hamburgers."

"Road trip!" I cried, like a college boy. "Theodore! Helena!"

"Helena!" the short cousin cried.

The big fellow knew what I was up to, I think, but said, "Yeah, Helena."

"Bye, little lady," the short one said, squinting to see into the house. The two of them slowly made their way to their car. It roared, starting, and they took a long time turning around and leaving. I followed them on foot, locked the gate behind them. I could hear their car roaring out of the hills for ten minutes.

When I got back to the cabin Juliet was dressed, had come out of hiding.

"You were so *scared,*" she said, shaking.

Saturday we had mule deer for visitors, and I felt like them, tentative, nervous, alert, as I fished, then wrote, then sat in the sun.

Later in the afternoon I heard chopping, not far away, and slunk through the trees and rocks to look. At our neighbor Jim's house, a quarter-mile downstream, a man was splitting wood. I walked boldly over. The man looked up, smiled easily. "You must be Bill," he said. "Theodore told me all about you guys." It was Jim himself. He was from New York, too, had spent eleven years there — plenty, he said. "Did he give you a gun?"

"He did. But he didn't say what for."

"Well, don't worry about that. This isn't New York!" We talked for a good long time. He said Juliet and I were welcome to use his sweat lodge and his beach and his well and his wood pile and his ranch pump and anything else we needed. He doubted he'd make it back much this summer. Too much work in Helena. "But any trouble at all, you come on over and stay here!"

Trouble?

*

Sunday morning I sat up in bed at the sound of an engine, or maybe two, followed it or them with my ears along the River of Promise road toward us, sure it or they would drive past. Over our hill they roared and stopped, goddamnit, stopped at our gate. Doors slammed. *Any trouble at all.* I heard very loud heavy-metal music for a moment, which suddenly clicked off. Then laughter, one engine starting, and a truck passing above us. Then nothing. I dressed and walked out there. At the end of our driveway, not blocking it, was a Jeep, empty, with Great Falls plates.

Back in the cabin, I didn't exactly forget about the Jeep, but went about the morning's work.

"It's just some fishermen," Jules said.

"Trespassing," I said.

"What do you care?" she said. I was torn between wanting to leave her in peace and wanting to make her see my worry. In the end I kept quiet so her peace could give me peace, and probably too so she wouldn't start in analyzing me.

Early in the afternoon, as we ate lunch at our picnic table in the yard, a man appeared, coming up from the river on our path. He was big and craggy-faced and blond, gravely unsmiling, wearing wet shorts. When he saw us he started, then just stood there, staring. I rose and fixed a fearsome gaze upon him, not inclined to appear the least bit pleasant until I knew what he wanted. "Yes?" I said.

Behind him up the path came a very muscular, handsome youth with no shirt. Then another man who was also quite big but who looked afraid.

"Who are you?" the first guy said.

"No, who are you?" I said.

"I'm Theodore Opalowski's attorney," the first one said sharply. "You're on his land."

"I've rented this place," I said equally sharply, "You're trespassing."

The attorney smiled. "Oh. Well, that's Theodore for you; he never mentioned it. Sorry. Some unfriendlys around here. Just making sure."

He and his two big friends came up and sat at the picnic table with us. "We've got a canoe on the river."

"What do you mean, 'unfriendlys'?" Juliet asked.

"Well, one in particular. Guy up the road, Bronco Slaughter. Two-bit cattle rancher. He attacked Theodore — jumped him from behind — broke Teddy's leg and hip — a very serious injury, five breaks. Ted'll limp for the rest of his life." The lawyer spoke slowly, laying all this damning evidence out with good, lawyerly flair. Then he switched back to tough-guy-on-the-river, speaking more quickly: "Over his fucking cows. He won't keep 'em off this land, or anybody else's, thinks the whole Promise Valley is his range. Theodore was the only one brave enough to stand up to him. We're suing, of course, the whole thing's pending. Big bucks, though it may be we get paid off in cows."

It was true: Theodore Opalowski limped. I spoke, in the casual tones of a client consulting with his attorney: "Do you think Juliet and I have anything to fear from this Bronco Slaughter?"

The attorney spoke back, taking me seriously: "Nothing. As long as you're not Theodore."

Juliet and I drove an hour down to Helena for groceries, stayed over with my sister and her husband. This saved me a long night of worrying that Bronco Slaughter (the name alone enough to call up evil images from every Western ever made) would mistake me for Theodore, since everyone else seemed to. In the morning, a perfect day, I called Opalowski to ask about his cousins, and ask about the lawyer, and ask about the shotgun, and ask about Bronco Slaughter, and ask if we were safe. Theodore wasn't home. The lady who answered said he'd be away for a week or two. I asked if two cousins had called or turned up looking for Theodore a few days earlier. She said no.

I bought a box of shells for the shotgun, and Jules and I headed home. At the cattle guard at the top of the River of Promise road there were two pickups parked, and a rangy fellow in a cowboy hat was just finishing a very professional repainting of the billboard-size property sign:

WARNING! THIS IS PRIVATE LAND. TRESPASSERS, VANDALS, THIEVES, ETC., WILL BE CAPTURED, PROSECUTED AND PUNISHED. NO PUBLIC SWIMMING. NO RIVER ACCESS. NO ONE ALLOWED. LAND OWNERS AND GUESTS ONLY. THIS MEANS YOU.

WE MEAN BUSINESS!

The old wording had been milder.

The man painting the sign put out his hand authoritatively to stop us. "You an owner?" he said neutrally, as I pulled up beside him.

"We're renting 4.5," I said. I was reluctant to say Opalowski's name. This man could be Bronco Slaughter, for all I knew.

The painter looked at me skeptically. "Whose place is that?"

"That's a nice sign you're making there."

"Oh. Why, thank you very much. Happens to be my line of work. Now whose place did you say you were renting?"

"Theodore Opalowski's," I said, and hurried to add: "But we're just renting it. We barely know him."

"Is he the construction worker?"

"I guess. But we don't know him well at all."

"Well, I seen your rig quite a bit and wondered who you were. Lot of vandalism last few months. Howdy, I'm at 6.8."

Next day was hot. Spooky voices echoed up from the river, shouting. When I crept down to investigate, I found out that there was a swimming hole up alongside the road under the cliff and that it was full of people, three of the year-round Promise Valley families, parents and babies, teens and kids, leaping off the big boulders, hollering and laughing. I found this comforting — all those kids: if they were safe, we must be.

Around noon the next day Juliet drove out to call a friend in New York. On the way back in on the dirt road, a high-suspension pickup truck got on her tail, right in her dust. Her impulse, being competitive, was to keep ahead of him, but finally, with the truck only twenty feet behind her, she pulled off into a Jeep trail to let him pass. He did, looking over at her. Now she followed him, past *3 so far don't UB 4,* amazed at his speed over the rotten road, choking on his dust. When she reached our gate, she was surprised to see that the truck had pulled in and that the driver, a big man, was fiddling with the padlock.

Her first thought was to keep going, but remembering that I was home with no car she stopped.

The man looked up, first at her face, then at her chest, then at her legs, then at her chest again, where his gaze remained. "Can I help you?" he said, not friendly.

"May I help *you?*" Juliet said.

"This is my house," the man said. "The question is, Can I help *you?*"

"It's my house," Juliet said, "so the question is, *May I help you?*"

"What do you mean it's your house? What'd that jackass do?"

"To what jackass are you referring?"

"None of your damn business." He opened the padlock, threw the barbed-wire gate down, climbed into his giant GMC rig and drove into our yard.

Up in my loft I'd heard his voice, then heard his big pickup truck whapping the boards of our little bridge. I fairly jumped down the stairs and out the door, wanting to meet him, whoever he was, while he was still in his truck where I could have him sitting down. I got to him as he was about to open his door. He stopped when he saw me and glared. I glared back, doing my best to look imposing, though I knew I looked like a perfect dork in my brand-new blue jeans and flip-flops.

"Yes?" I said, at his window. At that exact moment I stepped on a prickly pear cactus, the spines of which popped through the sole of my flip-flop. "Yow," I said, "what do you want?"

"This is my place."

"No, it's Theodore Opalowski's place, and he has rented it to us." I leaned down and pulled two long cactus spines out of my flip-flop and foot. Juliet drove in behind the guy, now.

"He rented it?"

"To us."

"Well, I'm his brother, Dick. Planned to stay up here for a night or two."

"Sorry. But thanks for the visit." I began to formulate a simple discussion of tenant's rights and landlord's obligations, but Dick suddenly smiled.

"Guess I could just stay over at Jim's."

"Theodore didn't say anything to you?"

Dick looked preoccupied. "Those fucking cows been around here?"

"Not lately."

"My bro' tell you about Bronco?"

"Not really."

"Well, watch out for Bronco. Dangerous man. Comes after me I'm going to shoot first, no shit." At that he lifted a clipboard on the seat next to him. Under it was a handgun, of a caliber I couldn't determine — something much bigger than a .22. "Blow his nuts off. You don't hurt my little brother, man."

Still behind Dick in our little van, Juliet honked, a New Yorker in the wild. "Oh, hey," Dick said, suddenly nice. "Take my card. Maybe one day you'll invest up here." He handed me a Century 21 business card with his photo on it: *Dick Opalowski. Specializing in River Lands.* He smiled a salesman's smile. "I'll leave you two alone in your love nest here. Be at Jim's. If you see any cows, shoot 'em. And if Bronco comes on this land, shoot him, too."

"I shall."

"Blam, blam," he said. He put his car in reverse, backed almost into Juliet's bumper before she moved, then followed her out, closely, as she backed in her tentative way until she was through the gate. There he blasted past her, jammed his truck into drive and was off, back up the hill. I heard him turn into Jim's driveway as Juliet put the gate back up.

"Who was that asshole?" she said.

"That was Theodore's brother, from what he says. His name is Dick."

"Does every drunk Dick in Montana have the combination to that lock?"

Next morning I felt good, I felt fine. The sky was blue, the river ran, the people in the pickup trucks were turning out to be landlord's brothers, well armed and staying within shouting distance. What was to fear? I took a notebook down to our rock in the river, swam, lay in the sun, sharpened my pencil on a stone, almost got down to business when I looked up and saw Bronco Slaughter's lead cow bumping the alders across the river, feeding. I found her picturesque at the very worst, but in my head I saw Dick Opalowski shooting her — *blam blam* — then Bronco coming to avenge the death, then Bjll (my own fragile self, looking fatally like Theodore) getting plugged, or beaten, or whipped, or whatever Bronco's latest *modus* was.

My placid morning fell hissing into the river and drifted away, fast.

At the rodeo in Helena a couple of nights later I sat with Ted Vogel (a clay sculptor, one of the residents at the Archie Bray Foundation) and his friend Drex from Utah. A man on a tame Brahma Bull opened the show with a bored, highly amplified, jingoistic speech about the flag and freedom and rodeo and God and the flag again and more freedom. Drex began to shout: "What about El Salvador! What about Harlem! You're full of shit, man! The same old shit!"

I slid away from him. The folks in front of us turned to look, four very tall, rangy guys in dusty cowboy hats. Drex addressed them directly: "He's full of shit, man, listen to this boob, will ya? Memorized every fuckstick flag-waving bromide in the book!"

I froze, ready for a brawl, but the cowboys just looked blank, turned back to look at the show. This was a lesson for me: even at the rodeo it was safe to be different, safe to be yourself, even if yourself was as obnoxious as Drex.

"So's it wild up there?" Ted said as Drex continued his harangue.

"It's nice," I said. "But people keep turning up and scaring me." I wasn't embarrassed to admit it.

Ted nodded. He'd been scared in places like that, too. He subtly changed the subject: "Has that lady in the camper turned up yet?"

"What lady?"

"This dancer lady. Rumor is, she turns up there every so often. A Gypsy lady."

"The Greatest Country in the World!" the cowboy intoned, riding his bull.

"What about education!" Drex shouted. "What about the banks! What about the water! What about the air! What about the fucking sky!"

"You'll find that Theodore Opalowski is a complicated guy," Ted told me.

Back on the river it was raining. But Dick Opalowski was gone, and that fact pleased me. Jim's house was safely empty again and at least one handgun had moved out of the neighborhood.

After two nights of steady downpour the sound of the river changed. The third morning Jules went down there and found the water the color and texture of chocolate milk. The river was rich with silt, its waves flattened, its movement thickened, its life invisible. At first I blamed Bronco's cows. They must have been upstream, kicking up the bottom. But the river grew browner, and thicker, and browner yet. I grew concerned for the trout. Surely they were used to muddy conditions, but they couldn't be happy down there, like living in the fog, if the fog were gritty. (Trout have a lateral line related to the stripe along their sides which is connected to their nervous systems in some mysterious way that allows them to feel their surroundings and the movement of prey. The trout adapt; they live, at least as long as their food holds out.)

The mud's from all the rain, I thought. The unusual amount of rain.

Next day, when Jules and I returned from a trip to the store, Theodore's car, a little station wagon much too small for him, was in our driveway. Theodore himself was sitting up at the picnic table in front of the cabin, just sitting in the rain, looking out over his land. "Don't mean to disturb you," he said in his high voice. "Golly. I've been two weeks in Seattle, and you've been here in your little Shangri-la."

"Hi, Theodore," I said. I was glad to see him.

"I'll not bother you. I'll stay over at Jim's. Just mean to have a swim and a sleep, and back to Helena for work in the morning. But, hey! I see you got a canoe! Maybe we could head down the river!"

"The river's full of mud."

"Those fucking cows been here?"

"No, but your cousins were. And the outhouse inspector. And the knapweed guys. And your brother. And your lawyer — that's his canoe."

"You sure those cows ain't been here?"

"Not that I've seen."

"What cousins?"

"Little short guy? Drunk as hell. Scared the shit out of me."

"Oh, oh. Norton. Crazy little gnome. Why, he's liable to turn up middle of the night in the middle of winter in the middle of a blizzard, middle of a bad dream. He's all right. I never shunned visitors, Bill. Golly, it's lonesome enough up here."

"And your lawyer told me about Bronco Slaughter and your leg and everything."

"Ah." He patted his bad leg.

"Theodore, are we safe up here?"

"Bronco Slaughter is my problem. He surely won't bother you!" At that, he reached in his shirt and unsnapped something. After a moment of struggle he pulled out a big handgun. "This is an eighteen-shot, semi-automatic .45-caliber pistol, Bill. I got her loaded up with dumdums. It's known as the last word."

I caught my breath, feeling as though I were in a rotten TV show. "Why do you carry that?"

"Personal protection."

"Do I need one?"

"What for?"

"Theodore, are we safe up here?"

"Safe as can be. It's a quiet place."

"Then why the handgun?"

"I'm the one needs that."

"Then why did you give me the shotgun?"

"Maybe a coyote. Once I had a rabid coyote come up here. Thing wouldn't let me out of the house. I had to beat 'im to death with my guitar — ugly, believe me. The shotgun's for the unexpected, is all. You can't live up here without a gun."

*

Later in the evening I hiked over to Jim's to fill our water jugs, had a visit with Theodore. I asked him about the incident with Slaughter, point-blank, so he'd have to answer. "Bronco Slaughter, see," he said, "thinks he can run his cattle anywhere in this valley, and he's wrong. Three years I lived here, and those blessed monsters showing up three times a week, wrecking the river, pounding down the land, eating up the woods. So I complained; I mean, I complained every time them cows set foot. And one day Slaughter, he's just had it with me. Crazy as popcorn on a hot skillet, he comes right over the fence, starts yelling at me. At which I turn my back and walk away. Next thing I know he's all over me, and I'm hollering in the dust, and he leaves me here to crawl out on my own. But you're fine. It's me he hates, and me alone."

" '3 so far don't UB 4'?"

"Oh, golly. Oh, Bill, you *are* scared! That's car accidents on the second hill, is all. People are always slipping off the cliff there. Barton McSweet's a sign painter. Golly, he'll put up a sign faster'n you can shit."

A day later the river began to clear. Hundreds of crayfish had crawled up to the river's edges and died, but now you could see the rocks again, and nearly see the bottom. I rejoiced, racing up the path out of sheer exuberance. At the top of the escarpment I stopped to look out across Theodore's oxbow meadow, only to see two teenagers at the very top of the taller of our two rock spires. They shouted with laughter and triumph after their difficult climb.

I made a point then of going about my business, of not worrying about the trespassing teenagers, of saying to myself, as Juliet might, that they were a couple of kids, no threat, a couple of kids on the river, having fun. It turned into a kind of mantra: couple of kids, couple of kids on the river having fun. I'd gotten to be afraid of everyone, for god's sake, and though I knew my fear was getting ridiculous, I couldn't seem to help it. I told myself to stop and think and relax: a couple of kids on the river, for crying out loud. A couple of kids having fun.

One day, heading down to the Missouri River to fish (two seventeen-inch rainbows, three pounds each, on caddis fly imitations that I had made), I stopped to pick up a couple hitchhiking. They got in the car without smiles, sat silently, a big-scale woman and a wiry little man, both in their late forties.

"You live here on the river?" I said.

"None of your business," the man said.

"We're going to the Promise Bar," the lady said.

I knew they lived on the river; I'd seen both of them in their ancient International Harvester pickup, coming and going from 2.6. "I live up at 4.5. My girlfriend and I are renting it."

"That the guru's place? The Polack?" the man said.

"I don't know him well," I said. "We're just renting."

"Curious fellow," the man said.

"As are Russians all," his wife said.

"Polack," the man said.

"He seems nice enough to us," I said.

"Our truck broke," the man said. "We are on foot."

"Why do you want to live here?" the woman said.

"It's too dry here for you," the man said. "Go live in Missoula."

I kept quiet, drove around the switchbacks up First Hill, looked out at the view.

"Danger everywhere," the man said. "I'd live in Missoula. College there and everything."

"What do you know about Bronco Slaughter?" I said.

"People avoid him like a swamp," the man said.

"He's got but one sheep," his wife said.

"Your artist friend got hurt over there one afternoon, I'll tell you that much. Went up there shouting and a-screaming about the cattle, which resulted in a scuffle."

"This happened at Slaughter's place?" I said.

"Yes, indeed," the wife said. "Medivac helicopter took your friend out."

"And the next week your friend's brother went up there threatening with guns and five guys big enough to hunt bears with switches. Now they got a lawsuit!"

"A *lawsuit*," his wife repeated.

"Terrible place to live," the man said.

"Too dry," the wife said.

We drove then in silence down the very long, very steep hill to the Promise Bar, near the interstate. In the dirt parking lot the couple got out. "Well, thanks," the wife said.

"Could just as easily have walked," the man said.

Jules and I headed for Helena. We closed up the house because after Helena we planned to go on up to Glacier Park for four or five days. I took out a crayon and made a sign and put it on the door:

THIS HOUSE RENTED BY BILL ROORBACH. THEODORE OPA-LOWSKI IS NOT HERE. HE IS IN HELENA. YOU MAY CALL HIM AT 442–6079.

Glacier Park was extraordinary. We drove through eight miles of beautiful burned-over forest to Bowman Lake, where we camped, drove over Going-to-the-Sun Road in a parade of RVs, made our way gradually to Many Glacier.

There we finally got out of the car and hiked in to Grinnell Glacier. The wildflowers up there were profuse and various and brilliantly colored. I carried the postcard of rings — safe in my hip pocket — to all our stops, but I never got an opening; somehow when the moment was right the mood was not; or when the mood was right the surroundings were off; or when the scenery was inspiring, Jules and I were fighting — time for lunch.

On the way home we passed through the Blackfeet reservation, then stopped below Choteau at a thoroughly eighteenth-century Hutterite colony to buy produce. At the Promise Bar, much refreshed, my head now cleared of fear and suspicion and paranoia, we stopped. Juliet made some calls at the pay phone outside the door: two friends in New York, her sister in San Francisco, her parents. While Jules stood in the sun and reported on our trip, I went into the gloomy bar and had a beer. The bartender was distinctly unfriendly. I sipped my beer and forwent the small talk.

Soon the bar's phone rang, an event in the quiet place. The bartender let it go fifteen rings, finally ambled away from his conversation to answer it. He listened a moment, then grew visibly agitated. "Why should I take a message after what he did in here!" More listening. "Of course they got no phone. Who's got a phone up there? What am I, the answering service?" More listening. "Well, awright. But you'd think I was the secretary around here." He hung up, huffing, then went back to his friends, chatted. After a long conversation he came down the bar, begrudged me another beer, then turned to the blackboard and with pink chalk wrote: DANNY SLAUGHTER BE AT WORK BY SEVEN OR ELSE.

I gulped my beer and strolled out of the bar, trying to be invisible, convinced I would run into Danny Slaughter outside — *after what he did in here*. Surely he was Bronco's son and as surely trained in evil. Surely he had been by the house and would recognize our van as an allied Opalowski vehicle. Juliet was still on the phone. To look nonchalant, I checked out a Geological Survey map of the Promise Valley that was posted on the entryway wall. One by one I found landmarks and each of our neighbor's houses. When I got to the tiny black square that represented our cabin, I found it was circled, thickly, in pencil.

I spent a bad night, thinking of all the connections. In the loft, after breakfast, I tried some breathing exercises that Jules had taught me, became relaxed, then set to writing. A couple of good hours of it, calming, then I heard the bellow of a cow on the road, close. I jumped to the narrow window in time to see Bronco Slaughter's cattle resignedly marching up the road. Behind the cattle was a man on horseback: Bronco Slaughter himself. It had to be him because it couldn't be anyone else. He was strong and thick and burly, shirtless and sweaty in the sun, his arms and neck tanned dark brown, his great breast and belly white as Moby Dick's. His hair was matted down and sweaty, but the hat was missing; he held it grimly in his hand. His chin was tanned, his forehead pale as his chest.

Behind Slaughter his sons, two gargantuan young men, also on horseback, bigger than their father, wearing home-sewn shirts and Stetson hats. All three wore red suspenders. I stared, fearstruck. Bronco Slaughter turned his head, looked down on his enemy's house, looked straight at me, saw me hiding there, looked straight into my eyes, held my gaze till he disappeared behind the cedars.

I'd done my best to handle my fears alone, to let Juliet live in peace, unworried. No more: I went to her and told all — all my fears, all my observations, Bronco, Dick Opalowski, the handguns, the lies of our landlord, everything. Juliet looked at me warmly, took my hands, looked into my eyes. "Bronco Slaughter is not interested in you," she said. "Bronco Slaughter is not interested in you one little bit."

Next day we drove out to the Missouri for some fishing and general noodling around. I felt better, felt fine, having unburdened myself to Jules. I knew she was right, of course; Slaughter was not interested in me. But still. Why did he look at me like that?

The Missouri was clear. This confounded my theory that the rain we'd had would muddy any river, not just ours. From the highway bridge we could see the River of Promise entering the Missouri. For a mile or so after the confluence there remained two rivers, the Missouri wide and green and clear and choppy, the Promise narrow and deep brown and still. After a mile, then two, the two rivers mixed, so that the great Missouri was silty, too.

Juliet and I fished and swam and drove around and made calls from pay phones, a day off from more productive pursuits. When we got back to the cabin (Jules dangling the dinner she'd caught, her first rainbow and a big one) there was a little Chinook camper in our yard. The license plate said DANCER, which I read as DANGER, which got my blood jumping, even after Jules had corrected me. Jules went about chores as if nothing were wrong, set up her easel and her paper and her pastels, began to draw a new bouquet of sunflowers. I made up some dinner, waiting for the next threat to appear. Pretty soon a pleasant-looking woman, fifty years old (at a guess), came up from the river, well tanned and stark naked except for a display of various wildflowers stuck randomly through her hair.

*

Still the rain kept coming. The river rose, growing louder and browner. Fishing was hopeless. Dancer was in our driveway, camping, and the truth was, after some initial displeasure, I was happy to have her there. I thought self-ishly that any bad people who turned up would get to her first, but assuaged my guilt over this thinking with the sure knowledge that her aplomb would get her safely out of any situation. She was warm and quiet, an old friend of Theodore's who wanted nothing more than to park her camper near someone she knew. She had tarot cards and practiced yoga, offered us high tech back rubs, had a book about conquering shame. She was nice to the bone and just about never wore clothes. Once, a long time before, she told us, she had lived up the road.

As soon as there was a lull in the conversation (and since I was asking *everyone*), I asked Dancer if she thought we were safe.

She tilted her head with concern for me, knit her brow, spoke soothingly: "I lived here for seven years, even farther up the river, and not one soul ever did one thing that wasn't friendly and helpful and loving and peaceful. Just once a crowd of teenage boys came through my land in canoes, you know, and I thought I was in trouble. You need to picture it: seven young fellows and me naked as driftwood in the midst of all those raging hormones. Handsome fel-lows all busting with muscles — all eyes, too — but they were very polite and said *yes ma'am* and *thank you* and *please* and simply climbed in their canoes and left, and I never really knew if I'd been threatened or had had a sexual fantasy of my own."

She giggled at her joke and her openness and I laughed to join her, then grew serious, asked if she'd heard about Theodore and his leg.

"Oh, Theodore. Theodore is known to get out of hand from time to time. Yelling at those poor cows! But he is a lovely friend."

Beginning to feel soothed, I told her my worry that Bronco might mistake me for Theodore.

"What if he does come? The whole affair is out of your hands. *N'est-ce pas?* You must free yourself from your fears! Fear is an addiction!"

Juliet and I ate out of cans, and ate spaghetti, and squash. There was no way to catch fish, our usual meal; the river was thick with mud. In seven or eight weeks, I thought, some of the silt would end up becoming part of the delta of the Mississippi River, way down in the Gulf of Mexico. Jules and Dancer and I bathed in the chilly chocolate water. Our hair looked like straw. There was grit in the creases behind our knees.

In the afternoon, while Dancer meditated in lotus on our rock in the river, Jules and I walked over toward neighbor Jim's to see what we could see. In the meadow the knap-weed plants were yellow, almost dead, and surrounded with perfect, yard-wide yellow circles of un-selective doom. At the pool under the swallow cliffs we spied an old couple bathing with their young grandchildren. We stood at the path surprised by them, watched awhile as the kids mucked around in four inches of new silt. Juliet looked at me. I looked at her. They must be the people who owned the cabin — always boarded up — between Jim's place and ours. We had not been seen, could have slipped home. "Hallo," I said, loud and friendly. The couple looked up, unhappily, as we approached. I kept my mouth moving so as not to scare them, explaining who we were and what we did, and how we had come to the River of Promise. Neither of them seemed impressed that we were renting from Theodore, rather scowled when I mentioned the name. "We own this beach," the wife said.

"Just wanted to say hi," I said.

"I hope you're not planning to write about this place," the man said. He was big and well weathered, sixty years old, I'd guess, or sixty-five. He looked at me long and hard. "Sorry," he said, meaning, *Sorry for being unwelcoming.* "I'm just mad as heck." He pointed at the river. "Kids have to swim in this muck." He asked how long the river had been up like this. I told him two weeks. He took me aside, as if the conversation were too delicate for the women and children, said, "The River of Promise has never held summer silt for more than a day or two in my life, and I, young fellow, have been coming here for fifty years. The River of Promise has never held summer silt for more than a day or two *ever,* and it's been here forty, fifty, sixty thousand years."

"What's happened?" I said, trying to be more concerned than intimidated. The man was heartbroken, and tough as he was he couldn't hide it. "The feds have let them do a clear-cut up in the Lewis and Clark National Forest. Some greedy and irresponsible logging company — and I don't blame the lumberjacks, but the company — has cut every single tree up there regardless of worth or catastrophe from the banks of the headwaters of our river. They used to leave a hundred yards by any river, any creek, any goddamn brook, even the worst of the bastards. You want to know what this is? This is a half a hundred thousand years of soil, bub, that's what this is, heading for Florida. This isn't Michigan. This isn't Maine. This land isn't made for clear-cuts. And you a writer: all that paper. If you think trees like the ones they took out of there are going to grow in what's left of the soil after next spring, you got a big fuck-you coming." At his own language, which he seemed to find shocking, he looked up at his wife, who watched the children, her back to Juliet.

"It only takes one asshole," he said, lowering his voice, "And the hell of it is, I voted for him."

We crossed our arms over our chests, stared at the river, helpless. After a long five minutes of silence I ventured to change the subject. "Do you know anything about the feud between Bronco Slaughter and Theodore Opalowski?"

"Fifty-fifty, I'd say. Bronco's had his ranch here a damn long time, and he's run his cattle up and down the river for just as long. He doesn't need goofballs living up here and bringing in one thousand and one goofball friends and telling him what he can and cannot do. And Dick Opalowski. He's the start of this mess. Mister Real Estate, selling the river off in parcels."

We held another long silence.

After a while his wife cleared her throat, looked at Jules and said, too loudly, "Maybe you could swim somewhere else."

The next afternoon I saw the larger of the Slaughter sons hitchhiking out of the valley on the Promise road. He dropped his thumb when he saw my van, a quarter mile away, turned his back on me, spit as I passed him by.

Dancer packed herself up and drove away. She had an addiction conference of some sort in Wyoming. Just after she left I saw a hawk fly over with a long snake dangling from its talons. I decided to make the sight into a harbinger of safety and security. An hour later Theodore turned up, accompanied by a very quiet young man, very tall. "Bean here went to Harvard," he said by way of introduction.

"Yes," Bean said, embarrassed.

"Any problems?" Theodore said.

"None."

"Cows?"

"None, but Dancer was here. And Reginald turned up next door."

"Dancer? Reginald? Golly, it's a regular convention." He drove his station wagon into the alders and covered it with branches. His friend from Harvard didn't help him, made gestures to show he thought it was silly.

"Why are you doing that?" I said.

"Camouflage," Theodore said.

"I mean, why are you camouflaging your car?"

"So no one can see it!"

He and Bean marched through the river with their shoes on, army style.

I had another bad night. What if Bronco had seen Theodore's car going by? Wouldn't he assume it was Theodore in the house? The next morning I woke up to shouts across the river. I leapt into my pants as Juliet groaned for quiet. I burst out the door to see Theodore racing around his meadow across the river, waving a shovel and hollering, chasing cows. The cows bucked and dodged, cut in behind him, stopped to graze when they'd got out of his way. Bean stood near the ponderosa stand where he and Theodore had slept in a pup tent, arms across his chest, clearly not impressed with his friend's activities, making a point of refusing to take part.

A couple of afternoons later my brother-in-law Mac turned up with his friend Jim and Jim's ten-year-old daughter, Fay. Along with Juliet they got in inner tubes, I got in the lawyer's canoe, and down the River of Promise we went, big Jim bumping his butt on every other rock (the rocks invisible, the river dense with mud) and Mac falling off his tube and me getting stuck in the riffles and having to get out and drag the canoe. Fay and Juliet hit it off well, and light as they were had no trouble with rocks, but floated peacefully through the canyon of the Promise. Two miles downriver we saw a cow in the underbrush, then another, then a sheep, then more cows, then Bronco Slaughter on his horse, suspenders crossed over his broad back.

Mac waved a jolly hello. Jim waved. Juliet shouted hello (she'd never seen him, after all). Only little Fay had the sense to ignore him. Slaughter did not wave back. He did not shout hello. He only glared. At me. Not at Mac. Not at Jim. Not at Juliet or at Fay. Bronco Slaughter glared at me, a blight on his river, sitting in Opalowski's lawyer's canoe.

On the afternoon of my balmy birthday Juliet and I went to Three Forks and saw the headwaters of the Missouri, took off our clothes in the state park there when no one was looking and swam at the place where the Jefferson River meets the Madison and the Gallatin. If there hadn't been four dams in between we could have floated home, though the 120 miles would have taken some days. I found a dozen perfect moments in which to propose marriage to Jules, but had forgotten the card of rings, and that small excuse was enough keep me quiet, though twice I made noises that with a tiny draught more boldness would have been the big old question itself.

Next afternoon, Maureen Kiritsy and her boyfriend, Craig, turned up at the River of Promise in their Volkswagen bus. Maureen had been Juliet's roommate in the minuscule apartment on Spring Street some years past. Now she lived in Santa Cruz, California. Craig was a Montana kid, home

from California, twenty-one years old, very polite and energetic, youthfully self-conscious, with long blond hair and
a two-cent beard, a fair analogue of myself at his age. His
license plate said CASSIDY; he had just read *On the Road* for
the seventh time.

He shrugged at my tales of fear and feuding. "Happens
all the time out here," he said. "So what? Has this Bronco
dude done anything to hurt you?"

I had to admit he hadn't. "But come on," I said, "it's not
nothing I'm worrying about."

Moe looked concerned.

"Bill's always been paranoid," Juliet said. "He started
college in 1971, you know."

They all nodded, as if that were a fine explanation.

Moe got a careful, caring look on her face, took a chance
with some advice: "Maybe something else in your life is
worrying you."

"Maybe teaching, or graduation," Juliet added helpfully.

Or maybe my notebook, hiding the card of rings, and
maybe the rest of my life, laid out in front of me in the map
of my imagination, the only map I could get, a map I knew
was faulty.

"I got something for you," Craig said. "Really works in
these cases." He went to his camper and rummaged around
for ten minutes, came back with two warm bottles of beer.
"Don't be so down on yourself," he said.

Down on myself?

"This is a damn fine place you got here, dude, don't ruin
it for yourself."

My sense of menace seemed to leave with Moe and Craig
and their bus named Cassidy (which we had to empty so it
could make it up the hills and out of the Promise Valley).

Juliet contentedly painted flowers and the scene across the river; we heated water in the sunroom and gave each other showers; I got back to fishing, using muddler minnows in the chocolate water and getting bolder and going farther downstream, walking back through meadows in the midst of Bronco's herd, only slightly breathless with fear of their owner. The cousins and the guns and the feuds and the vandals and the billboard-size sign of warning were all emblems of menace, it was true, but at last I'd figured out that they weren't any more actual menace than a person's worst worries were actual trouble. Like the grafitti artist's shadow figures in Soho, the guns and feuds and vandals were harmless if they didn't scare you. (Back in New York a short month later, I noticed that someone had painted the lurking silhouettes with skirts and bras and ties and clown hats, destroying all their power.)

Somewhere in the cabin was a mauled and horribly abridged tiny-print paperback of the journals of Lewis and Clark. Poking through it for mention of our river, I found page after page of harrowing escapes from Indians and awful injuries to expedition members and death by stampeding buffalo and rifle wounds and snake bites and drownings and general terror over a two-year trek through the unalloyed wild. In the midst of all this adventure a sentence by Lewis (the better writer of the pair) struck me. He's contemplating the rest of his journey through what he knows is hostile territory. No need to fear, he says: "I will believe in a good, comfortable road until I am compelled to believe differently."

Mule deer curled up in the tall grasses of our yard to sit out the daily storms. At night if I heard rumblings, I knew it was rocks in the river, and if I heard engines, I guessed it was the B-52s from Malmstrom. I'd met twenty of Theodore's friends and found they wouldn't harm me. I knew all the pickup trucks by now and expected children's voices from the river. Cows? I liked the goddamned cows; the herd had nothing to fear from me. If Bronco glared, I'd glare right back.

I'd gotten used to life in the quiet. I knew the creakings of the house, the scratchings of the mice, the calls of every bird. I liked the tapping rain on the tin of our roof, the quiet whisk of the wind in the pines, the river's lunky conversation, always coming by. And you just don't shun visitors on the River of Promise.

River of Promise

In the early morning of August twenty-first, 1989, safely at home in our cabin on the River of Promise, I got the postcard of rings out of my notebook once more, put it once more in my hip pocket. Only a week until we left Montana, only a week to enjoy the wild and woodsy part of our engagement — that is, if I pulled the engagement off. I was running out of room. Today pretty much had to be the day. The card was all wrinkly from previous attempts, but still colorful with its stack of seven rose-gold rings and their many-colored gemstones. And though the card was nothing more than an IOU, I had come to think of it as priceless.

Juliet was already out on the deck, setting up to draw the sunflowers we'd gathered on the road the previous evening as we came back from seeing off Maureen and Craig in their bus named Cassidy. Juliet clipped a piece of blue paper to her board, leaned it on a hefty ponderosa log and got out her charcoal. She walked around the flowers two or three times, adjusting them in the morning sun, then sat on the deck, one leg around the log, the other tucked beneath her. She squinted and waved the charcoal in the air.

"Let's take a morning hike," I blurted. "We'll work at ten."

Teasing me for my delivery, she blurted back, "That

sounds just fine." She made two strokes on the paper, then a third, then a flurry of strokes, the underdrawing taking shape. She stopped to drink her coffee, drank it very slowly, then very slowly finished blocking out the composition.

By eight we were pushing aside the alders on the banks of the River of Promise. At the water we took off our shoes and rolled our pants legs above our knees and crossed at a shallow riffle. On the far bank we found rocks to sit on while our feet dried in the sun. I felt the postcard crinkling against my butt on the rock.

We put our shoes back on, crossed the field collecting burrs in our socks and shoelaces, and made our way to our landlord's big hill, the volcanic escarpment that rose abruptly two or three hundred feet above the river and above the meadow and above the pointed tops of our two rocky spires. We climbed, following game paths, stopping twice to pick the burrs and needle grass out of our socks and sneakers. It was steep going. I thought of some of the serious differences we had: Juliet a city girl. I mean, what is the point of marrying a city girl? *She has brought me back to the woods.*

We climbed, picking our way through the loose rock and cactus, slipping on pinecones, grasping roots, growing warm with the effort, the sun on our backs. I thought, What if she isn't, after all, the right woman? What if we get home and I meet Ms. Right in one of those slow motion grocery-spilling encounters on the subway? *I will believe it a good, comfortable road until I am compelled to believe otherwise.* Juliet and I stopped to inspect evidence that a deer had slipped in the pine needles and fallen — I have always liked signs that deer are clumsy, too. Higher, we saw a fur-and-wee-skeleton-filled pile of owl droppings, but no owl in the tree above. The ponderosas up here were broken, scruffy, familiar, the same trees we'd been looking at from our front porch for five weeks. Close up they showed all the scars of their afflictions. A rock that from the cabin looked like a school bus was simply a pocked and crumbling volcanic upwelling. A tree that from home appeared to have fallen over had in fact exploded, blown to chips by a bolt of lightning. And what if she says no? *A good and comfortable road.*

At each level we stopped for a look back on our familiar valley. From the third ridge you could see the sparse relationship of the four neighboring properties: every fence, every woodpile, every wrecked snowmobile in the northern neighbor's woods. I spied an old truck up in the trees to the east behind Reginald's cabin, a truck I hadn't seen the other times I'd been up here. Jim's little cabin was turned to face the south, looked solid and important down there at the end of its drive. More to the west, our own cabin was hidden by our ponderosas, all except a portion of the tin roof, shining. Juliet pointed out our picnic table in the yard.

At the top of the hill, a stiff wind and a 360-degree view: mountains, meadows, a million pines, the River of Promise, the sky with its hundred clouds. I pointed down into the woods behind the hill we stood on, pointed and described earnestly until Juliet picked out the second homesteader's cabin, the one I'd found on my birthday. It was mostly collapsed, barely visible except for its sustained geometry in the midst of wildness. Once more I patted the postcard in my pocket as Juliet ambled away. I gave her a hard look, admiring the fine muscles of her legs and liking her dopey sun hat. Her hair escaped blondly from a faulty bun. "Let's go on over here," I said, as if casually, and rambled down over the loose rock.

Juliet followed, studying the view, stretching, bending, performing fragments of yoga. I didn't want to rush her, didn't want to give my plan away, didn't want to start a fight. The rock I was headed for jutted out over the river, was lower than the crest of the hill, offered a full view of our stretch of the river, and of our cabin, and of the dirt road that passed it. I sat down, careful to leave room beside me, surprised to note that I was as nervous as I'd been when I used to audition for bands, as shaky as when I first got up in front of a class to teach, as scared as if I were about to leap off the cliff and into the rocky river, two or three hundred feet below. I looked back, found Juliet sitting on the crest of rock above me. She held her hat in her lap and her hair blew in the wind, catching the sun, having escaped its bun entirely.

"Oh, come on," I called. "Come on down. Here's the river. It's perfect."

"Perfect for what?" she called back. "You come up here. Or better yet, stay down there." She threw pebbles at me.

"I've got something to tell you."

"Tell me up here."

I climbed.

By Juliet's side I grew nervous again and waited to catch my breath. The sun was upon us. When the wind stopped momentarily, I could hear the river. I didn't kneel, but put a hand on Jules' knee and got all serious, trying to think of one of the great new twenty-first-century proposals I'd thought of. Pulling the postcard out of my pocket I said, "Will you marry me?"

Juliet looked at me seriously, said, "Are you for real?" She took the card, turned it over and over as if it should have something more tangible on it than a picture, perhaps a note, an explanation. She turned away from me, her face flushing as she realized what I'd asked.

I said, "Sure, for real."

"Okay," she said. It was her turn to blurt: "Fine."

We looked out over the valley. Something dense had happened to the sunlight, and to the rocks and hills. The river seemed still, frozen into black crests and waves and turnings that reflected the sun, fraught and newly solemn.

Juliet put her hand on my shoulder, flushing more, looked out over the valley with me, but couldn't hold the silence for very long: she found it difficult to be both cool and excited at once. To avoid the subject of our sudden engagement she began to chatter, planning our nuptials (this would prove to be our longest sustained conversation on the topic, ever). She worked out a fantasy wedding, rejecting various dates, rejecting whole months, inviting all her grade school teachers and every old friend and serving them roast pig in a sort of pink glow in an unnamed field, then uninviting everyone and having a tiny service in a country courthouse in a little town by the ocean. We fairly danced with excitement, far more excitement than our modern and somewhat cynical expectations had prepared us for. We grew so excited, in fact, that we beamed and rose, could not sit still.

At the back of our hill was a cliff, cleft by a single crevice. Halfway down, we had to clamber around an enormous and undamaged old ponderosa pine; beneath it were so many pinecones and needles that we couldn't find footing but inched along like spiders, feeling the walls of the crevice. In the woods below we stopped to have a kiss, which we'd forgotten up on the hill. Juliet looked at me, grinned, flushed, frowned, said, "Now we're engaged?"

I said we were.

"We don't need a license or anything?"

I kissed her and she kissed me, and we kissed again and held each other, license enough.

We hiked downhill then, through thick pine needles to the homestead. The cabin had been built of logs, was ten feet square, no more. The homesteaders must have been short; the single cabin door was only five feet high. Rude additions, the children's rooms perhaps, had been built of planks, were now collapsed. The roof had caved in, and under its weight the floor had fallen in, too. Through the tangle of those rotting boards twisted a bramble of the homestead's mail-order roses, grown wild. Alone here on my birthday hike I had looked for treasures — potsherds, homemade nails, a wagon wheel hub, tools — but today I pictured the young couple, pictured them clearly, just kids, coming here with nothing but a horse and a cow and a few tools, getting started, facing the possibility of death every day. Somehow they'd survived here long enough to build a house, to build outbuildings, to have a family, to wear a road on the face of the earth.

Juliet and I hiked down to the river. To cross in this deep spot we took our shoes off, and our socks, then our pants and underpants, held them in the air, held our shirts up off our bellies and waded. The sun was hot. Downstream in the near distance, I could see neighbor Gunnarson and his wife on their roof, far enough away that the sound of the blows from their hammers didn't coincide with the strokes of their arms. When they stopped to rest, we heard two blows more. When they started up again, we watched two blows of silence before the beating began.

Bachelor Party

Just about twelve days before our wedding — on an afternoon when Juliet was at the seamstress' place getting the final fitting and stitching and bunching and tweaking done to her mother's wedding dress — I got the subtle urge to go fishing. Though I'd never even considered fishing in Manhattan before, I quickly evicted all the months of wedding plans from their chambers in my crowded brain, shoved them under the boxes arriving from Bloomingdale's, got my fly rod out of the closet, found my bass-fly box in a kitchen drawer, rode downstairs in the elevator carrying rod and flies, stepped through my lobby and into the great outdoors. Up West Ninety-third Street I hiked, trying to look and feel nonchalant, or even comfortable, marching along, carrying that eight-foot-long fishing rod, avoiding people with its tip, getting it caught in sidewalk canopies instead of forest branches, suffering the stare of the hot dog man on the corner of Central Park West. I headed for the boat pond.

Everyone stared, which happens whenever you carry anything slightly out of the ordinary in New York. When I was a small-time contractor, doing plumbing work and tiling, I'd get dirty as hell working in some dismal basement, get all sweaty and filthy, then walk down Fifth

Avenue, heading home, pushing my handtruck — grouty buckets and dropcloths and plumbing snakes on top of my milk crate full of tools — usually depressed about some aspect of the job. People stared from restaurants. Pity the poor homeless mental case!

So I carried my rod into the park, past all the Columbia Prep High School wastrels who lined the benches smoking cigarettes and cussing. They stared at my rod. The joggers looked at it, the cops, the six homeless men in their Bushville made of cardboard, two ladies on horseback, the skateboarders, the bicyclists, the lovers, the dog owners, the dogs themselves, the roller skaters, the old men, the pretty au pair girls in the playground, the little kids (who said *What's that?*, more to Mom or Dad or au pair than to me, but I answered: *Fly rod*), the nannies with snow-white babies, the Frisbee maniacs, the conga players, the gay male sunbathers, the fat lady who's always at the fountain — they all looked.

It was evening of a perfect June day, the kind of day that I hate in New York, for it only reminds me of the nicer places I might be: Colorado or Montana or Casey Key in Florida, Martha's Vineyard or Qualicum Falls or even the crazy Berkshires — anywhere but the city, with its steaming pavements and wedding plans, its noisy nights and (almost) in-laws. At the boat pond bridge (art deco cement) over what might once have been a brook, I stopped to watch the pond, something I had learned on rivers in the West: watch the water and determine — or guess — what the fish are eating, what the conditions are, where the hot spots are.

Over the head of a sleeping man in a suit and tie I watched the rowboats plying the sunny evening waters. Past the trees of the park the towers of Midtown rose: the Grace building, the AT&T building, the Gulf + Western building, the Central Park South hotels — buildings every-where, a cliff of buildings, a canyon with pigeons and sea gulls instead of swallows and swifts. On the pond, fish rose through the reflections of skyscrapers.

I marched on. A kid stared, said, "What's that?"

His dad said, "It's to kill fish."

"Why does the man want to kill fish?"

"He kills them and eats them."

The kid looked one hundred percent horrified.

At the lakeside gazebo across the street from Strawberry Fields I found an opening large enough to backcast over, but several people were already fishing. I watched as one fellow speared a worm and flung it out onto the water. Immediately his bobber sank and he pulled in a small sunny. He attended to it rather brutally, gripped it too strongly, then flung it back. A lady with a very short fade hairdo was fishing right from the gazebo. Nearby, two other gentlemen were pulling sharply back on their rods, striking every twitch of their bobbers. They were all talk-ing:

"Honey, that's a big one, there."

"I'll show you a big one soon enough."

"That'd be news."

"You watch or I'll catch me one of these and fry it on your flattop!"

They all laughed.

"Reel 'em on in there, blood!"

"Hi," I said.

The three men ignored me completely, probably wise behavior in Central Park, but the lady turned and eyed me. "What kind of pole is *that*?" she said.

"Fly rod."

"He's after flies," the biggest man said.

His friends and I laughed. But not the lady. "Well, come

an' fish," she said. Her bobber sank and she pulled in a sunny, surprised me by pulling forceps out of her shirt pocket. Very delicately she removed the hook; very delicately she placed the fish in the water, where it danced away, unharmed. "Show you something," she said, turning to me. She pulled on a thick string. Out of the murk a slow-moving *catfish* appeared, two pounds if it was an ounce, a solid foot long, fat and whiskered, but also scarred over its smooth, scaleless skin with big, white blotches characteristic of either ammonia or acid burns.

"What's with the spots?" I asked.

"He's beat up," she said seriously. Her name was Robin, as it turned out, and she had grown up in Far Rockaway where there was nothing but fish, as she put it, and where she fished like crazy as a kid. Her husband was not interested in talking to me. The other fellows were nice enough; one even went so far as to ask me about flyfishing, although it was clear that he wasn't too interested. Then, using a rapid kind of code language that I did not fail to understand, he let Robin know that flyfishing is something fussy that rich people do in mountains.

Robin smiled, very friendly. "We fish here every Monday. Come on and fish with us sometimes." The message was, *But don't fish here now.*

"Yeah, do," her husband said, not so sincerely as Robin.

I hiked on. Near a cattail bog I left the road and walked in the mud, and suddenly I was having sensual flashes from the wilderness. I couldn't see the buildings anymore; I couldn't see any people; I could only see cattails taller than I was. For that moment the *whoosh* of the cars on the park loop might have been the wind, the car horns the honking of geese. If there were sirens I didn't hear them, so intent was I on the water.

Something big under the surface was beating its way through the cattails. I watched its obvious path as it proceeded to my side of the bog. Through the murky water, I could make out the creature's form. It was a carp, a survivor, two feet long, very fat, twenty pounds (at a guess), slowly sifting through the muck on the bottom.

I slogged through the mud at the shore and over a pair of big rocks, then through some bushes where I ignored a man pissing and scaled a steep rock face behind another gazebo, where a couple was making out, possibly making love. Beyond the gazebo there was a stretch of clear shoreline and a rock in the water from which I might fish. As soon as I started to tie on a fly I was transported. The familiar pond looked new, looked fishy, looked wild. Suddenly I heard the bird songs, saw the water, smelled it, forgot the people and the distant fear of being mugged and beaten and robbed of my tackle. Across the water a snowy egret swooped low, an actual *egret,* and landed on some rocks. I couldn't see another person, although I heard the lady in the second gazebo giggling. Across the lagoon the carp were thrashing the reeds.

I started, as always, with a hare's-ear nymph, a little, fuzzy, buggy-looking thing that fish are supposed to mistake for the larva of an insect. I made my backcast up through a slot in the big maples, brought the rod forward, watched my line fall softly on the water. The nymph made a tiny plop, and I was in Connecticut again, my childhood. My wedding was not about to happen. The city was gone. I did not have forty-eight final papers to comment on. The neighbor's apartment had not just been burglarized.

First cast I felt nibbles, the sort of tiny hits that you get when baby sunfish grab at the fuzz on your fly. Second cast I hooked a feisty little sunny who wriggled wildly until I put him back. He was only a sunfish, but he was my first fish in New York City. I did a little jig. A bittern (a smaller member of the heron family) came bluntly through the sky and landed not fifty feet away from me. A ragged man muttering in Hindi (my best guess) came up behind me, head cocked politely, stared at the rod. As he didn't seem to pose any danger I kept fishing, trying to keep my backcast out of his very long hair, which stood up high enough to catch any errant fly I might throw. I fired a long cast over to the reeds — bassy-looking territory indeed. The ragged man's mutterings modulated, a distinctly positive jump in his commentary. I was finally consistently good at casting, and it was fun, and I was only twenty blocks from my apartment. I caught six more sunnies and a smallish bass, and cast to the many rises, growing peaceful and relaxed.

I fished into the dusk, then nervously hiked out. On the way I ran into a man with a spinning rod. Like unusually wary fishers happening upon each other in the backcountry, we stopped to chat in the park underbrush. His name was Marcus. Pomaded hair. Red-rimmed dark glasses. Nice clothes. Oxford accent. The manner of a slightly annoyed professor. "I'm an artist," he said. "Also a construction worker." All this work kept him too busy to fish much, he told me, but this summer he planned to make more time for fishing.

"Would you eat the fish out of here?"

"Why not?" spoken rapidly. "No reason not to. No sewage goes in here. No spraying is done in the area. No poisons except rat poisons are used, and these, of course, are buried in the ground. No runoff here, or very little. This pond is spring fed. The fish make good eating. Again, why not eat them?" He was getting angry, apparently believing he'd detected a racist element to my question.

"Yes, why not?" I answered.

*

A few glorious mornings later (in a week of glorious mornings, and afternoons, all of them too well made for New York), Juliet came home carrying a huge box that held the red pumps she'd be married in. She tried them on for me, then we checked over our endless list of things to do and calls to make, made some more lists, compared them, revised them. In two days we had to leave for New Hampshire, where the wedding would be and where we meant to spend a week getting everything organized. Juliet went through her lists finding things that absolutely had to get done while we were still in New York, then left again, down Columbus Avenue in search of presents for the women of the wedding party.

For my part, I was pretty sure I could find a seersucker jacket and nice gifts for my groomsmen next week in New Hampshire. Nothing else on my list seemed all that pressing either, so I called Kurt Carlson, who was about to be my best man. He's an architect in the city, was just starting to get interested in flyfishing. I'd known him from the first day of Miss Greene's first-grade class back in New Canaan, some thirty years before. "Fishing?" he said. Normally we went out for drinks or dinner, or sometimes walks. "*Fishing?*"

We made a date for six o'clock that evening — southwest corner of the Central Park boat pond. I said, "I'll bring the tackle."

About five-thirty, after writing notes on twenty-four more freshman compositions, I hiked out of my building, two rods in hand, past the private guard at the brownstones down the street. He told me an entire fishing story — he kept a house in the Berkshires, had a boat, owned seventeen rods, held the Western Massachusetts record for a smallmouth bass caught in a river — although he had never spoken to me in the three years of my walking past him, had never so much as nodded to my hellos. In the park I marched along with my rods, ignoring everyone except kids who asked me what kind of pole is *that?* I said the phrase *fly rod* eleven times between my house and the boat pond. I stopped again at the art deco bridge, then at the bog, watched the cattails getting thrashed by the carp. The egret was back. Seven mallard ducklings paddled in a courageous knot, alone. I heard — then spied — a red-headed wood-pecker hammering at an old beech tree.

At my spot, a rock across the lagoon from the cattail bog, I tied on a nymph. Here there was also a stretch of grass along the shore, plenty of room for Kurt when he came, though not much room for casting. I was ten minutes early. Kurt was nowhere to be seen. I perched on my rock. Be-neath me a good-size bass was visible, sitting on her nest, but I wasn't able to interest her. I tied on a popper, swam it past her face. Then a mosquito imitation. Then a gnat. Then a black ghost, which looked so much like a minnow swimming that *I* almost jumped in and ate it. The fish turned to look at the black ghost, but that was all. I stood directly over her, waving my rod — impossible in the wild. She was a New York fish, unspookable.

Then a man rode up on a mountain bicycle. He was dressed in a very expensive fishing vest, brand new, and carried a top-of-the-line Sage rod with a Billy Pate reel, several thousand dollars' worth of stuff. "You got the spot," he said. Hispanic, from the sound of his voice, a big fellow, on the fat side, missing both front teeth so he lisped with something of a whistle. "Hey, what's this? Two rods?"

"I'm waiting for a friend."

"Well, hey, any friend of yours . . ." He held out his hand and we shook. "I am Joaquin. I fish here every damn day.

I'm on disability, you know. Couple more months. Can't wait to get back to work. I'm a printing foreman downtown. Now, every day I fish. Took a six-pounder out of here earlier in the spring. Now the bass are spawning, so it's hard times. Who's your friend? A good fisherman?"

I told him that Kurt was new at it, but competent enough for the action I anticipated that evening.

"Like all of us," Joaquin said. As it turned out, he was from East Harlem. He was very excited about flyfishing — which was as new to him as it had been to me in Colorado — had just started tying his own flies, had spent every extra cent on equipment, even bought the bike to make it easier to get to the ponds in Central Park. "I never fished nowhere but New York City," he said, a confession. "Give anything to see a trout, man. Going up to the Catskills this summer." He kept casting his eyes down at my second rod. It seemed to bother him, as if he didn't believe I had a friend coming, had just brought it along as an excuse to get rid of someone like him. By now, Kurt was late.

I asked Joaquin my standard question: "Would you eat fish out of here?"

"Would I eat shit? Would I eat dog meat? No way, man. Also, I believe in catch-and-release."

We stood apart and proceeded to fish. He was good, sent his backcast up over the lower trees, up and into the gap in the maple boughs, shot his line easily and long over the water.

I fired my line in a different direction. Pretty soon a sunny leapt at my little beetle imitation, took.

"Stupid sunfish," Joaquin said as I brought the fish to hand and let it go. "Here. Try this. I tied it. It's what I call a Central Park Bugger. Really it's a woolly bugger."

He handed me a nicely tied woolly bugger, and I laughed

at his joke. I tied the fly on, threw it, and bang, I had a fish, and nothing tiny, either. It waited out in deep water, then came in, quite expertly, came right to shore where I could see how big it was, over a foot long and fat, a nice bass, a New York City largemouth. Close to shore it came to a halt, stonewalling me in the manner of an oft-caught veteran, sat rather than exhaust itself fighting. If I tried to pull it up cold my delicate tippet would break. The fish and I both sat tight, but the fish won: I pulled up on him, at which pressure he swam lazily between two rocks, then over a root, then back under the root, then back through the rocks. He jerked his head and my tippet broke nicely. He didn't even flee, just sat there in shallow water, plain sight, Joaquin's Central Park Bugger hanging off his lip, decoration for a few hours until his digestive juices could eat the hook away.

"These fat bastards are pretty wise, some of them," Joaquin said.

"I lost your Central Park Bugger," I said.

He handed me another. "Trade me something," he said.

I fished around in my box and pulled out an eccentric popper I'd tied, using carved cork from a wine bottle. It was something of a dog, in my opinion, but the only true bass fly I'd ever tied, the only fly I had that was worthy of the trade. "That's a Boat Pond Popper," I said.

Joaquin was not competitive and had a big heart. "That's the best fly I ever seen," he said.

Just then Kurt walked up in his suit and tie, carrying his raincoat in the handle of his briefcase. Joaquin looked at him with disdain. "This is your *friend?*" he said to me. "Shit." He handed me another Central Park Bugger and walked away, barely acknowledging jaunty Kurt, stopped several hundred yards away and began to fish off the riprap along the sidewalk from the boathouse.

Kurt said, "Did you frisk that gentleman?" which was comical because Joaquin looked so utterly harmless in his fishing duds, even in the middle of Central Park, where strangers are not always friends. Kurt tied on a nymph I gave him and in no time managed to catch himself a sunny. We kiddingly made much of his first New York catch. And we carried on, into the dusk. It wasn't quite fishing we were doing — more like talking and flinging flies and untangling knots while looking over our shoulders for trouble.

After a while we could hear a group of youngsters coming from way off. Soon they were upon us. Two came over and asked me questions while three hung back next to Kurt's briefcase. He shuffled over to protect it, keeping his line in the water.

The three kids came up on the rock, crowding me, yammering:

"Why you doing that?"

"How much that pole cost?"

"Is that a fish?"

"Let's not fall in," I said. At that the biggest kid, maybe eight years old, pushed the littlest kid, maybe five, who twirled his arms desperately and fell in the lake before I could catch him. He went completely under. The other kids all took off. I dropped my rod and pulled the boy out of the water, managed not to fall in myself. He was very small, just a stick, really. I stood him on his feet on the rock. He very badly would have liked to cry, it was obvious, but could not. "Kick his butt," he said, starting to shiver. He stayed in my hug a long minute, dripping, then ran off after his companions.

Kurt walked downshore. He fished with his briefcase between his knees now, but nothing was biting. Kurt and I were far enough apart that Joaquin decided it was time to amble back. He stood near my rock so we could talk, cast my popper out over the water, let it fall, and sit. I felt ashamed, since I knew the popper was kind of a lumpy effort, wished I had better flies in my box. But when Joaquin began to retrieve there was a big boil in the water under the popper and something took. The fish fought for a moment, then swam to shore, found a good rock, broke Joaquin's tippet.

"Every motherfuckin' time," he said.

I gave him another eccentric little popper, feeling suddenly proud of my handiwork. A sweet older couple came and stood behind us, watching. She had a big purse and was clearly not the least bit worried about it. The old man explained what we were doing as we did it, knowledgeably.

"Always someone in the way," Joaquin said loudly, back-casting brazenly over them. "Yesterday some guy in a nice *suit* comes up and tells me he likes to fish in *Montana,* like he's proud he knows Spanish, you know? And every day some kid'll come up and ask what the *fuck* are you doing, you know? Those kids tonight, right? They bug you? Little peckers."

I told him how the littlest kid got pushed in.

"I prefer the *kid* falls in the water than all the trash people throw in. At least with the kid you *know* someone's going to come and drag him out, dead or alive, whereas with the cup or the paper plate or what-have-you, that shit's just going to lay there."

Kurt got something on and managed to land it: a medium-size largemouth bass. Forgetting his briefcase for the moment, he came over with the fish, pleased, smiling wryly. "Dinner for two," he said. A stranger might not know he was kidding. Joaquin was grudgingly impressed, exclaimed over the bass, guessed its weight, helped unhook it, watched as Kurt put it back in the water. "You got a good heart, man," Joaquin said, referring to Kurt's careful catch-and-release. "But I never saw no one catch *anything* wearing a tie." He shook his head, thinking about it. "Next time you see me, I'll have a tie on, too, as it seems to work."

Later, at dinner, in an Irish bar just six blocks away from the boat pond, my best man and I debated, trying to decide if Joaquin was kidding about wearing the tie. Then our talk turned to Juliet and her red shoes and heirloom dress. In nine days I'd be wed.

A Wedding on the Water

Think of the density of the relationship between brothers, between sisters, the awful spirit of emulation, love and combat one and the same; consider the tension and denial between siblings of opposite sexes, the tumult beneath the jolly hello, hug and a kiss; consider the waves of projected hopes, the guilt and sadness, the exalted, crushing joy between parent and child. Consider friendship, too, friendship in every form and level and meaning, its re-enactments of family arrangements and pathologies, its many motives, many pleasures, many masks — its wondrous layers of support. And think of the differences between families of in-laws, the tectonics of their neighborliness: the shock of subtly altered customs, the mountain ranges thrown up, the many dormant volcanoes waiting only to explode.

At a wedding, love's all there, sweeter than the cake, louder and more bored than the band, tastier than the food, fatter than the caterer, wetter than the lawn, bigger than the tents, tall as the ancient oaks over the gazebo roof, as dark as the clouds that come from nowhere, as refreshing as the rain, a blessed, hulking, uninvited guest that the hired cop can't see to bounce.

Jules and I had gotten through the autumn and winter of our engagement in our little apartment in Manhattan. Her drawing table was in the living room, my desk in the bedroom, and those were all the rooms we had. She stepped over my books to go to bed, I stepped on her drawings to get to the kitchen. One or both of her parents called every day with a question about the wedding, called through September and October until we'd had enough and told them to stop. My own parents' strategy was to remain distant and rather vague about the whole affair, except occasionally to express dismay that this drunken, debauched and probably uncontrolled event had to be in New Hampshire at *their* summer house.

In the meanwhile Juliet painted every day at the Art Students League, full time, and waited on weddings at night and weekends, working for caterers. She saw perhaps thirty weddings that fall, thirty big-budget, big-family extravaganzas, some costing in the hundreds of thousands of dollars (four bands, twelve hundred guests, jugglers, strolling mimes, choice of cuisine, a tambourine, silly hat and potted plant at every table setting). She reported invariably that the bride looked unhappy and coerced, that the guests looked crazy, that the parents seemed dull and brutal. I, in my meanwhile, taught logic and rhetoric at Columbia, attended graduate classes as a student, wrote furiously on my master's thesis, due in March. The weather in June, the size of the pure white tents, the price of the ice, the personality of the band, seemed but distant calculations.

Also, I had begun to worry about death. Something about getting married had unleashed the terrible truth about mortality, my own in particular, but everyone else's, too, and the earth's (only a few billion years left!), and Juliet's. We would all die. What brought this on, friends explained in various ways, is that one rite of passage implies the next.

✳

One autumn weekend Jules and I had driven up to New Hampshire to case the joint, promising her parents that we'd call caterers and listen to bands and interview photographers. Instead we hiked. We made the top of Mount Cardigan in an hour and a half of hot stomping and looked from its bald top at the nearby peaks of the White Mountains of New Hampshire and Maine, and across the Connecticut River to the Green Mountains of Vermont, and past those placid peaks to the distant Adirondacks of New York. Too bad the maples had dropped their leaves, but still the mountains around us and the valley below were quilted in pointillist color. The locals let us know that we'd missed the peak of the foliage, but that meant we'd also missed the peak of the foliage crowd, so things in New Hampshire were very quiet and therefore soothing.

Lake Mascoma stood before my parents' red house in perfect silence each morning, throwing a mild mist as we waited for the sun to come up over the ridge to the east across the lake. Jules and I started in on the annual fall chores (anything to avoid starting in on the wedding chores). We took down screens, put up storm windows, drained the bunkhouse pipes, brought in the raft and leaned it on the seawall, dragged the old Aquacat by rope to the carport, raked a few leaves, then paddled the leaky old canoe as far as the pinched waist of the lake at the Shaker Village (once a real Shaker settlement, then a monastery — all commercial now, condos blooming, but picturesque still with its lush stripe of meadow climbing the hill, greenly). We trolled for perch and bass and hoped for pickerel, and wondered at the growing population of sea gulls, watched the flights of geese and ducks come in over the mountains to the north, watched them take off and disappear over the valley to the south, felt the clear, still air, listened for loons, smelled our own and our neighbors' wood smoke, absorbed the melancholy lilt of fall.

At the end of our long weekend, having failed to talk to a single caterer or photographer (but having looked at pictures of tents in a rental catalogue at Blood's Catering and Seafood), Juliet and I stopped very briefly at the landward side of the Shaker Inn, a single mile from my folks' house. Our date, June 23, 1990, was open. Well, there. We reserved the entire place for our guests and for ourselves, felt a great sense of relief: We'd done something. We had a look at their chapel (built by the Franciscan monks after the Shakers died down below the level of sustainable potency), a garish but gloomy stone mausoleum, Jesus everywhere — on eight big windows, on crosses in every corner, on wall hangings and paintings and drapes from the pulpit, on alms boxes and tapestries and on the very face of the organ — and made the next decision: we'd be married at the house, on the lawn, rain or shine, in tent shade or sunlight, out there where God could get a look at us (if he wanted) with no competition from his putative son.

Later that fall, Jules negotiated a family moratorium on wedding plans, wedding talk, wedding worries, wedding phone calls, any mention of our wedding or anyone else's, any mention, in fact, of June, or large gatherings, or misshapen New England states of any description whatsoever. We would open the subject again in January, and not before. Under cover of this moratorium we all made it through the solstice holidays (first my folks', Connecticut, then hers, New York, our first Christmas entirely together) with no great discussions, no great battles, no weepy soulsearching (though much innuendo passed under our raft).

In mid-January, amidst a great flood of warnings issued by both sets of parents about the lateness of the hour, Juliet and I drove up to New Hampshire for a week's break in winter. We had lists of flower arrangers, caterers, ecumenically minded clergy, photographers, musicians, Porto-san providers, and tent renters, all somehow gathered from the distance by Juliet's mother. I felt swamped, amazed that a simple cookout on a simple lawn wasn't going to be as easy as we'd imagined back in August, sitting in the warm sun high over our river in Montana (then I'd seen myself flipping burgers and mixing drinks — a host, not a *groom*).

We hiked. Mascoma was solidly frozen (the January before some friends and I had drilled the ice with an antique auger, found it to be twenty-eight inches thick), so there was a new route to walk — just outward — out across the frozen lake, hearing it sizzling with fissures, cracking and booming, a kind of slow, wet lightning emitting soggy thunder.

The lake in winter seemed small, the red house large. Juliet and I dragged mattresses out to the living room and sat up late in front of big fires in the glass fireplace, trying to tame the wedding plans, trying to tame the wedding itself, no idea where our simple dream had failed us. One problem seemed to lie in the tension between her inward, private nature and my more outward, strongly public nature (qualities we admired in each other, our differences part of what we teach each other). Her childhood wedding fantasies featured elopements and secret pacts; mine called for great convocations of people. Juliet's fantasies had been reinforced by the nauseating spectaculars of her catering career (always ending with garbage pails filled with uneaten food in the heart of the capital of homelessness), but I still pictured my wedding as a gloriously medieval and theatrical hippie spectacular, a *happening,* wherein the best elements of every wedding I'd ever been to would spontaneously ignite, where one generation would dance with the next, where death and all other forms of doom would be held at bay for hours, for days, for weeks, with never a problem or an empty purse, with never a harsh word from anyone, or a worry, and none of this rude elbowing by thoughts of mortality.

Out on Mascoma we hiked, working out our compromise, the wind blowing hard and cold across the snowy and quite temporary gray ice, the notion of impermanence riding my shoulders as the wind whipped us home.

In March, Juliet and I went to talk to the leader of the Ethical Culture Society in New York to see if she'd agree to marry us. Early on we'd innocently mentioned the phrase Justice of the Peace to my mother (she used the initials, JP, couldn't bring herself to say the whole phrase), who then spun into her only fury of this campaign. Her father had been a minister, both her living brothers were ministers — JPs were for the lawless, the godless; for elopers, runaways, outcasts, orphans; for gamblers in Nevada. The fact that Juliet's parents had been married by a justice of the peace held no romance for my mom; the fact that they had been married *twice* by a justice of the peace (once in his legal jurisdiction, for the books, once outside it, for the guests) was unknown to her. Juliet and I needed to find some form of willing clergy to save the peace and to assuage my mom, who deserved it. At a catering event, Jules heard a ceremony she liked and recognized the person performing it — Jean Kotkin, leader of the Ethical Culture Society in New York, a friend of her dad's. We made an appointment.

Jean was brisk and honest and straightforward, asked us

about the quality of our commitment, seemed impressed by the fact that Jules and I were going on eight years together, outlined some of the troubles we might face, introduced (to my thinking at least) the idea that we were about to create a new family, a family of two. Jean knew the Karelsens well from the Ethical Culture Society and was willing to perform an ecumenical service that would draw on the traditions of many cultures without mentioning Jesus and without asking too much of God. She said she would call the attorney general of New Hampshire to get permission to perform a marriage there. She'd had experience with clerks in small towns like Enfield, clerks who could not be expected to have heard of Ethical Culture, who could not be blamed if they thought of it in the same category as Scientology, or the Church of the Exquisite Agony, or that Jim Jones Kool-Aid bunch down in Guyana.

Jules and I made a spring trip to New Hampshire, just two weeks after the same journey by the parents Karelsen, who had found a caterer and who had arranged lodging for themselves and their entourage away from the Shaker Inn, which was handsome but perhaps too rustic for most of their friends. Jules and I were to meet with and okay the caterer, to find a band, to talk to a flower lady her parents had met, to find a photographer.

But we hiked. Having canceled the first of our appointments with the prospective caterer, we crossed the road and hiked in the mud of spring up to Smith Pond. We had to leave the trail for the mile where it coincided with a four-wheeling road; the mud was knee deep. In the forest the woodpeckers were back and knocking at the boles of dead hardwoods, robins cocked their heads at worms; sunlight fell through new leaves to dry the forest floor. Juliet and I stopped for a very long time at one of the still-excellent canals the Shaker brothers had dug, watched the clear water rushing past in deep silence (both we and the water, deep silence), and stopped for a very long time at each creek crossing to listen to the roaring over the rocks, to watch the airy tumble of clean and leaf-redolent water climb over the snags of winter. We found baby fire newts in puddles in the trail. And but slowly made our way to Smith Pond.

Smith Pond is a spring-fed beaver impoundment couched in a half-mile depression at the top of Shaker Mountain (or Shaker Hill, or any of a number of other names for the ridge we'd climbed, the name depending on whom you asked, or which map you consulted). The Shakers improved on the beaver dam with rock and cement, enlarged the pond to store water for their settlement on Lake Mascoma below. (The beavers of Smith Pond are extinct now and the Shakers only a single old woman who may yet have died, the huge carp in Mascoma the one living reminder that they'd been there at all.) The dam had been remodeled by the Franciscans, who'd signed their work by embedding pebbles in the fresh cement — Br. Isaiah, Fr. Francis — and added horseshoes and bits of glass.

The pond was serene in the sun, the single cabin more thoroughly vandalized than I remembered. "The thing is," Juliet said, "I'm really really in love with you. *Dearly* in love." She'd never phrased it this exact way, so it touched us. Forget the caterer and the family and the photographer and the guests, each of them in turn. Did you need a formal transition to be your own family? What was it that a wedding was supposed to offer?

The planning went on too long, assumed onerous proportions, causing logistical fights that masked the real issues: my mother was losing her last unmarried son, Juliet's father losing the first of his daughters, and these rather bromidic observations became real to us. The feelings of loss came complete with the emotions associated with grief. It's a kind of death, and parents, we discovered, really do feel it that way: every fork at the rehearsal dinner becomes an emblem of this special grief, and every petal in every fading flower arrangement becomes a daughter falling forever away, and every word of the wedding ceremony twists into every parent's (and grandparent's) heart and burns. The problem is mortality: these kids were babies just yesterday, these kids are us, and we are an adult's life older than when they were born. The problem is that birth itself implies death, that life is death. The solution to the problem (and many cultures know this) is that death is life, too.

How Jules avoided the appointments to alter her mother's wedding dress, to make it her own!

Late in April, Juliet's folks threw an engagement party so we could meet and greet their friends. My father and Juliet's father jousted with barbed, poison-tipped jokes at every encounter, and laughed so hard they choked. In another era they would have used spears and clubs, and left each other bloody and gasping.

I stood amongst strangers, lifted champagne glass after champagne glass of beer, painfully and almost ridiculously aware that all of these well-wishers would be dead very soon, their gifts tarnished or dust. Death, for the moment, had become my work; I'd contracted to write a long article on the subject, was in the midst of interviewing dozens of morticians and morgue workers and emergency room people. I rode with a New York City ambulance crew, saw death happen. I watched doctors in emergency rooms, aware that at times they had to fail. I stared at cadavers, amazed. I just wanted to figure it out: how could a man think about marriage when death was the ultimate reward?

A week before our wedding day, Jules and I drove up to New Hampshire with her sister Eva, maid of honor (or best woman, as we preferred to call her), all of us cheerful and excited and glad to get out of New York. From that fine town (in the midst of fishing expeditions to Central Park and other pleasing tumult, including my graduation from Columbia) I'd hired a New Hampshire fiddler named Dudley on the basis of his tapes; a photographer on the word of Juliet's folks, who had found him; a caterer who took care of acquiring tents and portable toilets (these to protect water quality in the lake by preventing the overflow of the cesspool). My own parents had hired a cop. I was aghast. What kind of hippie spectacular wedding needed a *cop*?

My dad had arrived ahead of us. He was worried about the looks of the house and about its ability to hold our trimmed-down list of guests. He had a basketful of projects for us — painting, rebuilding, cleaning, raking, assembling — and we hove to. My dad and Eva worked like farmers. I worked in a haze of indolence brought on by nerves. Juliet didn't work at all: stressed and riven by the vision of herself at the very center of the imminent meeting of everyone she knew and everyone she was related to, she referred to herself as the bride and disappeared easily each sunny day for oppressed and anxious naps.

My own favorite view of Lake Mascoma on those clear, hot days before the wedding was from the hammock, looking north. In a composition as elegant as any artist's, the dark branches and sparse leaves of a leaning birch crossed my view of the two green and granite humps of Moose Mountain, two thousand feet high, which stood far at the end of the lake, slightly veiled by the mist of distance, rolling in hills down to Enfield, whose tidy graveyard made a vague and mysterious grid on a great lawn near two partly hidden church spires and a handful of houses.

Across the lake the shores were covered in great old oaks, younger maples, birches and beech, leaning hemlocks and solitary pines, all surrounding and hiding the summer houses close on the water, each house with its dock and its flotilla of small boats and rafts, each beach with a kid fishing, each yard with an old man in a hammock, each chimney puffing wood smoke. Families, histories, weddings, births, doom. (I was still focused on the doom part, of course.) On the water, oak pollen floated in scummy islands, marking the water lines of my parents' own assortment of small boats and making a yellow veil at the beach. Under the pollen the water was astonishingly clear and stained (as always) orange-brown by the tannins of a billion oak leaves. And acorns floated, bobbing, and here and there an oak gall, and after a windy night many bunches of oak leaves and many twigs and branches.

All around the lake were monumental slabs and piles of granite, some drilled and dynamited by the Shakers to make their stoic buildings, the rest remaining naturally cracked and positioned and covered in lichens, sturdily at rest in geologic time and heedless of Algonquins or Shakers or Franciscan monks or weddings on the water. In the mornings the lake stood still, a mirror erupting with rings from the feeding of fish.

My best man, Kurt, arrived on Wednesday — three days to go — and we all worked till midafternoon, then hiked and swam and fished and sailed, looked for turtles in the river's mouth. At the Enfield town clerk's office I explained that Jean Kotkin had been approved by the attorney general of New Hampshire himself, that Ethical Culture was legitimate — like Quakers, I said, to help the process along. At mention of Quakers the clerk nodded her head and signed the forms, and Juliet and I were licensed to be wed.

Friday evening we rehearsed on the lawn, then ate the rehearsal dinner at the Shaker Inn. Juliet and her party of striking bridesmaids stayed on the grounds in a yellow mansion with a turret and many porches, the former home of the high priests of Enfield. Jules had decreed that no men would be allowed, and so the maids' boyfriends huddled in the sparely furnished rooms of the Great Stone Dwelling (the Shakers' austere housing, later dormitories for the lowest of the monks, now plain rooms for the most budget-conscious of the inn's guests). I along with my party of married geezers and their families stayed far from Juliet's yellow manse, hundreds of yards away across the grounds of the inn — back near the museum, next to the store, past the chapel — in a plain Shaker building with a kitchen and much bare wood.

The bride and her retinue threw a party for all the women who'd arrived. The groom by default had a party for all the men, which broke up late, but not so late that as I went to sleep I didn't jealously hear great commotion and hilarity from the bride's party, those many hundreds of yards away. Next day I heard that the women had taken off their clothes in fits of shouting and laughter and danced death away till dawn.

On Saturday morning, June twenty-third, 1990 (this date engraved inside our rings), there was an extraordinary downpour. No one had ever seen a rain like that one. No one even said it would be good luck, it came down so hard.

The sky was low, and black, and pure rain — ropes of rain, buckets of rain, cauldrons of rain. The circus tents drooped with puddles, which dumped onto my father's head and onto his new driveway, turning it into a mud swamp. Valiant Pop dug drainage ditches under the tents, trudging quixotically around the tables with a garden shovel, dripping from the eyebrows, limping from a fall in the mud, his bifocals askew. Many little girls, our flower bearers, danced in the rain in bathing suits, turning blue. My friends stood around me, my brothers, my sisters, watching, amazed. The lake tossed in squalls, the trees on the far shore bending and twisting, the oaks around us groaning.

But early in the afternoon the rain stopped, leaving a dense and textured cloud cover. The groom ate lunch and retired to the bunkhouse for a nap, having not seen the bride since dinner the night before (as planned — tradition!), the first night Jules and I hadn't been together for more than five months. Up from my nap, I showered and dressed (white pants and bucks and suspenders I'd bought for another wedding, seersucker jacket from a store in Hanover). With one half hour to go I opened the bunkhouse door to mayhem, and the full results of the nuptial accretion. Friends of family. Acquaintances. Many children. The neighbors. Phone calls from those who couldn't be there. The caterer and her staff. An accordion player looking for the fiddle band. Jimmy with the beer from the local brewery. The iceman. Wind in the treetops. Wine up from storage in the basement. Old roommates. Old neighbors. My brothers. Their wives. Mud. Cater-waiters. Flowers in boxes. Heavy metal babysitters. Babies. Wary parents. My sisters — one pregnant — their mates. Our surly photographer. Unfamiliar, hand-shaking cousins. Juliet's brother, his wife, pregnant. Liquor in quarts and half gallons. Nieces with kisses. Jeff Young in dreadlocks, setting up his synthesizer and amp away from the old-timey fiddle band in the corner. My groomsmen casting lures over the lake with the fishing rods I'd given them as gifts, pulling in bass, throwing them back. Death wasn't in the picture, not in the picture at all. Death had gone on ahead.

Down amidst the granite blocks by the lake I stood with Kurt and Jim and Jon Zeeman and Chris and Vince waiting for a signal from Jean Kotkin. We all wore African daisies in our lapels, five different colors. Zeeman checked the sky for signs of more rain, wearing the natty white pants he'd bought at a thrift shop that morning. Down here we were more or less hidden from the guests, and Kurt handed me a paper bag that he'd been carrying gingerly. In it was a Manhattan in a nice glass from the inn, complete with ice, swizzle stick and cherry. "Your last drink as a single man," he said solemnly. I drank, watched the McAnns' house next door, where Juliet and her bridesmaids and best woman and eleven assorted children were preparing to walk up the McAnns' driveway through the white birch trees, around the stand of stately firs that border the field, then back down my family's driveway, under the tents and through the aisle running between the many chairs set up on the lawn, and to a spot under the oaks next to the gazebo where the flower lady had placed pots of flowers to define, not an altar, exactly, but a place to be wed.

I climbed the slippery hill, then Kurt climbed it, then Jim and Jon and Chris and Vince (that order occurring naturally, and only later one of us realizing that it was the order I'd met them in over the years), dropping their fishing rods one at a time to follow while Dudley and his second fiddle sawed away at some wedding music. The five of us knights lined up.

Pretty soon one of my nieces was visible in the trees up the hill, holding the hand of a second cousin of Juliet's. They marched down the driveway holding African daisies, grinning, beaming, marched under the tent and came down the aisle. Now a couple of unhappy little boys, sons of cousins, came shuffling, poking each other. Now my mother's wee, arthritic poodle, unannounced, stiff but regal. Now Eva. Now each bridesmaid in turn, in unmatched dresses that by grace of fortune were complementary. Now the several daughters of friends and my other niece, all dressed in Sunday best and giggling round the bride, who smiled uncertainly and wouldn't catch my eye. Wearing a crown of flowers, Juliet marched slowly toward me.

The kids lined up in front of us, fidgeting and giggling and fighting. Juliet stood beside me and faced all that grinning love — our friends and our acquaintances and our families. A long, long pause in front of the lake beside the swaying oaks, everyone watching the sails out there, the dense, poignant clouds, a motorboat passing, shouting skiers. Someone in the crowd made a joke about that morning's downpour, and everyone laughed. Juliet smiled, slowly, just as the clouds broke (the clouds honestly broke, as in the worst B movie), and the sun came through in rays for one long minute, shining on fair Jules.

While Jean married us I felt Juliet shaking beside me, trying to cover her nervousness with a brash resistance to any gaze I tried to give her. She looked into the crowd and never at Jean; she looked for a young face that would beckon her away from all this, beckon her back to hamsters and beach houses and the private bosom of her imagination.

When Jean said we could kiss, Jules turned to me and smiled. Then she frowned. We kissed. Juliet smiled again, then frowned again, then hugged me. We kissed more emphatically, to hoots from the littler guests, and that was it.

We everyone danced to the fiddle and accordion music, clogging in rows on a plywood dance floor poised over the mud. The contra dancing made every guest a partner to every other guest, at least for a moment. We danced in a circle, then two circles, then three; we danced in squares and in rows, in small groups and large. "Change your partners," Dudley called, and "Change your partners, round and round." I took the hands of my nieces, and the hands of the bridesmaids and the hands of the women and girls. I bowed to my brothers, bowed to my groomsmen, bowed to the father of the bride. I spun round with my sisters, spun round with Eva, took my new brother-in-law's hand. At the end of every song I was back beside Jules, and we waited, sweating — exhausted, really — for more. And Juliet took my brothers' hands, and bowed to my sisters, and bowed to my mother in turn; she spun round in her heavy wedding dress, took the hands of my father, danced in a circle of friends. At the end of every song she was back beside me. And together under the arches of many arms Juliet and I sashayed, danced lively down the line to the tune as it swelled — accordion, fiddles and flute — danced lively as the music lifted up through the trees, out over the lake, and into the deep blue night.